Behind the Angel of History

Behind the Angel of History

The *Angelus Novus* and Its Interleaf

Annie Bourneuf

THE UNIVERSITY OF CHICAGO PRESS *Chicago & London*

The University of Chicago Press, Chicago 60637
The University of Chicago Press, Ltd., London

For more information, contact the University of Chicago Press, 1427 E. 60th St., Chicago, IL 60637.
Published 2022
Printed in China

31 30 29 28 27 26 25 24 23 22 1 2 3 4 5

ISBN-13: 978-0-226-81670-8 (cloth)
ISBN-13: 978-0-226-81671-5 (e-book)
DOI: https://doi.org/10.7208/chicago/9780226816715.001.0001

This publication is made possible in part from the Barr Ferree Foundation Fund for Publications, Department of Art and Archaeology, Princeton University.

Library of Congress Cataloging-in-Publication Data

Names: Bourneuf, Annie, author.
Title: Behind the angel of history : the "Angelus novus" and its interleaf / Annie Bourneuf.
Description: Chicago : University of Chicago Press, 2022. | Includes index.
Identifiers: LCCN 2021031020 | ISBN 9780226816708 (cloth) | ISBN 9780226816715 (ebook)
Subjects: LCSH: Klee, Paul, 1879–1940. Angelus novus. | Luther, Martin, 1483–1546—Portraits. | Benjamin, Walter, 1892–1940. | Quaytman, R. H. (Rebecca H.) | Jewish art and symbolism—Germany—20th century. | Expressionism (Art)—Germany—20th century. | Angels in art. | Underdrawing.
Classification: LCC N6888.K55 A62 2022 | DDC 704.9/4864—DC23
LC record available at https://lccn.loc.gov/2021031020

∞ This paper meets the requirements of ANSI/NISO Z39.48-1992 (Permanence of Paper).

For my family

Contents

CHAPTER 1

2015

In 2015, the artist R. H. Quaytman made a startling discovery about another artist's work, one created almost a hundred years earlier: Paul Klee's modest picture of a bird-footed creature titled *Angelus novus* (1920) (fig. 1.1).[1]

This "new angel," now in the collection of the Israel Museum in Jerusalem, has become one of the best known of the modern Swiss-German painter's works by a delayed and circuitous route: through its prominent place in the writings of its first owner, the German-Jewish critic Walter Benjamin, and especially his use of it to describe "how the angel of history must look."[2] In preparing for a show at the Tel Aviv Museum of Art, Quaytman visited the *Angelus* in the Israel Museum's prints and drawings study room and saw that it incorporates an old engraving of someone in a dark robe (fig. 1.2).[3] The work, she saw, is made of three layers: Klee had glued his watercolor paper onto a slightly larger engraving, and that onto a still slightly larger piece of cardboard. Determined to find out what, and who, it was, Quaytman emailed me; my book on Klee was about to be published.[4] But I had no idea that there even *was* an engraving in it. I felt a bit embarrassed until I confirmed that it had never been mentioned in any of the many published discussions of the famous work.

If you look at the work closely—in person and in decent light, as I did in Jerusalem some months later—about a finger's breadth of the engraving is plainly visible all around: its fine engraved lines, "LC" or "CL" monogram, 1520-something date, and folds of drapery against a dark ground, indicating someone's torso, are not hard to spot. Why hadn't anyone mentioned it?

The engraving is part of Klee's work: pressed between the watercolor paper bearing his drawing and the cardboard mount he inscribed with the title, the engraving serves as a dark inner frame or border of the kind he often made for his works on paper.[5] But in most reproductions, the engraving is invisible. Sometimes its details drop out so it looks like another one of Klee's many dark watercolor or ink borders; only in reproductions does the print's dense network of lines appear homogeneous even when viewed up close. In his essay "The Work of Art in the Age of Its Technological Reproducibility," Benjamin mentions the ability of a photographic reproduction of a work to "bring out aspects of the original that are accessible only to the lens (which is adjustable and

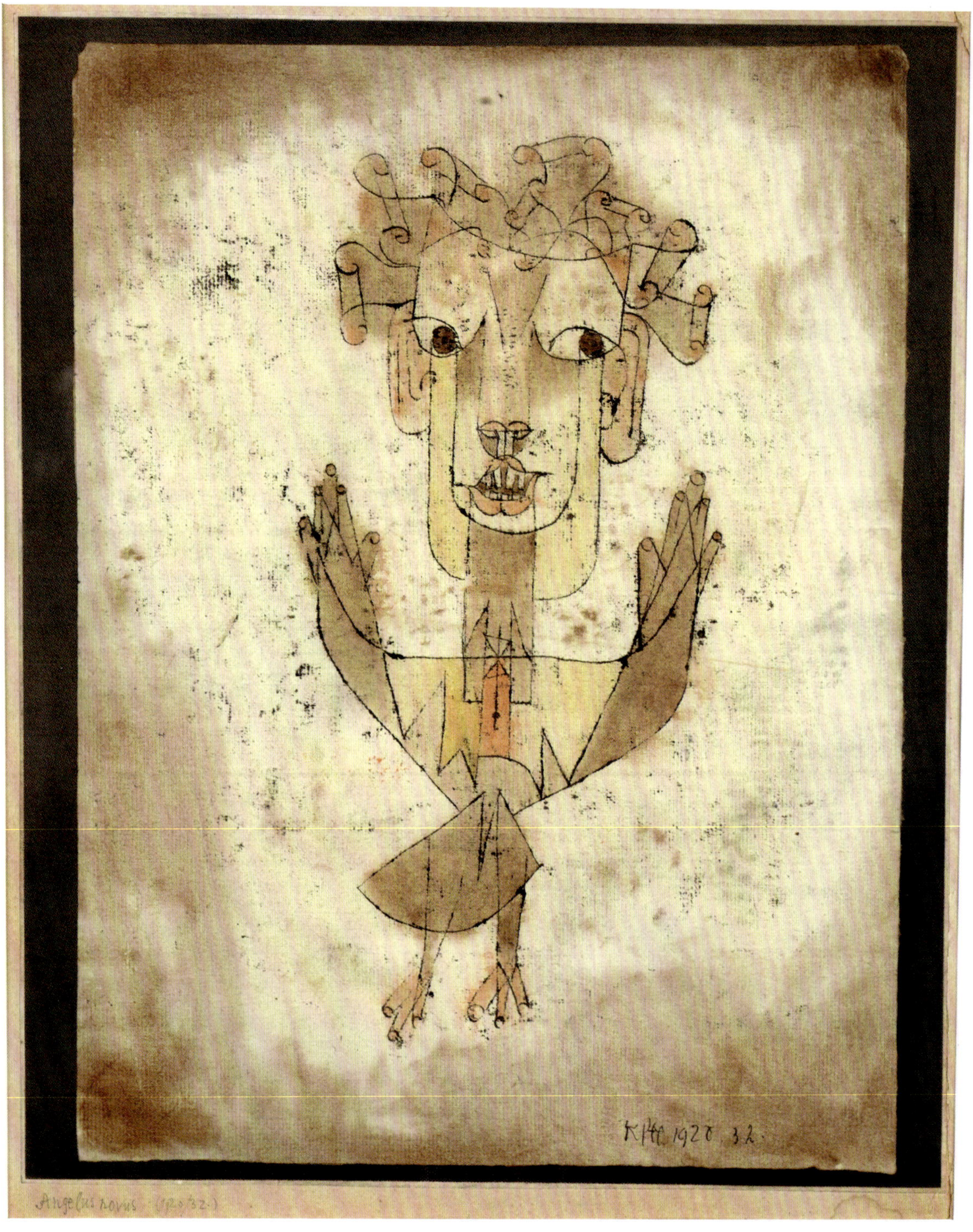

FIGURE 1.1 Paul Klee, *Angelus novus*, 1920, 32. Oil-transfer drawing and watercolor on paper on engraving on cardboard, 31.8 × 24.2 cm. The Israel Museum, Jerusalem. Gift of Fania and Gershom Scholem, Jerusalem; John Herring, Marlene and Paul Herring, Jo Carole and Ronald Lauder, New York, Accession No. B87.0994. Photo: The Israel Museum, Jerusalem, by Elie Posner.

FIGURE 1.2 Paul Klee, *Angelus novus*, 1920, 32, detail. The Israel Museum, Jerusalem.

can easily change viewpoint) but not to the human eye" among the causes for the waning of the authority of the original, but, as it happens, an important aspect of Klee's *Angelus novus* is considerably more obvious to the latter.[6] Reproductions often crop off the engraving altogether; since the first books on Klee were published in the early 1920s, reproductions of Klee's pictures have often omitted their important mounts and borders (figs. 1.3, 1.4).[7] In reproductions of the *Angelus* in particular, the combination of halftone and the fine, regular parallel lines of the engraving (of a newer and an older method of printing tone) can create moiré patterns, again camouflaging the engraving—or, very plausibly, providing a reason for cropping it off.[8]

In any case, Klee didn't arrange the picture's layers to attract attention to the engraving at first glance or from across the room. Klee repeatedly emphasized that the kind of looking he sought to create a place for in his art was a durational roving of the fovea centralis.[9] The *Angelus* rewards and ensnares that closer, longer look, revealing both articulation where you wouldn't expect it and, with the same blow, concealment, *showing* that the support of the drawing of the angel hides someone else.

I was lucky to be in touch with Quaytman during the final months of her quest. In the end, she succeeded by going on the clues that Klee left visible, plus untold hours of sifting through digitized print collections and some luck. Luck was necessary, for the print was, as it turned out, both commonplace and obscure. Quaytman discovered that the mystery image was—of all things—a portrait of Martin Luther.[10] Comparing their details, it is certain that the print interleaved in the *Angelus* is an impression of an 1838 engraving of Luther by the little-known Dresden-based engraver Friedrich Müller (fig. 1.5).[11] A very

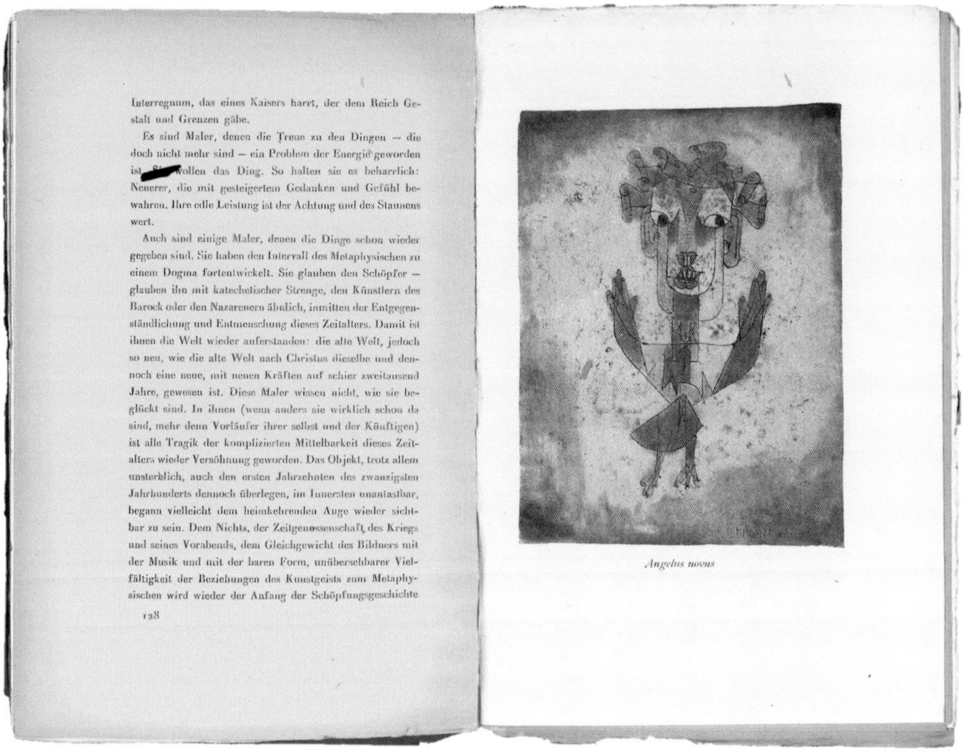

Interregnum, das eines Kaisers harrt, der dem Reich Gestalt und Grenzen gäbe.

Es sind Maler, denen die Treue zu den Dingen — die doch nicht mehr sind — ein Problem der Energie geworden ist. [redacted] wollen das Ding. So halten sie es beharrlich: Neuerer, die mit gesteigertem Gedanken und Gefühl bewahren. Ihre edle Leistung ist der Achtung und des Staunens wert.

Auch sind einige Maler, denen die Dinge schon wieder gegeben sind. Sie haben den Intervall des Metaphysischen zu einem Dogma fortentwickelt. Sie glauben den Schöpfer — glauben ihn mit katechetischer Strenge, den Künstlern des Barock oder den Nazarenern ähnlich, inmitten der Entgegenständlichung und Entmenschung dieses Zeitalters. Damit ist ihnen die Welt wieder auferstanden: die alte Welt, jedoch so neu, wie die alte Welt nach Christus dieselbe und dennoch eine neue, mit neuen Kräften auf schier zweitausend Jahre, gewesen ist. Diese Maler wissen nicht, wie sie beglückt sind. In ihnen (wenn anders sie wirklich schon da sind, mehr denn Vorläufer ihrer selbst und der Künftigen) ist alle Tragik der komplizierten Mittelbarkeit dieses Zeitalters wieder Versöhnung geworden. Das Objekt, trotz allem unsterblich, auch den ersten Jahrzehnten des zwanzigsten Jahrhunderts dennoch überlegen, im Innersten unantastbar, begann vielleicht dem heimkehrenden Auge wieder sichtbar zu sein. Dem Nichts, der Zeitgenossenschaft, des Kriegs und seines Vorabends, dem Gleichgewicht des Bildners mit der Musik und mit der baren Form, unübersehbarer Vielfältigkeit der Beziehungen des Kunstgeists zum Metaphysischen wird wieder der Anfang der Schöpfungsgeschichte

128

FIGURE 1.3 Wilhelm Hausenstein, *Kairuan; or, A Story of the Painter Klee and of the Art of This Age* (Munich: Kurt Wolff, 1921)

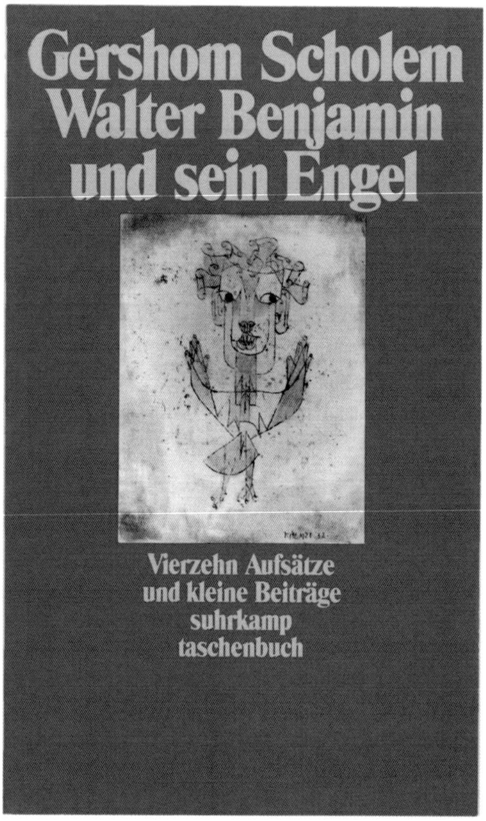

FIGURE 1.4 Cover of Gershom Scholem, *Walter Benjamin und sein Engel: Vierzehn Aufsätze und kleine Beiträge* (Frankfurt: Suhrkamp, 1992)

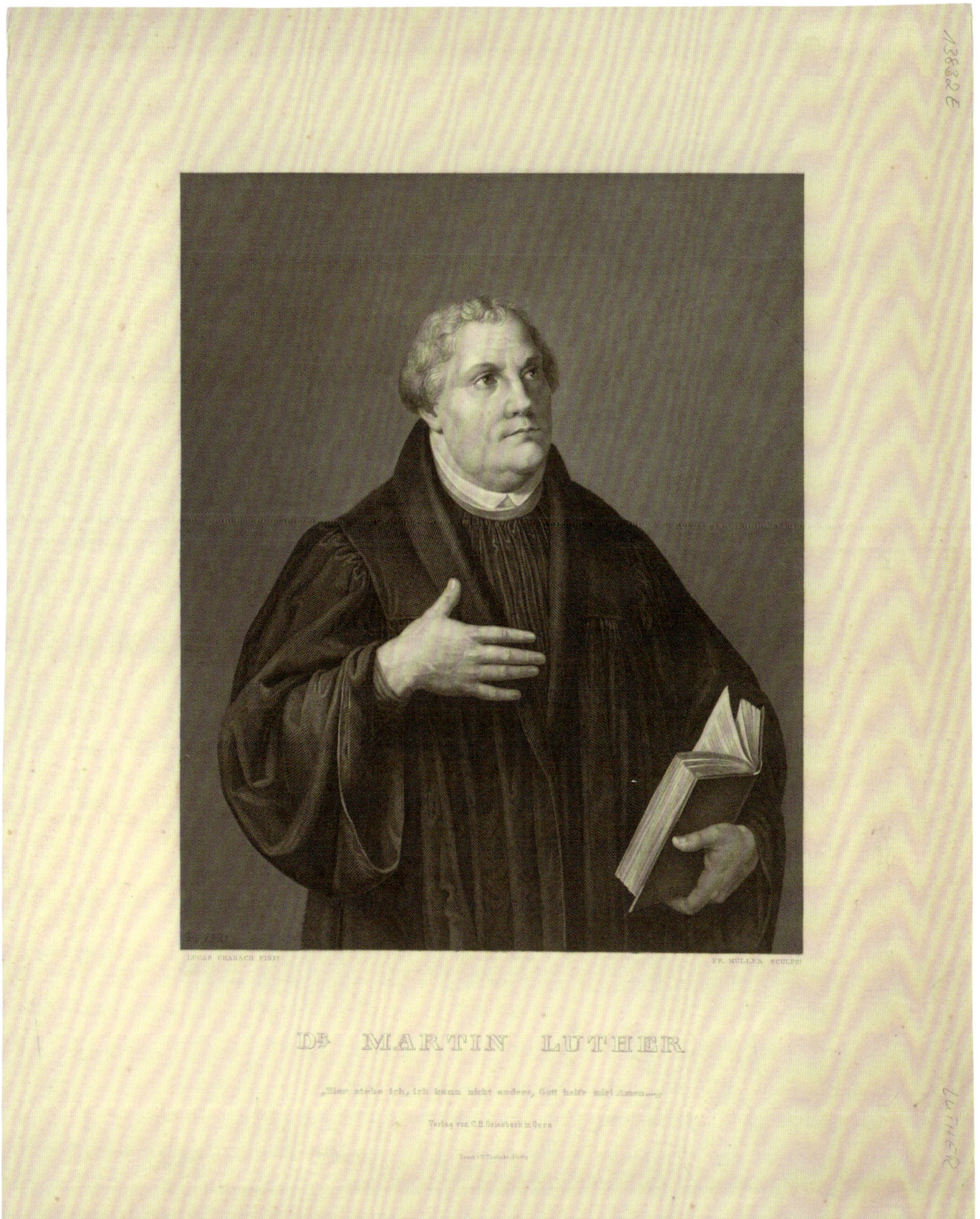

FIGURE 1.5 Friedrich Müller, *Dr. Martin Luther*, 1838. Engraving, 33.4 × 27.2 cm (plate). Collection of R. H. Quaytman.

ordinary print, it might have hung in any Lutheran home or schoolroom.[12] The inscription in small letters just under the engraved image—cut off by Klee or a previous owner—reads "LUCAS CRANACH PINXT" on the left and "FR. MÜLLER SCULPST" on the right; the date at the lower left is 1521. It presents itself as reproducing a 1521 painting by Lucas Cranach the Elder, Luther's chief portraitist, and is inscribed with the bold words with which, according to legend, Luther refused to retract his heresies at the Diet of Worms that same year: "Here I stand, I can do no other, God help me! Amen."[13]

In her thought-provoking essay on her discovery, Quaytman expresses regret. She writes: "My curiosity took over and the obvious was forgotten—that Klee didn't intend us to know who lay behind. That alone should have stopped me. If the Angelus defaces Luther, am I defacing the Angelus? The meaning of an artwork cannot, by its very nature, be hidden from view. How can I morally situate this exposure?"[14] Quaytman's unexpectedly positive identification—her search could well have petered out in resonant uncertainties—certainly might be seen as intrusive, even destructive. Because of its role in Benjamin's writings, in the late twentieth century, long after Klee pasted these pieces of paper together, the *Angelus* became, in Otto Karl Werckmeister's phrase, an "icon of the left."[15] How could this new knowledge sit alongside Benjamin's writings about the picture?

Did Klee want anyone to see this "Easter egg"? Is it a private joke? A secret confession? If Klee had wanted us to *know* what the engraving was, he wouldn't have covered up so much of it. But the amount the picture reveals certainly invites viewers to wonder who lurks behind the angel. In contrast, Klee sometimes used an old print's backside simply, it seems, as a cheap piece of pretty good paper.[16] He was thrifty. But this is another matter: the engraved interleaf is partially on display, and however cheap it was, it would have been even cheaper to omit it, to use its backside for another work.

And did Benjamin suspect Luther was hiding behind his angel? It seems unlikely that a window mount or something of the sort hid the interleaf while it was in his possession; careful visual examination of the light-sensitive work reveals no differential light damage. Benjamin praised art-historical work on seemingly "insignificant" and "inconspicuous" aspects of individual works; Ernst Bloch admired his "sense for the peripheral," his "unique gaze for the significant detail, for what lies alongside."[17] The teasing margin Klee left visible might help explain why Benjamin was so interested in this particular work by Klee. Yet no textual evidence suggests that he guessed what lay beneath.

In any case, the work as a whole poses itself as a picture puzzle, drawing the attentive viewer into a guessing game. And I think that in Germany circa 1920, the "fine minds" Klee said he saw as his public would have enjoyed putting together the clues Klee left them to guess that this was a print of one of

Cranach's many Luther portraits.[18] Unlike Quaytman, they would never be able to nail down which particular one, and they couldn't be at all sure they were right. But for the cultured early twentieth-century German viewers Klee envisaged, monogram and date would suggest the famous German Renaissance master Lucas Cranach; the dark robe a sober churchman rather than a noble; and, turning from the engraving's visible margin to Klee's drawing, the angel's jowls and curls recall doctrinally significant attributes of Luther that Cranach emphasized in many of his well-known portraits. Just how widespread Luther portraits were in early twentieth-century Germany—how familiar they would be to such viewers—is suggested by a later Nazi decree issued in Oldenburg in 1936 that ordered schools and other public buildings to remove them.[19]

Cranach and Luther themselves made the massive circulation of Cranach's Luther portraits a major component of the Protestant Reformation's media strategy.[20] Beginning in the late 1510s, the large Wittenberg workshop run by Luther's friend Cranach, the Saxon court painter, churned out enormous numbers of paintings and prints of Luther. The art historian Joseph Leo Koerner has described as follows the task of such images in sixteenth-century churches and schools: "On the one hand, they indicate, by means of portrait likenesses, that faith is a decision, an inner conviction individually confessed by empirical persons in their historical and biographical specificity. On the other hand, these likenesses . . . organize the surrounding spectacle of obedience to a collective."[21] In the nineteenth century, Luther portrait prints after Cranach had a huge circulation—Müller's was one of dozens. The image of Luther was deployed on an enormous scale in Imperial Germany; Luther was seen as a "German hero, a powerful early manifestation of German culture and national identity, which, finally, had rendezvoused with political destiny in 1871" (fig. 1.6).[22] Just a few years before Klee made the *Angelus*, the German government had tried to use the four hundredth anniversary of the Reformation in 1917 to boost the war-weary public's fighting spirit.[23] While Klee didn't intend us to know who lay behind, I think he would expect us to guess.

The passage on the *Angelus* and the "angel of history" in Benjamin's "On the Concept of History" (1940) made Klee's picture an "icon," but not only of the left. Benjamin's friend Scholem, the scholar of Jewish mysticism, used it to exemplify what Benjamin's leftist admirers failed to countenance in Benjamin's thought.[24] The critic Adam Kirsch has proposed that the *Angelus*—as "a work by a non-Jewish artist that has been permanently inscribed in Jewish culture by Walter Benjamin's messianic interpretation of it"—could point toward a new conception of Jewish art, defined not by the artist's identity but by "a Jewish way of seeing and talking and writing about art," locating it "in a universe of Jewish discourse about the power and danger of the image," engaged with

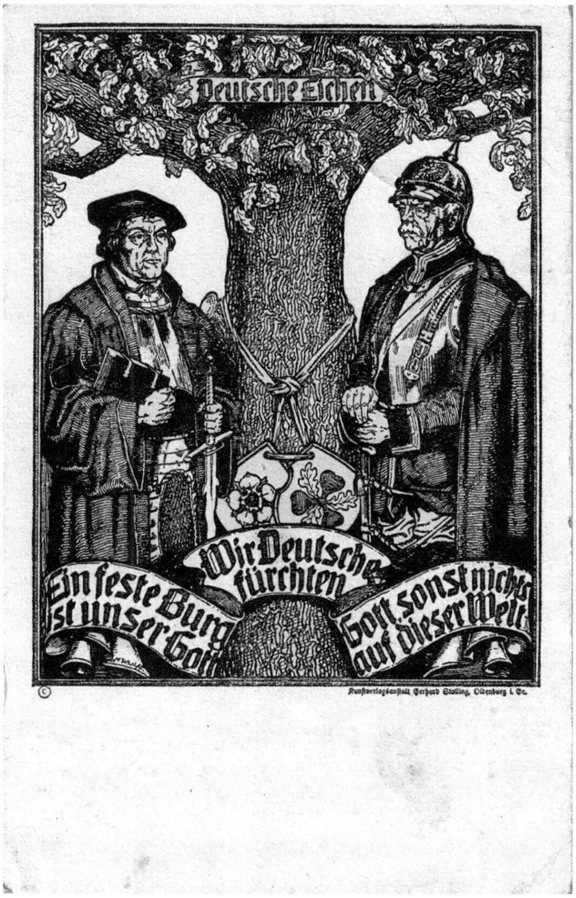

FIGURE 1.6 *Feldpostkarte* (field postcard) of Luther and Otto von Bismarck as "German oaks," 1914

"the connection between the image, which the Torah mistrusts so deeply, and the word, which has always been the source of value and law for Judaism."[25]

The ninth of the numbered "theses," as Benjamin himself termed them, comprising his "On the Concept of History" begins with an excerpt from a poem in the angel's voice that Scholem wrote in 1921 as a birthday present for Benjamin.[26] Here is the thesis in its entirety:

> My wing is ready for flight,
> *I would like to turn back.*
> If I stayed everliving time,
> I'd still have little luck.
>
> —Gerhard Scholem, "Greetings from the Angelus"

> There is a picture by Klee called *Angelus novus*. It shows an angel who seems about to move away from something he stares at. His eyes are wide, his mouth is open, his wings are spread. This is how the angel of history must look. His face is turned toward the past. Where a chain of events

> appears before *us*, *he* sees one single catastrophe, which keeps piling wreckage upon wreckage and hurls it at his feet. The angel would like to stay, awaken the dead, and make whole what has been smashed. But a storm is blowing from Paradise and has got caught in his wings; it is so strong that the angel can no longer close them. This storm drives him irresistibly into the future, to which his back is turned, while the pile of debris before him grows toward the sky. What we call progress is *this* storm.[27]

I will say a little more about this complex and celebrated passage in this book's epilogue. For now, I merely want to note that it is in conjunction with this passage that the picture became a logogram for Benjamin, for the Frankfurt School, for modern Jewish intellectual history, for critical historiography, for memory (see, for instance, the sheer frequency with which the *Angelus* appears on the covers of books devoted not to Klee but to these and adjacent subjects.)[28]

What, then, to make of Luther *here*? Under, as it were, Benjamin's ninth thesis, beneath Klee's drawn angel, we find this hero-image of German nationalism—as Quaytman writes, Müller makes Luther a "Teutonic alpha male, a triumphant warrior of his beliefs."[29] The reformer meant many different things in early twentieth-century Germany: the national hero, the creator of the German language, the great Bible translator, the initiator of modernity, the man of conscience, the devoted family man. In 1920, when Klee sandwiched Luther's portrait into his work, the reformer was often seen as the defender of social order, the personification of authoritarian counterrevolution, as he sided with the nobility against the peasants who revolted against them and as Lutheranism granted the state, as Ernst Troeltsch put it in 1912, a "certain semi-divinity."[30] From the perspective of 1940, when Benjamin cited Klee's picture in "On the Concept of History," there is no avoiding the Nazis' use of Luther. No hostility toward the image of the reformer should be extrapolated from the Oldenburg order; the Nazis made lavish use of him, especially foregrounding Luther as author of the treatise *On the Jews and Their Lies* (1543) and a protagonist in the long and violent history of Christian persecution of Jews.[31] A poster produced on the occasion of "German Luther Day" in 1933 features a picture joining a portrait of the reformer resembling Müller's (based on related portraits from the Cranach workshop) with a swastika and yoking together in a rhyming couplet Hitler and Luther as protectors of the German people (fig. 1.7).[32]

With this in mind, we might be tempted to say that, in contrast to Benjamin's "angel of history," the drawn *Angelus novus* literally turns its back on catastrophe. Many of Klee's works involve complex temporal layering, making visible to the viewer the process and duration of the making of the work, whose past stages remain visible in the finished work so that it may be grasped as

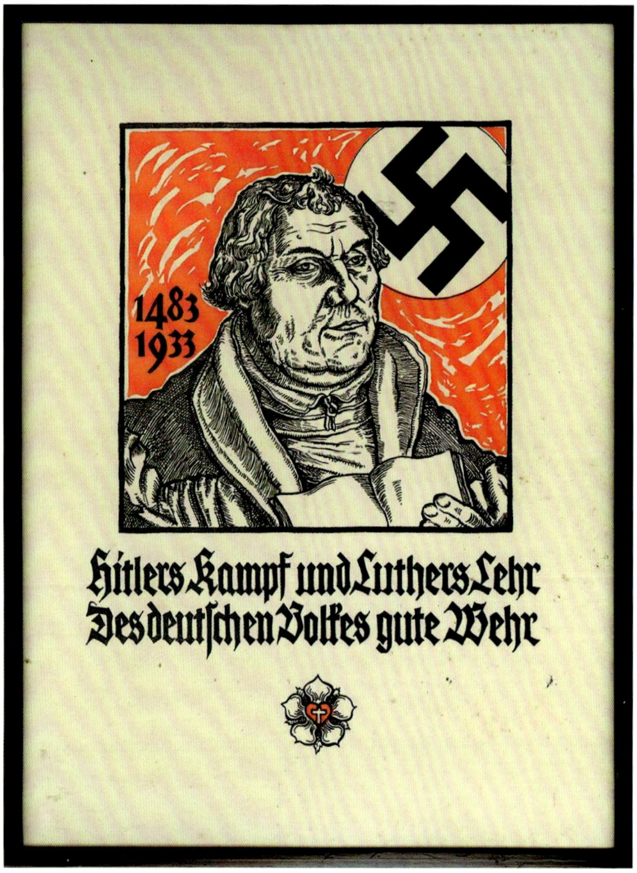

FIGURE 1.7 *Hitler's Struggle and Luther's Teaching Defend the German People Well*, 1933

dynamic formation rather than static form; this is one of the great emphases of his writing and teaching.[33] In his 1924 lecture "On Modern Art," Klee wrote, "To each dimension that evanesces in time we should say, 'You will now become the past; and yet every now and again as we pursue our new dimension, we will stumble onto a critical place, perhaps a fortunate place, which will restore your present to you.'"[34] In this case, Klee leaves visible a stratum that shows not only an earlier moment in the history of the making of this single work but also earlier moments in larger, longer, and far more vexed histories of religions, languages, national identities, and politics.

After Quaytman got in touch with me, I went through my shelves to examine reproductions of the *Angelus*. The best one I could find was a splendid, uncropped, full-page color reproduction published in the second edition of the widely used college textbook *Art since 1900*.[35] In it, the engraved border is entirely visible—monogram, date, drapery, and all. It's in a chapter I've assigned my art history survey students; the text on the facing page is covered with my own penciled notes.

Quaytman visited the *Angelus* in 2013 on a research expedition to Israel, preparing for her Tel Aviv exhibition. Mark Godfrey, the exhibition's curator, accompanied her; the angel's overexposure was on both of their minds. As Godfrey wrote, while the *Angelus* was "without doubt the most significant European 20th-century artwork in Israel, as much for its qualities as a drawing as for its provenance," he doubted that Quaytman would do anything with it "because it was so iconic, so obvious."[36] As Quaytman wrote, the picture "stood symbolically at the center of my interest: the correspondence between Walter Benjamin and Gershom Scholem and their differing perspectives with regard to the image and its relationship to words. However, I feared any approach to the *Angelus* I could possibly pursue would be overwhelmed . . . by both its historical and contemporary contexts (coincidentally during the installation of my exhibition, Okwui Enwezor deployed the *Angelus novus* to announce his concept for the Venice Biennale, and only yesterday I saw that Hito Steyerl made use of it in a video)." Most of all, she couldn't imagine working with the picture because she "simply didn't like Klee," blaming him, she writes, "for a plague of faux-naive, self-cuddling artworks across wide swaths of amateur modernists."[37]

But in the prints and drawings study room at the Israel Museum, Quaytman noticed the engraving right away, and that caught her. In her essay, she describes the iconic nature of the *Angelus* as deflecting her attention away to its edges: "After experiencing a familiar combination of shyness and repulsion towards this image, so weighed down by history as it is, my focus naturally scurried back to the materiality of the artifact."[38] As she wrote, "Clearly visible were the overlapping initials CL, a date of 152? (or was the 1 a J?), and black pleats from a gown suggesting a portrait of a priest, nun, or monk."[39] She had almost too many reasons for noticing the print and, crucially, for staying with it. Not only was she looking carefully (as Klee would have wished), but edges and the superimposition of images are both of central importance to her own art: "I believe," she writes, "that it is often at the edge of an image that a painting's self-awareness is unconsciously situated."[40] She collects engravings, images of which she sometimes uses in her own work: she is specifically interested in the character of the engraved mark as a cut, "graven like those images we don't worship," distinguished by "the constraints of systematic precision and the counteracting pressure of the plate."[41] She has noted that engravings might be considered a kind of middle ground between words and images; the relations between the two are of deep concern to Quaytman, whose art is structured by analogies and disanalogies between books and paintings.[42] In 2001, Quaytman established a set of ground rules for her art, a generative set of limitations to follow and violate. Every exhibition of her work is conceived and titled as a "chapter"—the exhibition in Tel Aviv was her *Chapter 29: Haqaq*—so as to "situate primary legibility outside the boundaries of the individual unit," so that one individual painting has something of the status of "an engraving that has been torn from a book."[43]

She asked the staff at the museum what the engraving in the *Angelus* was: "To the astonishment of us all, it turned out that they didn't know because the question seemed never to have been asked."[44] Michael Maggen, head of paper, prints, and drawings conservation at the Israel Museum, "seemed confident that the engraving had been put there by Klee simply to protect the . . . paper from buckling while drying."[45] But as Quaytman writes: "Does not a 16th century print situate the subject within a specific temporal history? Was the *Angelus* paying homage to or defacing what it obscured? Suddenly I was utterly engrossed in Klee. Even if the angel looked innocent, I felt it wasn't. I wanted more than anything to find the answer."[46]

Quaytman's art often converses with that of the early twentieth century—with Kasimir Malevich, Katarzyna Kobro, and Hilma af Klint, whose first US solo exhibition, *The Secret Pictures of Hilma af Klint*, Quaytman installed in 1989.[47] In a 2016 catalog essay Juliane Rebentisch meditates on how and why Quaytman's art cites "iconic works of modernist and postmodernist art," sometimes by means of silkscreen, discussing one of the paintings riffing on the *Angelus* that Quaytman made after visiting the Israel Museum:

> Both the silkscreened quotation and the handmade remake are quite emphatic about the distance that separates them from their sources . . . the artist has . . . in one version of *Angelus novus*, applied thick layers of urethane foam to the picture, obscuring the motif save for a small detail. If at first glance these are gestures of appropriation, their primary purpose is not to stamp a woman artist's name on icons of (a masculine) modernism—Quaytman in fact discourages this reading. . . . Indeed, her adaptations are not so much appropriations as expropriations: the aim is to extricate the source material from its familiar interpretations in order to initiate a fresh examination of what modernism meant and means. In the perspective of this inquiry, modernism is not a settled affair. The question of the import of modernism—its legacy as well as its future—ultimately also touches on the intersections between art and politics. The consequences for the philosophy of history of Quaytman's recent discovery that Klee glued his *Angelus novus* on top of an engraving showing a portrait of Martin Luther (!) are hard to gauge; in the framework of her own project, it merely adds a facet to her insistence that the history of modernism is incomplete—that, for our future's sake, it remains to be (re)discovered, (re)interpreted, (re)written.[48]

To make the figure of the *Angelus novus*, Klee used oil-transfer drawing, a duplication technique he used frequently at the time: he coated one side of a piece of paper with oily, tacky ink or paint so he could use it as if it were carbon paper, to transfer a drawing onto a new surface by retracing its lines.[49] As Tamara Trodd has written, Klee's artisanal process of image reproduction can be understood as his way of "simultaneously preserving and 'consuming'" a drawing: this watercolored oil-transfer picture has, as many of them do, a double—a pencil drawing also called *Angelus novus* (1920, 69) (fig. 1.8)—that Klee kept, while the watercolor went to his dealer.[50] The drawing does not appear to be scored or damaged, suggesting that in this case, as in others, Klee made a tracing of the pencil drawing, placed that tracing over the face-down sheet of paper covered with ink, and retraced the tracing's lines with a stylus to transfer the image onto the Ingres paper of the oil-transfer *Angelus novus* (1920, 32). As Trodd writes, although Klee's oil-transfer technique resembles "established techniques used by artists to avoid the reversal of a composition in transfer and print processes," some of Klee's oil-transfer drawings reverse the original drawing and others, like the oil-transfer *Angelus*, do not.[51] Klee's layering of the face-up watercolor paper over the face-up engraving in the *Angelus novus* suggests the stage in the production of the oil transfers in which the face-up drawing is placed on top of the paper that will become its face-up transfer, suggesting that the old engraving might be seen, preposterously, as a copy or transfer of Klee's drawing.

In the 2014 painting Rebentisch discusses (fig. 1.9), Quaytman used Klee's oil-transfer technique to duplicate his angel onto one of the plywood panels she consistently uses as supports, "hoping to learn more through the making of the thing."[52] Then she covered up almost all of her own remake of Klee's angel with a thick, tumorous blob of foam, bulging in profile and surrounded by a border nearly as wide as the almost occluded central image, a pattern of closely spaced black and white zigzags that vibrate and dazzle, echoing but amplifying the engraving's parallel lines. Quaytman added pink and yellow-green fluorescent paint along the top beveled edge of the plywood support; the viewer cannot see them directly, but only the colored glow that they bounce off the wall, a Day-Glo pseudo-halo.[53]

In pondering what it is to hide something in a picture, Quaytman's painting reenacts with Klee's own drawing Klee's covering over of an older image. Quaytman's painting subjects Klee's to a kind of analytical splitting, demonstrating the distance between source and remake that Rebentisch notes: her painting separates out from one another the acts of copying, hiding, framing, and haloing compacted together in Klee's picture. Yet there is also a closeness between the two: Quaytman's expropriation also draws attention to the procedural similarities between crucial maneuvers of her own work—citation, superimposition, attention to the edge—and the way the *Angelus* was put together.

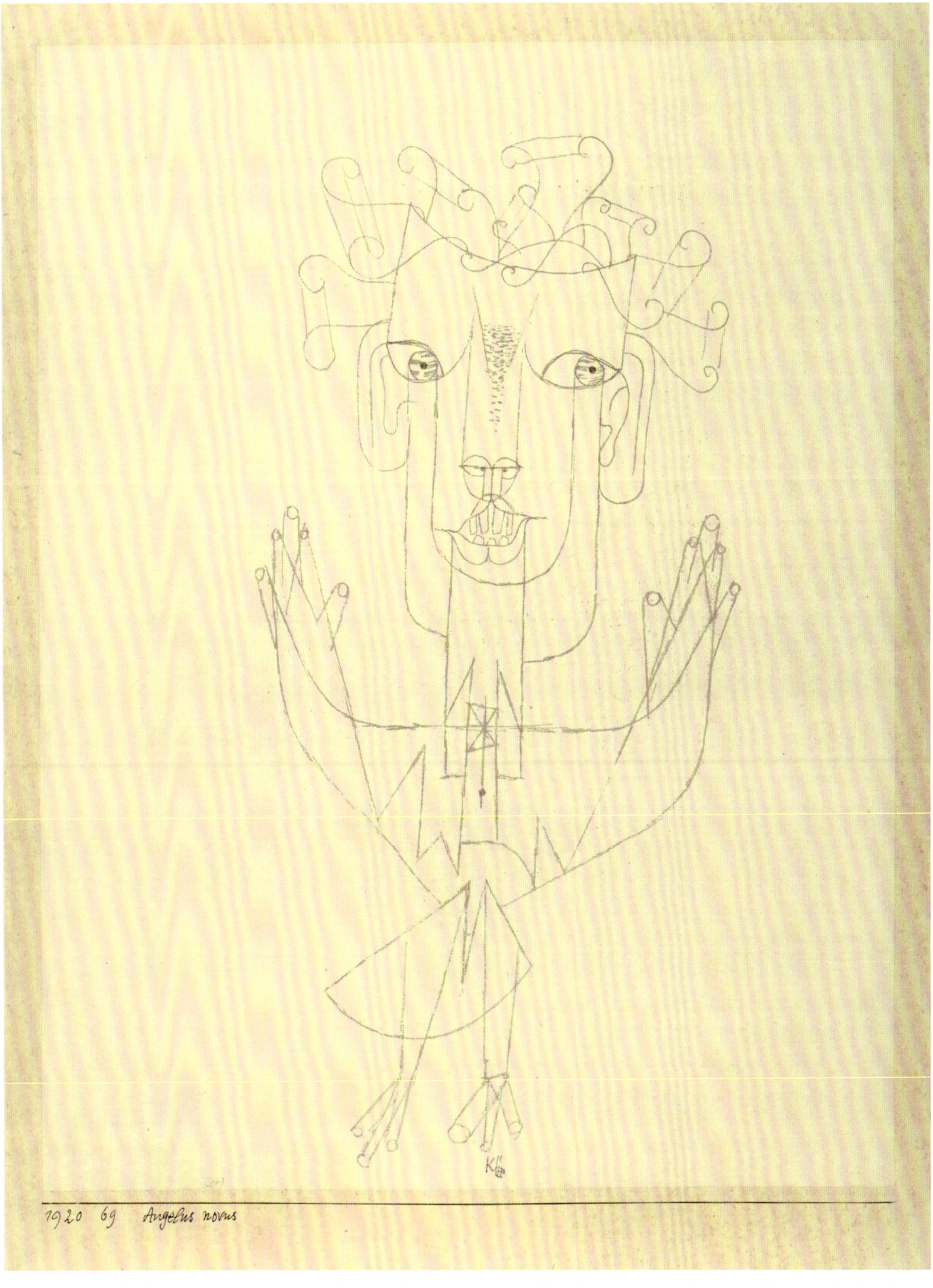

FIGURE 1.8 Paul Klee, *Angelus novus*, 1920, 69. Pencil on paper on cardboard, 30 × 22 cm. Private collection, Switzerland. Photo: Zentrum Paul Klee, Bern, Archiv.

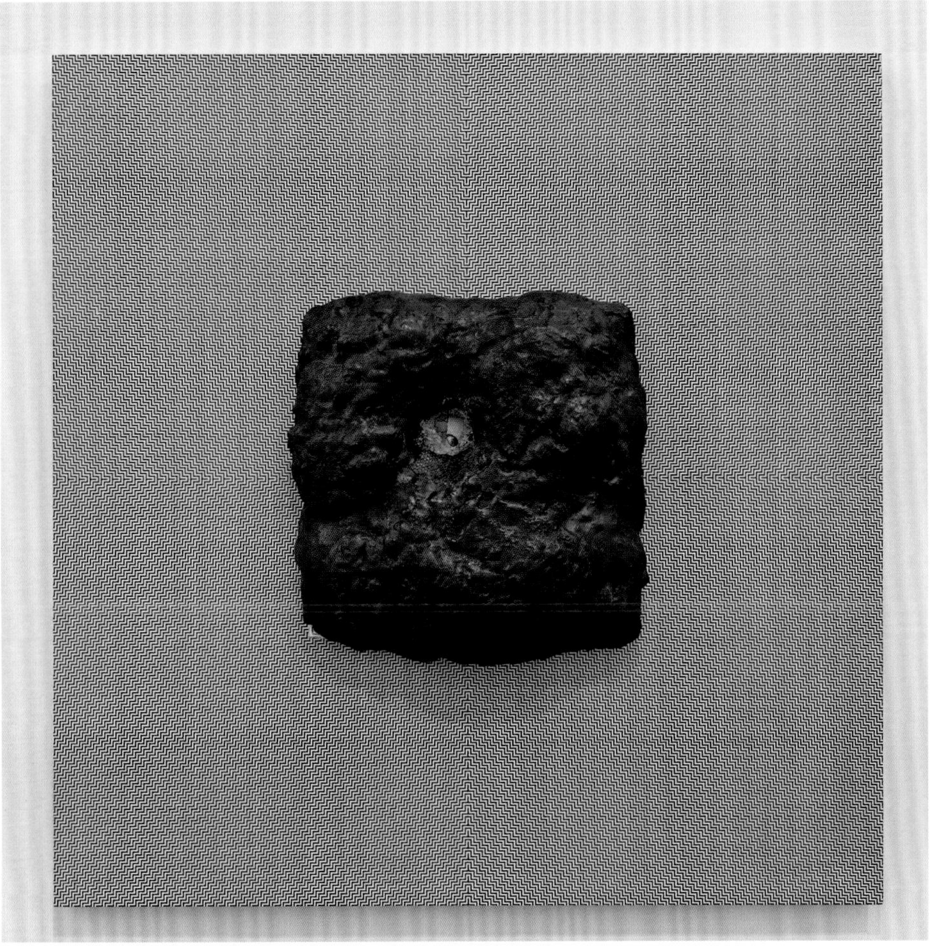

FIGURE 1.9 R. H. Quaytman, *O Tópico, Chapter 27*, 2014. Encaustic, oil, gouache, urethane foam, silkscreen ink, and gesso on wood, 82.2 × 82.2 cm. Courtesy the artist, Miguel Abreu Gallery, New York, and Gladstone Gallery, New York and Brussels. Photo: David Regen.

One moment of Quaytman's search got caught by Christine Smallwood's 2015 *T Magazine* interview with Quaytman and the poet Susan Howe, Quaytman's mother: "Quaytman had recently returned from Rome, where she has been preparing for an upcoming show in Tel Aviv. She had noticed that Paul Klee's *Angelus novus* was mounted onto an engraving, and she wanted to know what the engraving was. She had scientists in Rome scan the mount, only to find the engraving obscured; Klee had rolled printer's ink over the back of it. Howe, who loves the *Angelus*, was excited that mysticism was getting into Quaytman's process. 'It's actually not getting there,' Quaytman laughed. ''Cause it didn't work.'"[54] Quaytman pursued many technological approaches in collaboration with the Israel Museum; the conservation department there X-rayed it, tried infrared reflectography, and finally sent it to Rome to try infrared thermography.[55] As Quaytman writes, the museum granted her permission to use any images generated by these processes: "That same year, I had made a painting using an X-ray of Malevich's *White on White* in MoMA's collection, so I was primed to use scientifically generated optics as the basis for a silkscreened painting."[56] None of this, however, yielded information that helped identify the engraving.

Benjamin's 1937 essay "Eduard Fuchs, Collector and Historian" uses the work of the socialist writer Fuchs on caricature and erotic art, inter alia, to construct a historical materialist approach to the art of the past. Although my book cannot claim to follow such an approach, the Fuchs essay contains a remark on the "after-history" of a work of art that is highly relevant for considering the *Angelus*. From works of art, writes Benjamin, the historical materialist learns "how their function outlives their creator and how the artist's intentions are left behind. They demonstrate how the reception of a work by its contemporaries is part of the effect that the work of art has on us today. They further show that this effect depends on an encounter not just with the work of art alone but with the history which has allowed the work to come down to our own age."[57] Benjamin then cites a sentence of Goethe that applies well to the *Angelus*: "Nothing that has had a great effect can really be judged any longer."[58] It is especially obvious in the case of this picture that its present effect is tethered to its reception. While works escape the intentions of their makers willy-nilly, Klee, incidentally, particularly welcomed this process.[59] But although the phrase "the reception of a work by its contemporaries" might seem to imply public discussion, the early audience of this work, in private hands for most of its existence, was tiny—that "great effect" was primarily on one person. And, in this case, "allowed" seems much too generous a word for much of the "history which has allowed the work to come down to our own age": the Nazi persecution of Jews shaped the itinerary of the *Angelus* along with its first owner's.

Benjamin's death in 1940, some months after his composition of "On the Concept of History," has mattered for its reception; it is not only a major work but his last major work, and it reflects on the political situation at the beginning of the Second World War that would soon claim its author as a victim.[60] As a German-Jewish exile who fled Paris as German troops advanced, heading south into collaborationist Vichy France, which had promised to deliver such refugees to the German authorities, the danger Benjamin faced impelled him to attempt crossing into Spain without a difficult-to-obtain French exit visa, in hopes of ultimately reaching the United States.[61] Benjamin, in failing health after the arduous journey, took his life after the Spanish authorities told the small group with whom he was traveling that they would be returned to France.

In 1940, as it happens, Klee died as well, of a debilitating disease in a hospital in Switzerland, where he had lived as a child. The Nazi seizure of power prompted both Klee and Benjamin to leave Germany in 1933, but their situations as exiles were very different. Klee was not Jewish; his family belonged to the Evangelical Reformed Church of the Canton of Bern.[62] (A Nazi newspaper called Klee a "typical Galician Jew"—a misrepresentation to which he decided not to respond because, as he wrote to his wife, Lily, "even if it were true that I was a Jew and from Galicia, that would not affect the value of myself or my achievement one iota."[63]) The Nazis targeted him as an avant-garde artist with a position at the Düsseldorf Academy; his house was searched and his teaching position suspended.[64] But Klee found a safe and familiar refuge in Switzerland.

Benjamin's Klee picture first became famous as the pictorial counterpart of Benjamin's ninth thesis in the wake of the surge of interest in Benjamin beginning in and around the student movement in West Germany and bound up with its attempts to reckon with the National Socialist past, in a postwar, post-Shoah world that neither Benjamin nor Klee knew.[65] In Werckmeister's words, "A dozen lines of printed text, conveniently focused on one picture suitable for incessant reproduction, have become a venue for drawing out a string of fundamental contradictions between revolution and religion, activism and resignation, political partisanship and historical detachment."[66]

In dealing with the *Angelus*, the necessity of a sense of the picture's itinerary after it left Klee's studio in 1920 is clear. It is bound up with the circumstances of Benjamin's life and the question of his legacy in the narrow sense (to whom should his property—in this case, "his most important possession"—go?[67]), inflected with the question of his legacy in a broader sense.

The most important sources are the writings of Benjamin himself and of Scholem, who, beginning in the 1960s, wrote in detail about his long friendship with Benjamin, in which the *Angelus* played an important part.[68] (In none of them is an explicit mention of an interleaved engraving in the *Angelus* to be found.) Scholem's writings on Klee's picture play a decisive role in its afterhistory: not only did Benjamin cite Scholem's poem ventriloquizing the angel in his 1940 passage on the "angel of history," but also Scholem's writings are very much involved in the events of 1972 that initiated the era of the picture's most frequent reproduction.

In 1972, Siegfried Unseld—head of Suhrkamp Verlag, the publisher of Scholem and Benjamin after the war—had many reproductions of the *Angelus* made for a celebration in Frankfurt am Main marking the eightieth anniversary of Benjamin's birth and the beginning of Suhrkamp's monumental project of publishing Benjamin's *Gesammelte Schriften* (Collected Writings), which would eventually extend to fourteen bound volumes.[69] (*Angelus novus* was also the title of the second of Suhrkamp's volumes of Benjamin's selected writings, published in 1966.) At this event, Scholem gave a lecture on "Walter Benjamin and His Angel," studded with recollections of his own imbrication in Benjamin's relationship to the picture, which was then published in the volume

On the Actuality of Walter Benjamin: On the Occasion of the 80th Birthday of Walter Benjamin, edited by Unseld.[70]

After the Frankfurt celebration, Unseld handed the picture over to Scholem, who brought it back home with him to Jerusalem.[71] The picture had been hanging in the Frankfurt home of Theodor and Gretel Adorno. Its route from Paris, where it had joined Benjamin in exile, to the possession of the Adornos is not entirely clear. In "Walter Benjamin and His Angel," Scholem wrote that, in 1940, as German troops advanced, Benjamin fled the city after entrusting Georges Bataille with two suitcases to hide in the Bibliothèque nationale, containing the *Angelus* "cut . . . out of the frame and stuffed . . . into one of the suitcases" along with his papers.[72] But Rolf Tiedemann attests that the Adornos told him many times that in fact they received the *Angelus* in New York in 1941 along with the group of manuscripts that Benjamin instructed his sister Dora to send them.[73] In any case, I strongly suspect that Scholem's verb "cut" here should not be taken literally; while I have seen Klee works on paper damaged by the cutting of their cardboard supports, the *Angelus* does not appear to have suffered such an injury.[74]

One way or the other, the *Angelus* "made its way to Adorno in America and later in Frankfurt," when the Adornos settled there in 1949, as Scholem writes.[75] It hung in the Institute for Social Research and later in the Adornos' living room.[76] In 1969, not long after her husband's death, Gretel Adorno wrote to the Swiss dealer Eberhard W. Kornfeld for an estimate of the value of the *Angelus*, which, she wrote, she had in her Frankfurt home as a "loan" from Stefan Benjamin, "the son of the philosopher Dr. Walter Benjamin."[77] She informed Kornfeld that the work in question could be found reproduced in the critic Wilhelm Hausenstein's *Kairuan; or, A Story of the Painter Klee and of the Art of This Age* (1921) (fig. 1.3) and in a 1963 book by the Germanist Herman Meyer. (Meyer, incidentally, reproduces the picture from Hausenstein and in the context of a discussion of Rilke and modern art—there is no mention of Benjamin.[78]) But Benjamin had left the picture to Scholem in a will he made while contemplating suicide in 1932, which Scholem found in the German Central Archive in Potsdam; Benjamin's son, Stefan, however, contested the validity of the will.[79] When Stefan died in February 1972, Unseld played a key role in helping Scholem secure the picture, prevailing on Stefan's widow to recognize Scholem's claim and receiving the picture from Gretel Adorno.[80] So, after his lecture, Scholem brought the *Angelus* to his Jerusalem home, where it stayed until, after his own death in 1982, it was given to the Israel Museum.[81]

Scholem's essay "Walter Benjamin and His Angel" uses Benjamin's relationship to and writings about the *Angelus* to show *pars pro toto* the shortcomings of the understandings, or misunderstandings, of Benjamin's work that had taken hold as it became well known in the wake of the student movement in the Federal Republic, spread by Benjamin's "Marxist commentators among the New Left."[82] Scholem discusses the angel as a recurring motif in Benjamin's corpus, acquiring new traits and associations, ever more complexly interrelated, over the course of his friend's life, from playful correspondence of the 1920s to the Karl Kraus essay of 1931 to "On the Concept of History." Scholem especially emphasizes Benjamin's enigmatic, private, and previously unpublished "sketch about himself" titled "Agesilaus Santander"—written in two versions in exile in 1933, both linking Klee's picture with the "fiction that at [Benjamin's] birth his parents gave him . . . two additional and thoroughly peculiar names" that he might use as "a literary pseudonym without directly being recognized as a Jew": Agesilaus Santander, an anagram ("sealed as it were with a superfluous 'i'") of "Der Angelus Satanas" ("The Angel Satan").[83]

Scholem argues that Marxist interpreters err by neglecting both how Benjamin's writings, including those that seek to annex historical materialism, are, at their core, mystical and theological and how many conceal "personal, indeed most personal, experiences which by projection into the objects of his works disappeared or were put into code, so that the outsider could not recognize them."[84] At the outset of the essay, Scholem makes the first claim in a manner especially interesting in the present context, with particular reference to Benjamin's style of writing and its effects, pointing out in it the "gesture of the esoteric writer"—the latter defined as "the producer of authoritative sentences," that is, "sentences lending themselves to quotation and interpretation."[85] Daniel Weidner has argued that some of Benjamin's and also some of Scholem's writings might usefully be seen as "esoteric" in this special, rather poetological sense. Weidner aims to direct interpretation of Scholem's writings away from attempts to find in it indications of "esoteric" content in the sense of clues to "hidden things like theology, messianism, and other dark affairs."[86] Instead, he shows how some of Scholem's writings lend themselves to citation by their "poetic closure and overdetermination which seems to urge the reader to come back to them time and again, since what they express cannot be expressed in other words but only repeated verbatim."[87] The repertoire of the "esoteric writer" also includes, as Scholem discusses in Benjamin's case, a gesture of hiding, the withdrawal of contextualization.[88] Perhaps one might see—although Scholem does not—the *Angelus* itself as an esoteric image in this sense, as a small stack of motions of making citable and of hiding.

The *Angelus novus* enjoyed a brief public life shortly after Klee made it in the winter or spring of 1920, before the opening of the exhibition of his work at the Hans Goltz gallery in Munich in May or June of that year, an important show that Benjamin did not see.[89] The next year, the picture was reproduced in the first truly substantial book about Klee, Hausenstein's *Kairuan* (fig. 1.3), which it seems Benjamin did not read.[90]

Benjamin's interest in Klee can be traced back to the artist's breakthrough exhibition at the Sturm gallery in Berlin in 1917, and he had acquired his first work by the artist in July 1920, when his wife, Dora Sophie Benjamin (née Kellner), gave him *The Presentation of the Miracle* (1916) (fig. 1.10).[91] Mentioning the gift in a letter to Scholem, Benjamin wrote: "Are you familiar with Klee? I really love him and this is the most beautiful of all his paintings I have seen."[92]

In June 1921, Benjamin bought the *Angelus novus* from the Goltz gallery, arranging for his friend Ernst Bloch to bring Goltz one thousand marks for it.[93] (As it happens, Bloch at this time was working on the Reformation. Later that year, he published his book *Thomas Münzer as Theologian of Revolution* on the preacher, initially inspired by Luther but siding with the peasants and against Luther and the princes in the German Peasants' War of 1524–1525—a book Benjamin criticized in a letter to Scholem.[94]) Benjamin asked Scholem, who then lived in Munich, to hang on to the picture for him until his own living situation in Berlin firmed up; it was almost half a year later, in November, that Scholem sent the picture to his friend.[95] In Berlin, Klee's picture "hung in the study of his residence at Delbrückstrasse 23, over the sofa, and later in his last residence at Prinzregentenstrasse 66."[96]

Before Scholem sent the *Angelus* on to Benjamin, it hung in the Munich apartment that Scholem shared with Elsa Burchhardt (the couple would marry in 1923), in her room, "a fact to which Benjamin referred in several letters."[97] The *Angelus* was personified in the friends' correspondence—the angel first figures in Benjamin's writings in the fabric of playfully elaborate, in-jokey banter, often mock solemn, connecting the two couples. In fact, in this early correspondence, the *Angelus* is linked above all with Burchhardt, and allusions are made to "his" long stay in her room; Benjamin remarks, in the tone typical of much of this badinage, on the *Angelus*'s "connections to Miss Burchardt, which are notorious."[98] The *Angelus* can even take on her form. In a letter from both Benjamin and Burchhardt in Heidelberg to Scholem in Munich, Benjamin writes: "You will have taken note of the fact that the Angelus has taken flight. Don't be alarmed. He has landed here in the handsome form of Miss Burchardt . . . I have now taken the Angelus to the leading café here where, surrounded by entente diplomats, he slurps nectar and ambrosia that I have selected for him."[99]

Remarkable in the characterization of the *Angelus* throughout this earliest correspondence is the emphasis on, to borrow Benjamin's words in a 1922 letter to Scholem and Burchhardt, "what a good Jew he is."[100] In a June 1921 postcard from the Benjamins to Scholem—the earliest published bit of correspondence in which the *Angelus* is mentioned—Dora wrote that "A. N." signifies the "newly created protector of the *kabbalah*."[101] Hebrew words tend to crop up around him; indeed, Benjamin calls him the "liege lord" of the "fertile fields of Hebrew."[102] The playful letters drew on the friends' conversations on "Jewish

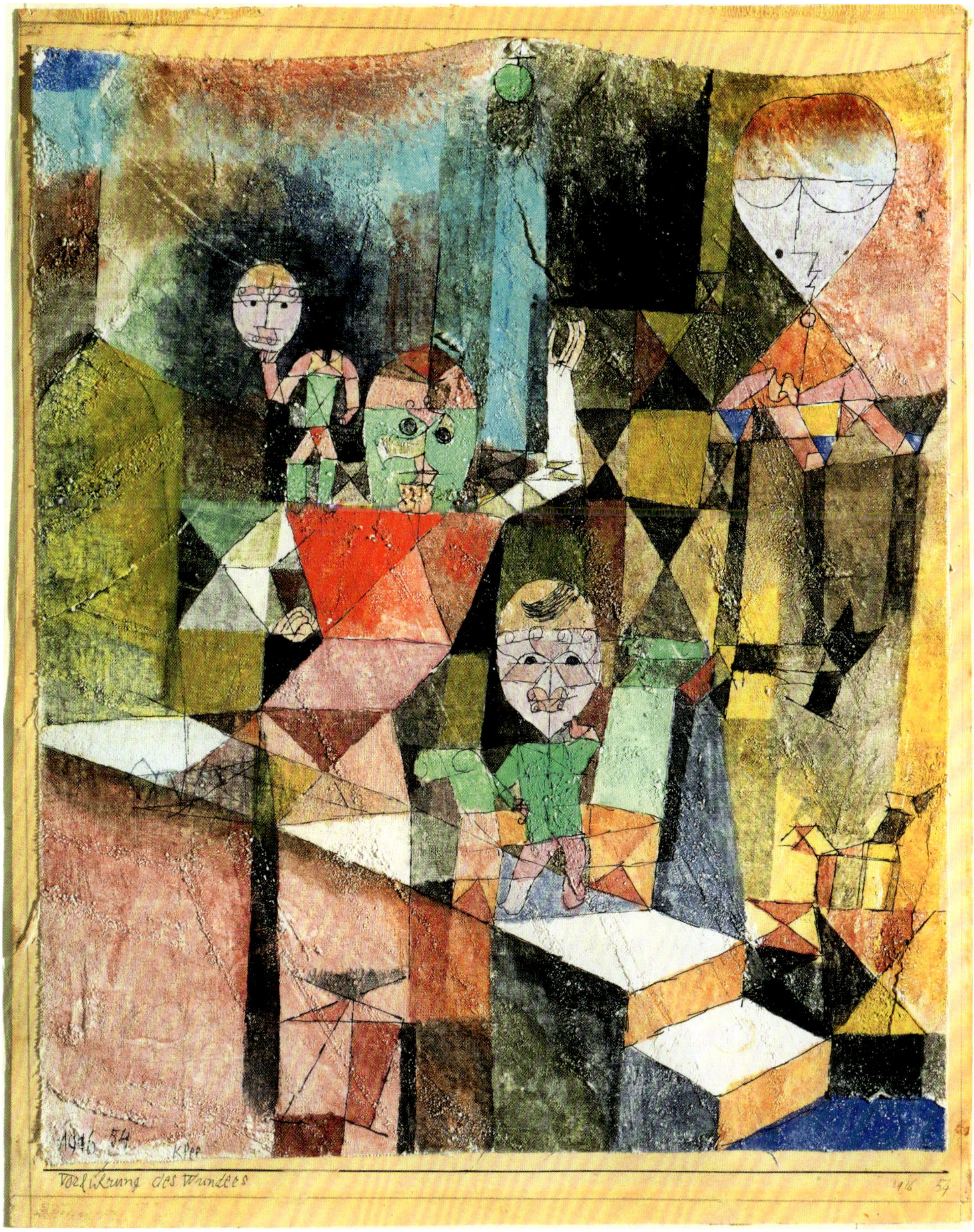

FIGURE 1.10 Paul Klee, *Presentation of the Miracle* (*Vorführung des Wunders*), 1916, 54. Gouache, pen, and ink on plastered fabric, mounted on board, 29.2 × 23.6 cm. The Museum of Modern Art, New York. Gift of Allan Roos, MD, and B. Mathieu Roos. Digital Image © The Museum of Modern Art, New York / Licensed by SCALA / Art Resource, NY.

angelology, especially of the talmudic and kabbalistic kind," which, as Scholem explains, derived from his own work at that time on a critique of Meir Wiener's book *Lyric Poetry of the Kabbalah*, a review that included "a detailed account of the hymns of the angels in the representations of the Jewish mystics."[103]

As Sander Gilman explains, in the early twentieth century, German-speaking Jews began to identify "the assimilated or acculturated Jew" as "the prototypical 'bad' Jew," in contrast to "a new model for the 'good' Jew in those very qualities despised by the Enlightenment" (usually "the Eastern Jew," who became a figure of authenticity and of intact tradition), inverting an earlier valuation.[104] The way in which the *Angelus* figures as a "good Jew" in this early correspondence should be understood in relation to the larger project, illuminatingly analyzed by Michael Brenner, undertaken by many Jews in Weimar Germany to gain, or to regain, knowledge of Hebrew and traditional Jewish texts, knowledge seen as "gradually lost during the nineteenth century," a project at once "restorative" and "innovative, because both the means of transmission and the conditions of reception were far removed from the world of premodern Jewry."[105] The four correspondents—all born into bourgeois German-speaking Jewish households, households representing a wide variety of political affiliations (for instance, Kellner's father was a prominent Zionist, while Scholem's was a member of the Central Association of German Citizens of the Jewish Faith)—might be located variously in relation to this larger project.[106] As Brenner notes, Scholem can easily be seen as "emblematic" of such a "search for a lost Judaism"—he was living in Munich at the time because he was writing a translation and critical edition of the *Sefer ha-Bahir*, an early kabbalistic source, as his doctoral dissertation at the University of Munich.[107] Benjamin, in contrast, had recently completed his dissertation on German Romanticism and never learned more than a smattering of Hebrew.[108] The association of the Angelus with Burchhardt in particular may not be as irrelevant as it may seem in this context: she was the only one of the four to have grown up in the neo-Orthodox minority, which continued to use Hebrew for prayer (at this time, she sometimes wrote to Scholem in German sprinkled with Hebrew, as in, for instance, the letter she and Benjamin wrote him from Heidelberg).[109]

The *Angelus novus*, with its Latin caption, does not seem to especially invite its identification as in some sense "Jewish." Other pictures of Klee's, though, might. The six-pointed star—which became favored in the nineteenth century among German Jews as a readily legible sign of Jewish identity and was adopted as such by the Zionists in Basel in 1897—appears in many of Klee's pictures, including Benjamin's other Klee, Kellner's gift, *Presentation of the Miracle* (fig. 1.10), in which one with black points and a yellow center stretches between the two of the figures.[110] Klee's 1918 watercolor titled *Angelus descendens* (fig. 1.11), whose titular angel is roughly similar to that of the *Angelus*

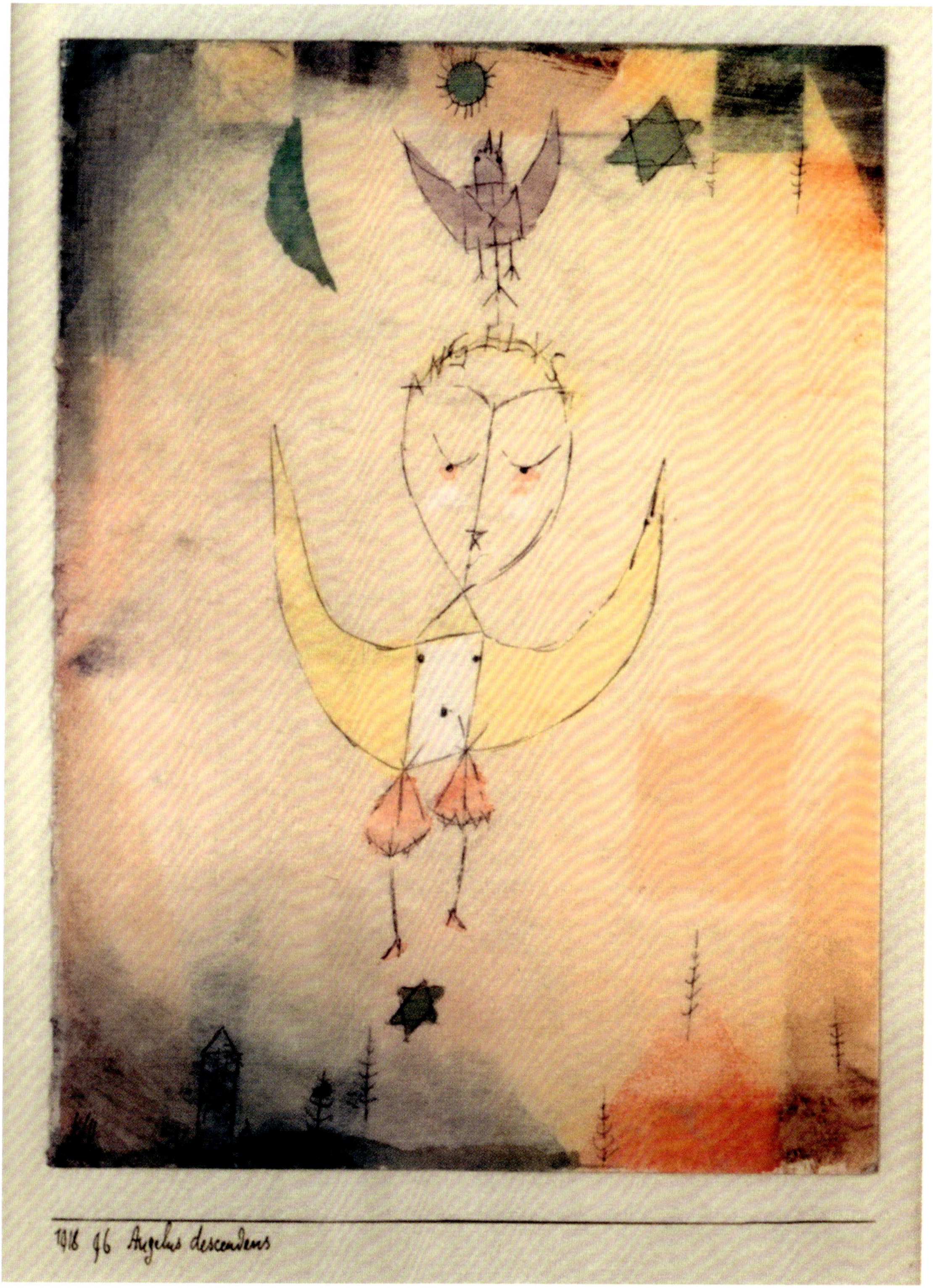

FIGURE 1.11 Paul Klee, *Angelus descendens*, 1918, 96. Pen and watercolor on paper on cardboard, 15.3 × 10.2 cm. Private collection, Great Britain.

novus in shape and pose, features two, and they are much more obvious than that of *Presentation of the Miracle*, which, in contrast, is enmeshed in figure-ground paradoxes.[111] Klee's frequent use of the sign likely played into the fact that he was called "Paul Zion Klee" in a newspaper article opposing his proposed appointment to the faculty of the Stuttgart Academy in 1919, which in fact failed.[112]

There was another artist who, like Klee, was associated with the Expressionism of the Sturm gallery in Berlin in the 1910s, where Benjamin likely first saw Klee's work, and used the Magen David liberally: the poet and artist Else Lasker-Schüler often deployed it in her drawings and illustrations as a mark of Jewish identity.[113] In Klee's art of this time, six-pointed stars are a prominent member of a repertory of small, schematic signs—along with crosses, crescents, hearts, suns, eyes, birds—a set of pseudo-hieroglyphics that he used, as I've argued, as a playful materialization of an art-critical hobgoblin, an art that approaches the condition of hieroglyphic writing, as discussed, for instance, in Baudelaire's "Philosophical Art" (1859).[114] Klee seems to have been fascinated with these simple arrangements of lines that are also immediately readable as referring to something other than themselves: this was part of his exploration of the relations between visibility and legibility.

Perhaps Klee's use of the Magen David has little to do with Benjamin's use of the *Angelus* as a figure of the "good Jew"; Benjamin seems never to have identified *Presentation of the Miracle* as somehow "Jewish."[115] In any case, the Angelus as a character in Benjamin's correspondence is very choosy in the field of contemporary German-Jewish culture. While he is very pleased with Scholem's German translation of one of S. Y. Agnon's Hebrew stories, Benjamin writes of him trying to decline, with "unattainable gestural symbolism," an issue of the journal *Der Jude* (*The Jew*); both Benjamin and Scholem often voiced scathing criticisms of Martin Buber and his monthly.[116] The poem that Benjamin wrote to Scholem as, it seems, a reminder to mail him the picture ("Scholem does not send the Angelus / To the place where he must go") ends with this rhyming couplet on the Angelus: "He is bedded on stalks of roses (*Rosenzweigen*) / But he'd rather remain hovering," an obvious punning reference to Franz Rosenzweig, about whose *Star of Redemption* Benjamin makes some cautious comments in the same letter.[117]

Less than two months after the first mention of the Angelus in the correspondence, Benjamin accepted a publisher's offer of the editorship of a new journal, which, Benjamin decided, would be called *Angelus novus*.[118] The Angelus as a kind of fictional character then began to play a role in Benjamin's only partially successful attempts to secure Scholem's collaboration in this endeavor (the latter's lack of enthusiasm strained their friendship).[119] Benjamin's 1922 announcement for the journal does not explain the source of the title, but it ends with a paragraph that glosses it as pointing to the journal's hoped-for ephemerality and contemporaneity (*Aktualität*) as follows: "According to a legend in the Talmud, the angels—who are born anew every instant in countless numbers—are created in order to perish and to vanish into the void, once they have sung their hymn in the presence of God."[120]

The journal never came to fruition, but Benjamin cited the picture that hung over his sofa in the years to come, in the "Karl Kraus" essay (1931), the two versions of "Agesilaus Santander" (1933), and "On the Concept of History" (1940). In the early 1930s, Benjamin's descriptions of it stressed its inhuman quality, which at times he speaks of in terms of Jewish mysticism: "The Kabbalah relates that, at every moment, God creates a whole host of new angels, whose only task before they return to the void is to appear before His throne for a moment and sing His praises. Mine had been interrupted in the process; his features had nothing human about them."[121] But elsewhere, Benjamin speaks of Klee's figures in general as inhuman in technological rather than mystical terms: "For just like any good car, whose every part, even the bodywork, obeys the needs above all of the engine, Klee's figures too seem to have been designed on the drawing board, and even in their general expression they obey the laws of their interior. Their interior, rather than their inwardness; and this is what makes them barbaric."[122] When Benjamin fled to Paris after the Nazi seizure of power, he left it behind but had it brought to him in the mid-1930s.[123] Scholem reports that, when he visited his friend in Paris early in 1938, "it was again hanging in his large room at 10 Rue Dombasle."[124]

The work's itinerary from Paris to New York to Frankfurt am Main to Scholem's Jerusalem home to the Israel Museum has already been discussed. While it is no longer secluded in a private residence or office, it nevertheless makes itself scarce; this work on paper is light sensitive and the Israel Museum is rightly protective of it. To spare the original, the museum has a photographic facsimile of the *Angelus* that it loans to exhibitions. The infrequency with which the work itself travels, combined with the peculiar nature of its fame, has led to some curious phenomena. For instance, the 2008 exhibition curated by Armin Kerber and Juri Steiner at the Zentrum Paul Klee in Bern made a spectacle of the very measures by which the museum sought to protect the picture: as the original was going to be on display for only five days, the museum stayed open around the clock for that short period, and, as light levels had to be carefully controlled, the *Angelus* was displayed in a dark room—surrounded by images of violence and terror from the First World War through 9/11, or, in Kerber's words, "more than 150 films, collages, pictures, photo series, installations, and sculptures as a cabinet of catastrophes of the twentieth century," envisioning Benjamin's ninth thesis as a walk-in mise-en-scène.[125] Such an exhibition hardly encourages viewers to look at the picture; instead it might be seen as exemplifying how the famous picture has been overlooked.

Quaytman's first email to me, early in 2015, included a good photograph of the lower left corner of the *Angelus*, displaying the fine engraved lines, the monogram, the three-quarters visible date, and the folds of the dark robe. Over Skype the next day, I said something despairing, along the lines of "But it could be anything!" No, countered Quaytman: the plain dark robes led her to suspect it was a portrait of a religious figure.[126] As she said, despite its sixteenth-century date, it did not look like an Old Master print; as she later wrote, she had the "impression that it was not an important or rare engraving but rather mass-produced. The way the lines were engraved gave that away . . . [they] seemed drawn mechanically with a ruler. It is also rare to see the background treated as a flat plane in 16th-century prints."[127] For the same reasons, a photomechanical reproduction of an Old Master print, which would render its linework faithfully, seemed unlikely. Moreover, a sixteenth-century print, unless badly damaged, would likely be too valuable a thing for a thrifty artist to interleave in one of his works.

At that time, my twins were newborns and I couldn't do legwork. Anything I could think to do at home on my laptop, I did. I emailed colleagues and combed the literature I could get. As I wrote in a short catalog essay for Quaytman's *Chapter 29*, the working hypothesis was that it was "a 19th- or early 20th-century reproductive print of a 16th-century painting (possibly by Lucas Cranach the elder)."[128] I finished the essay before her discovery, although it was published afterward; we printed it unchanged as a document of process, as the Tel Aviv exhibition itself, which opened two weeks before her discovery, grappled "with the engraving as an unanswered question."[129] The hypothesis was based on the appearance of the thing: the logical explanation for the apparent discrepancy between the 1520-something date on the probably much more recent print was that it was a reproductive print. Dark, flat backgrounds are customary in painted Northern Renaissance portraits (van Eyck, Cranach, Holbein) but, as Quaytman said, less frequent in prints of that time. Those engravings of the period that do have such a background, like Dürer's *Sudarium Held by Two Angels* (1513) or Cranach's portrait of Martin Luther with a doctor's cap (1521), look quite different; the hatching, as Quaytman said, does not have the mechanical uniformity of the one that Klee used. It seemed probable, then, that this was a later reproductive print after a sixteenth-century painting, probably a fairly well-known one. While monogram dictionaries turned up plenty of artists with a monogram that more or less matched the engraving's (Luca Ciamberlano, Lodovico Cardi, Leonardo Corona, Conrad Lauwers, Caspar Luyken), only Lucas Cranach worked with what certainly looked like a 1520-something date.

I told two scholars of Northern Renaissance art, Peter Parshall and Jennifer Nelson, about the mystery; intrigued, they generously helped, looking through their books, telling me where else I should look and whom I should contact. It seemed I was barking up the right tree; when I forwarded Quaytman's photographs to Parshall, he wrote back, "It looks like an engraved reproductive print with a Cranach the Elder signature and a date (1521/27/29) showing some draped figure, perhaps a standing religious figure or a portrait."[130] Both felt that finding a conclusive match between a particular Cranach painting and the engraving would be difficult at best, because of the nature of the production of the Cranach workshop and its reception. "As you have probably already noticed, there are approximately a gazillion Cranach copies and variants floating around," wrote Nelson.[131] "It is a needle in a haystack given the history of loose attributions etc.," wrote Parshall.[132]

My role in the history of Quaytman's discovery is peripheral. I wasn't there when she found either her question or her answer; I could and did assure her that no one knew the answer or had even asked the question in print. (In conversations since then, I've spoken with two art historians who did notice the engraving, and wondered, but, not seeing any promising way of pursuing the question, very reasonably dropped it.) What I did was egg her on. As she wrote: "After hanging the show in Tel Aviv I returned to my studio. Annie Bourneuf and I had continued our email correspondence, both of us still feeling the urge to figure this problem out. We would send websites back and forth and exchange ideas about how to keep looking."[133]

Quaytman is not the first in recent decades to claim the discovery of some kind of hidden image in the *Angelus novus*. For instance, in connection with Benjamin's ninth thesis, Beatrice Hanssen has written that "behind the Klee picture hides another . . . a picture, moreover, that could well be regarded to be the Renaissance counterpart or mirror-image to Klee's modernist watercolor, namely Dürer's engraving *Melencolia I* from the year 1514" (fig. 1.12).[134] Here the preposition "behind" is, of course, figurative: Hanssen is speaking about Benjamin's writing and not about the actual artifact Klee made. Nevertheless, it is striking to consider the connections that can be drawn between Quaytman's and Hanssen's hidden engravings that bear early sixteenth-century dates, although Dürer's enigmatic *Meisterstich* of a winged being personifying melancholy would be valued infinitely higher than the pedestrian reproductive Luther portrait. The Cranach workshop produced at least four direct ripostes to *Melencolia I*. It is easy to imagine Benjamin wondering about his own *Angelus* as he read about Dürer's rebus-like print in the studies by Giehlow, Warburg, and Panofsky and Saxl that he would cite in his study of the German Baroque *Trauerspiel*, or play of mourning.[135]

The art historian Johann Konrad Eberlein's claim is of a different nature. In 2006, Eberlein published a short book arguing that Klee's drawn angel refers

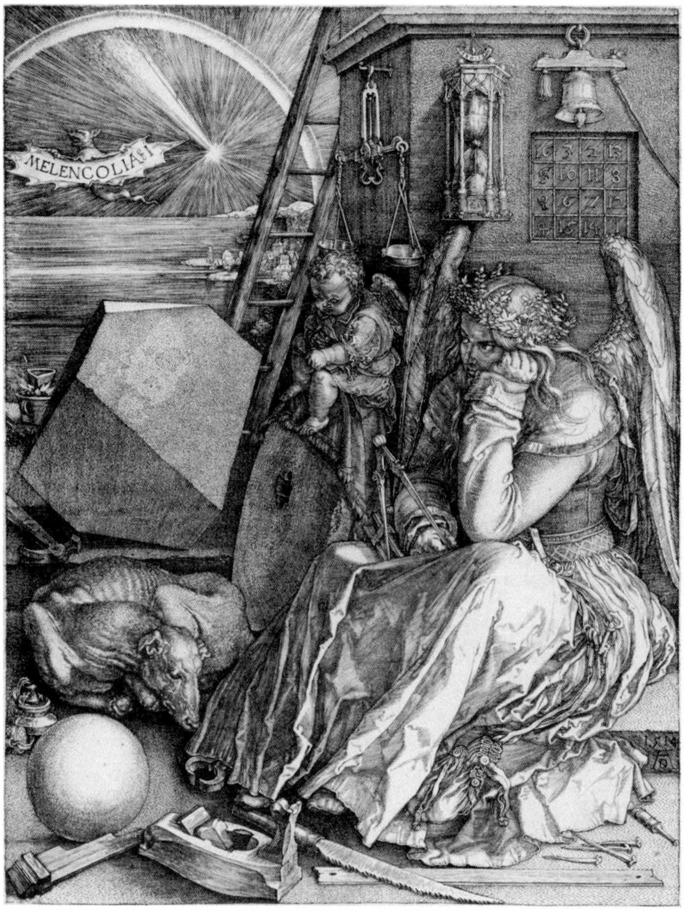

FIGURE 1.12 Albrecht Dürer, *Melencolia I*, 1514. Engraving on laid paper, image: 23.8 × 18.4 cm. Brooklyn Museum, Gift of Mrs. Horace O. Havemeyer, 54.35.8. (Photo: 54.35.8_PS9.jpg).

specifically to Adolf Hitler's appearance and characteristic dress—Eberlein singles out the cinched waist of the angel's body and that of the trench coat habitually worn by Hitler—and that the *Angelus novus* should be seen as Klee's critical and foresighted response to the budding demagogue, aiming "to clarify with irony, and thereby repudiate, national-conservative messianic claims."[136] Some of Klee's pictures of the period do caricature contemporary "types" (take *Portrait of an Expressionist* [1922, 240] or *Christian Sectarian* [1920, 4]), and, less often, specific persons—there is a little group of works of persiflage directed at the Kaiser Wilhelm II, complete with *Pickelhaube*, such as *The Ranting Kaiser Wilhelm* (1920, 206) and *The Great Kaiser Armed for Battle* (1921, 131).[137] However, the titles of all of these pictures, which Klee visibly inscribed on them, play a crucial role in specifying their targets. And although both Klee and Hitler lived in Munich in early 1920, nothing suggests that Klee was the informed observer of the city's far-right milieu that he would have had to be to caricature Hitler at that point.[138] Eberlein is right to connect the *Angelus novus* with the interplay of religion and politics in counterrevolutionary Munich, as I argue in the next chapter, but no such connection can be made by finding a reference to Hitler's personal appearance in Klee's drawn angel.

While Eberlein describes the *Angelus novus*'s interleaved engraving only as "a dark brown ground," perhaps the picture's presentation of itself as a picture puzzle is in some sense at work in his curious interpretation.[139] At times, Benjamin and Scholem referred to the picture as appearing to withhold something. Soon after the *Angelus* arrived in Benjamin's Berlin apartment, Benjamin reported to Scholem that "just as before, he disdains to whisper suggestions—like the oracle."[140] It seems that the last stanza of Scholem's 1921 birthday poem for Benjamin alludes to the picture's air of keeping back some secret to riddle out by explicitly denying the latter's substance: "I am an unsymbolic thing / and signify what I am / you turn the magic ring in vain / for I have no meaning."[141]

Quaytman titled her 2015 Tel Aviv show *Chapter 29: Haqaq*, explaining, with reference to the "linguistic-mystical cosmogony" of the *Sefer Yeẓirah*, that the "word means 'engrave,' 'law,' or 'rule' in Hebrew and was the method God used to hew 32 paths to creation (22 letters + 10 numbers = 32)" and was also linked to her "more immediate interest, the ancient Judaic prohibition against the graven image."[142] As mentioned earlier, she has said that part of the work that the bookish term "chapter" does for her art is to counteract the tendency to take a painting as a self-sufficient unit, giving it instead something closer to the status of "an engraving that has been torn from a book."[143] But above all, she seeks to do this by means of her sequencing and spacing of the paintings in relation to one another and their surroundings.

In Tel Aviv, she had the walls of the gallery reconfigured to make two right angles, a smaller one nesting within a larger one, and the arrangement of the paintings was often striking: one was hung across the inner corner of the smaller right angle—some rest on shelves, sometimes one leans on another, partially covering the one behind it—two abut an outer corner, such that a frontal view of one reveals the plywood thickness of the other.[144] Silkscreened photographs populating the panels included images of the *Angelus* in various forms, some derived from the scientific probing of the work that Quaytman initiated, some digitally manipulated. In one, Klee's linear creature has vanished while the engraved edge has widened: a luminous void is surrounded by an emphatic array of margins and their markings, such as dates and authorial marks (fig. 1.13).

At the end of her essay on *Chapter 29*, Quaytman turns the excised caption on the Luther portrait toward a consideration of her chosen medium: "Luther takes the image's alibi. . . . Like an Ad Reinhardt cartoon, I imagine a painting

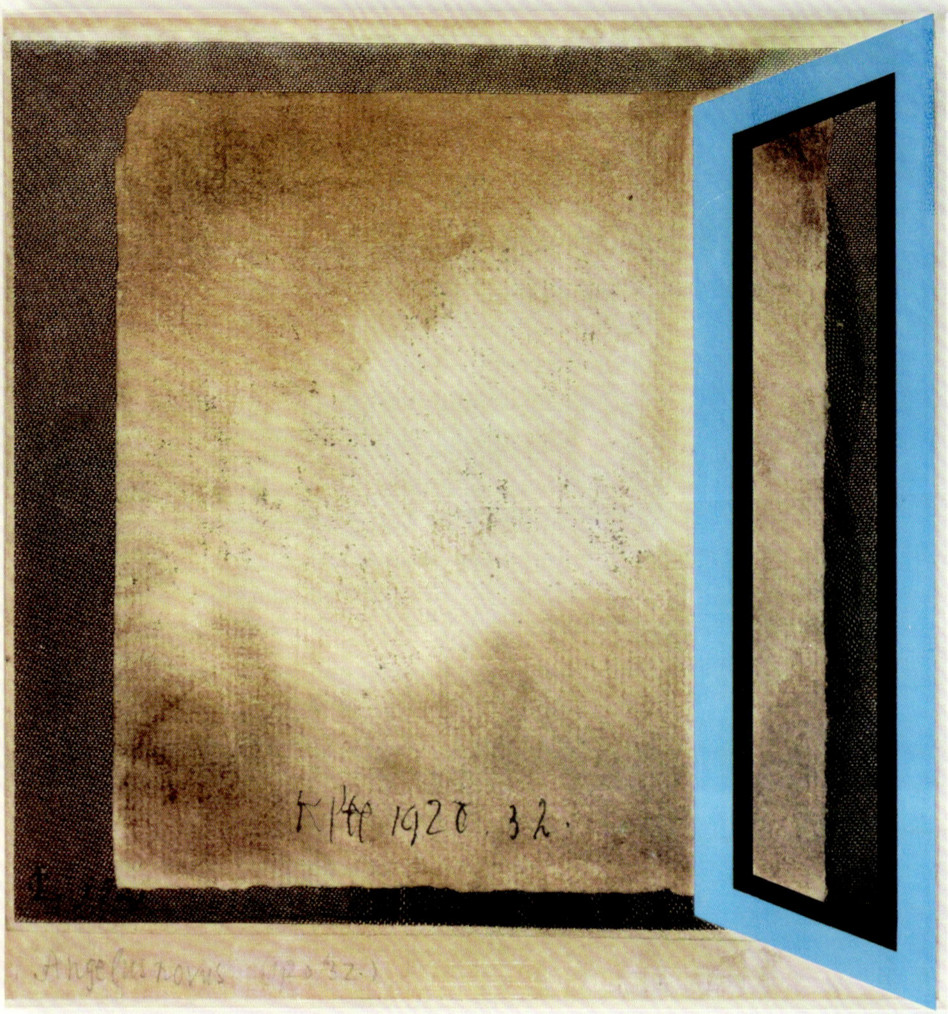

FIGURE 1.13 R. H. Quaytman, *חקק, Chapter 29*, 2015. Silkscreen ink and gesso on wood, 62.9 × 62.9 × 1.9 cm. Courtesy the artist and Miguel Abreu Gallery, New York, and Gladstone Gallery, New York and Brussels. Photo: Christian Erroi.

saying: 'Here I stand. I can do no other.' But I don't accept that plea bargain because the image, like Luther, is not innocent. It does many things, most of which are unintended. . . . Painting is a form that has inherited a hope of escaping, paradoxically, my own innocence. These images are never innocent and this is why I chose painting."[145] She proposes that this chapter suggests a new reading of the past few chapters of her own work, taking shape as "an artist's art history" that hinges on aniconism: "I realize my focus was turning more clearly to the injunction against graven images. . . . The paintings do their job best when they sacrifice the representations they also support."[146]

Michael Baxandall discusses a quality of description in modern art history and criticism that he calls "ostensivity": how writers use words "in tandem with the object, the instance," assuming the objects they discuss to be available to their readers, "really, or in reproduction, or in memory," and therefore not aiming to tell the reader what it looks like but pointing out what is interesting to notice about it.[147] Since the Renaissance, writes Baxandall, there has been "an accelerating shift from discourse designed to work with the object unavailable, to discourse assuming at least a reproduced presence of the object"—while much of Vasari's writing exemplifies the former, around 1800 Johann Dominico Fiorillo added footnotes "specifying the makers of the best engravings after the pictures he is discussing," and twentieth-century writers habitually assume "the presence or availability of the object" at least by means of photographic halftones.[148]

Perhaps only two of the sentences that Benjamin wrote with reference to the *Angelus novus* even seem to be in this ostensive mode—the brief description of the picture in "On the Concept of History" ("It shows an angel who seems about to move away from something he stares at. His eyes are wide, his mouth is open, his wings are spread"). In contrast, take Benjamin's reference to his own watercolor in a piece of writing that circulated broadly, his 1931 article on Karl Kraus in the *Frankfurter Zeitung*, a well-regarded liberal newspaper: "One must have . . . seen Klee's *New Angel* (who preferred to free men by taking from them, rather than make them happy by giving to them) to understand a humanity that proves itself by destruction."[149] In Benjamin's notes for the essay, Benjamin does refer to a visible feature of the *Angelus* that goes some way toward explaining why one might see it as taking rather than giving—"the clawed feet [*Krallenfüße*] of Klee's Angelus novus" might indeed suggest how a raptor seizes.[150] But in the final version, this gesture of pointing has vanished, and the title, inscribed under the reproduction of the watercolor in Hausenstein's 1921 book (which Benjamin might or might not have known), has been altered. Benjamin knew perfectly well that only a handful of his readers would likely remember the picture he mentions, exhibited once ten years earlier, the picture "one must have . . . seen . . . to understand a humanity that proves itself by destruction"—his friends. In "The Work of Art in the Age of Its Technological Reproducibility," Benjamin characterizes the viewing of paintings in "the churches and monasteries of the Middle Ages, and at the princely courts up to about the end of the eighteenth century," as taking place in a "manifoldly graduated and hierarchically mediated way."[151] Something similar might be said of Benjamin's handling of the unassuming *Angelus*.

Indeed, in a 1931 letter to Scholem, Benjamin mocks himself roughly along these lines in a report on the décor of his Berlin apartment: "Not everything is up yet, but to my horror I already have to answer for the fact that only saints' pictures (*Heiligenbilder*) are hanging on the walls of my Communist cell." Benjamin enumerates them: various objects of Christian art ("the old three-headed Christ . . . a reproduction of a Byzantine ivory relief; a trick picture—three different representations of a saint depending on the perspective from which you view it—from the Bavarian forest; a Sebastian") and the two Klees, the *Angelus novus* and *Presentation of the Miracle*.[152] Benjamin counts his Klees among his *Heiligenbilder*—saints' pictures, holy pictures, devotional images or *Andachtsbilder*, a term used primarily for Christian representations of sacred figures, from Byzantine icons to the pocket-sized chromolithographs of popular Catholicism. One might well see Benjamin's letter as elaborating on the parodying of holy pictures in both of his Klees, starting with their titles' gestures toward the sacred (an angel, a miracle). Brigid Doherty has suggested that *Presentation of the Miracle* can be seen as an "ironic reconfiguration" of Raphael's Sistine *Madonna*, reworking the celebrated painting's "revelation of the incarnation as a carnival side show."[153] Benjamin distinguishes the *Angelus* from the rest of the pictures as the "only messenger of the Kabbalah": it is, as it were, oddly enough a Jewish *Heiligenbild* outnumbered by its Christian confreres.

The humor in Benjamin's odd term *Kommunistenzelle* is perhaps missed if translated as "Communist cell."[154] Instead, it is a communist's cell or cella, evoking the rather absurd idea of a closed-off chamber for communist ritual or contemplation, as in a monastic cell, or the cella or sanctuary of a temple in which images are kept.[155] In this letter, Benjamin makes fun of himself as a character a bit like Leo Naphta in Thomas Mann's *Magic Mountain*, a kind of communist pseudo-priest with an apartment stocked with devotional images.[156]

Some formulations in his later work on the artwork essay echo Benjamin's self-mockery in this letter. In the artwork essay, Benjamin uses the Latin form of the word "cell": "Cult value as such tends today, it would seem, to keep the artwork out of sight: certain statues of gods are accessible only to the priest in the cella."[157] The context here is Benjamin's assertion, in the course of his argument, that "technological reproducibility emancipates the work of art from its parasitic subservience to ritual," that the history of art "might be seen as the working out of a tension between two polarities within the artwork itself"—its "cult value and its exhibition value."[158] The former, Benjamin explains, is linked to ritual and magic and tends to keep the image hidden ("what matters is that the spirits see it"), the latter to public presentation, the possibilities of which technological reproduction so extended.[159] In the third version of the artwork essay, Benjamin adduces the Sistine *Madonna* as exemplifying an "oscillation" between a mode of reception emphasizing "cult value" and another emphasizing "exhibition value"; Doherty has suggested that Klee's *Presentation of the Miracle*, in its parody of Raphael's picture, might be seen as both "an instantiation and a travesty of something like an oscillation between cult value and exhibition value" and "an invitation to speculate about that oscillation."[160] It is certainly tempting to see the *Angelus*—not only as Klee made it, or as Benjamin may have seen it, but also in its career through the short twentieth century as we can trace it now—as also instantiating, travestying, and certainly as inviting speculation about such an oscillation.

Benjamin's usually nonostensive—or, better, anti-ostensive—manner of writing about the *Angelus* has encouraged some commentators to suppose that he was a poor observer or perhaps had little opportunity to look at it.[161] What he writes about the picture often seems to have precious little to do with its appearance; the gap between the picture and the words of commentary is very wide. But this gap might be seen as opening up not only between Klee's object and Benjamin's writing but also within Klee's object.

Consider the title *Angelus novus*, inscribed by Klee on his cardboard mount, along with the date and the catalog number (32—part of Klee's own system for ordering his work, corresponding to the sequence of a picture's entrance into the catalog he used to track his production). The Ingres paper bears a linear figure with the enormous head and shrunken body of a caricature, crooked teeth, birdlike feet, and an ambiguous pair of raised winglike arms or armlike wings (rather than the separate pairs of arms and wings usual in depictions of angels). There are no obviously angelic attributes (e.g., haloed head, trumpet). It is not so much that we have first a picture of an angel that is then, as it were secondarily, titled "Angel," but rather that the visible title and the curious linear figure together make this figure legible as an angel.[162] In Klee's *Angelus descendens* (1918) (fig. 1.11), the inseparability of picture and writing is even more obvious and programmatic—this being, likewise sporting a single pair of arms-*cum*-wings, is not only labeled by the title on the mount at lower left, but the very contour of its head is inscribed "ANGELVS." The interplay of writing and drawing was a central concern of Klee's.[163]

Although Benjamin never says so explicitly, perhaps this is one of the reasons he so valued Klee's art.[164] In this period of his work, Klee typically mounted each of his watercolors on a piece of cardboard inscribed with a suggestive title that often relates to the image rather obliquely, serving as a starting point for speculative interpretation (consider *Presentation of the Miracle*).[165] The *Angelus novus* extends an invitation to textualizing speculation that one might say Benjamin accepted. Klee's picture cannot be said to invite Benjamin's particular rewritings of the image, but it does invite this kind of activity on the viewer's part. In its very veering away from the picture, Benjamin's writing around it might on another level be seen as responsive to it.

In the weeks after her exhibition opened, Quaytman pressed the Israel Museum to continue the investigation. She had some leverage, for, as she wrote apropos of the *Angelus*'s trip to Rome, she had "agreed to donate a painting to the Israel Museum" to compensate for the expense of pursuing the mystery.[166] But the museum staff felt that the possibilities for looking under the watercolor paper without damaging the object were exhausted. Back stateside, we corresponded about how to go on. I followed some hunches that did not pan out, looking at nineteenth-century print catalogs and magazines reviewing reproductive prints.

One day, Quaytman sent me a web page displaying images of tinted engravings from Carlo Lasinio's *Raccolta di 324 ritratti di artisti eccellenti* from the 1790s; this engraver's initials could work with the monogram, and the *ritratti* featured many isolated, dark-robed figures against flat, dark backgrounds. I objected because of the date. She appended to an email a series of remarkable images she found browsing through the engravings accessible through the site on which she had found Lasinio's, the regional government of Lombardy's searchable cultural heritage portal consolidating digitized holdings of prints from archives, libraries, and museums: a handless, footless baby riding a centaur—a horse-drawn wagon plummeting from the sky as the nymphs it is about to fall on gesture in alarm—a muscular man who appeared to be gathering asteroids in flaming urns—a study sheet of gesturing arms.

When I checked my email late the next day, I found a series of emails from Quaytman written within half an hour of each other. She had copied me on an email to James Snyder, director of the Israel Museum, urging the museum to continue investigating, perhaps by analyzing the paper. "I'm sure it's something like this," she wrote, and, as she says in her essay, she dropped in an image from the same Lombardy cultural heritage portal, one that "seemed to have similar dimensions and the correct type of robes," as plenty of engravings do, this one from a large collection of engravings held by the Biblioteca Morcelli-Pinacoteco Repossi, in Chiari, a small town not far from Brescia.

Another email contained the same image again and a URL linking to the photograph and basic information about the engraving (http://www.lombardiabeniculturali.it/stampe/schede/3y010-00352/?view=ricerca&offset=1132) and the subject line "could it be? Luther." The other, with "the subject line: '!!!!!!!!,'" contained the same image and URL, plus a superimposition of the same image and the *Angelus*.[167] As I later read in her catalog essay, she thought: "'Just for the hell of it, let's see what happens when I overlay it in Photoshop with a high res image of the *Angelus*.' And boom!!! It slid right on like Cinderella's slipper."[168] Although the JPEG on the website was small, it was clear that it was an exact match.

The next day she announced her discovery in an email to almost twenty people involved with the inquiry. In Munich in 1920, Klee had one impression from Friedrich Müller's 1838 plate: others now rest in boxes in collections not only in Chiari but also in Vienna, Massachusetts, Rhode Island, and no doubt elsewhere. According to the Lombardia Beni Culturali website, the engraving Quaytman found was left to the Biblioteca Morcelli upon the 1888 death of Ferdinando Cavalli, landowner and senator active in the Milan-based Society for the Encouragement of the Industrial Arts.

Certainly, it is testimony to Quaytman's sheer tenacity and hard work—sustained in part, it seems, by the pleasure she took in the haystack itself—that she, against all odds, was able to answer the question she had posed. And obviously, thanks are due to the efforts of the Biblioteca Morcelli-Pinacoteco Repossi (and of so many other collections, large and small) to digitize their holdings. But it should be noted that overlay is one of the basic moves of Quaytman's art. In this case, she was reenacting in Photoshop what Klee did with paper in 1920.

Now she made a few paintings in which the full Luther engraving (not only the visible border, which already figured prominently in the Tel Aviv pictures) became a further element to manipulate, often in conjunction with the image of the *Angelus*. These were exhibited at the Miguel Abreu Gallery in New York in October 2015 alongside some of the Tel Aviv pictures. A couple of them play with the proximity of the head of the engraved figure and that of Klee's angel, something one suspects looking at the *Angelus* itself. In one, there is a new composite figure, with the reformer's robes and the angel's scroll-like coif and all four of their eyeballs, almost aligned with each other, overlaid with the thick black stripes of the cover of Benjamin's *Trauerspiel* book, as first published by Rowohlt in 1928 (fig. 1.14). In a couple, the margins of the Luther portrait print, snipped off almost entirely in the *Angelus*, come into play, with Luther's words: "Here I stand, I can do no other, God help me! Amen" (fig. 1.15).

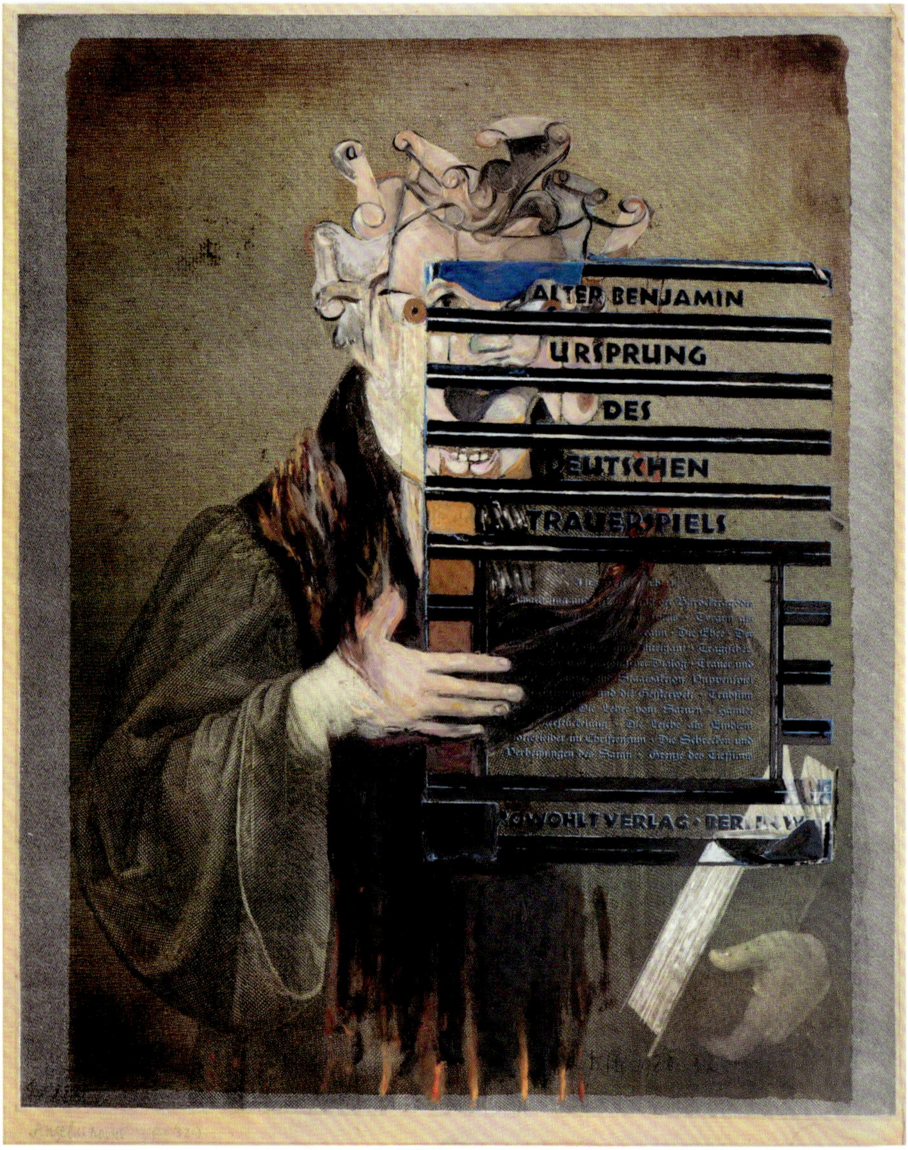

FIGURE 1.14 R. H. Quaytman, *חקק, Chapter 29*, 2015. Oil, silkscreen ink, and gesso on wood, 94.1 × 94.1 × 3.2 cm. Courtesy the artist and Miguel Abreu Gallery, New York, and Gladstone Gallery, New York and Brussels. Photo: Christian Erroi.

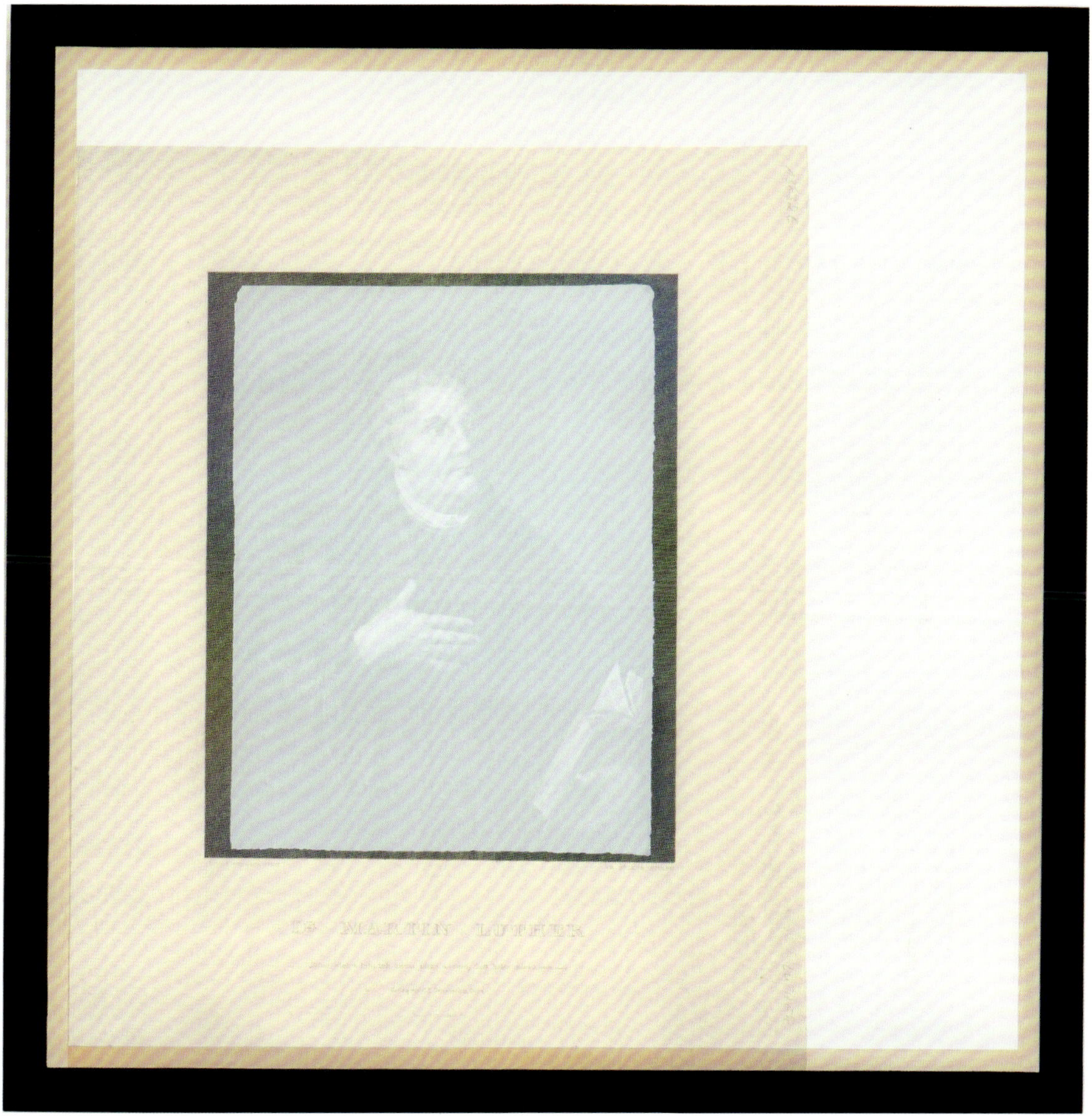

FIGURE 1.15 R. H. Quaytman, *חקקק, Chapter 29*, 2015. Silkscreen ink and gesso on wood, 62.9 × 62.9 × 1.9 cm. Courtesy the artist and Miguel Abreu Gallery, New York, and Gladstone Gallery, New York and Brussels. Photo: Christian Erroi.

CHAPTER 2

1920

What difference might this long hidden face, this portrait of Martin Luther, make for the interpretation of Klee's *Angelus novus*, the picture within which it is sandwiched? This is the question this chapter tackles by contextualizing its layers, showing how and suggesting why Klee's compound work sets up ramifying comparisons and contrasts between the drawn angel and the engraved reformer. While Benjamin's dealings with the *Angelus* are the subject of the next chapter, here I set them aside to keep the focus squarely on the picture Klee put together in 1920.

One could see Klee's layering of his watercolored drawing of an angel over the Luther portrait as destructive, as, to borrow Quaytman's apt word, defacing the underlying image.[1] Or one could see the *Angelus* instead as protecting the old engraving, perhaps even smuggling it into places where it would not be welcome undisguised. But little suggests that Klee had strong feelings about Luther in any direction. He does not present his unbelief and criticism of Christianity as hard-won; his family, in Switzerland, belonged to the Evangelical Reformed Church of the Canton of Bern but did not especially emphasize religion.[2] A letter to Oskar Schlemmer of November 1919, not long before Klee made the *Angelus*, confirms Klee's sense of distance from the Christianity of his upbringing. Responding to a newspaper critic's use of antisemitic language against the proposed appointment of "Paul Zion Klee" to the Stuttgart Academy faculty, Klee wrote to Oskar Schlemmer, the leader of the campaign supporting his appointment: "Paul Zion is not right, rather entirely mistaken, not that I can see any shortcoming in Judaism. All the same, my legitimate forefathers were Protestants."[3] Responding to an attack Klee assumes is racist, he counts his forebears as Protestants, but, it seems, not himself. The few times Klee mentions Luther in his letters, it seems that he is simply a figure of cultural history: in 1902, Klee admires Cranach's portrait of Luther at the Uffizi; in 1906, he praises Rabelais and contextualizes him as a "contemporary of Luther's . . . reform-minded, but going far beyond stupid Luther."[4]

Judging from his art, Klee appears to have observed the religious revival of the immediate postwar years with both curiosity and detachment: some pictures that Klee made between 1919 and 1921, such as *Christian Sectarian* (fig. 2.15) and *The Saint of the Inner Light*, might be seen, as Eberlein suggests, as "critical-ironic figures" caricaturing those caught up in the revival. Along somewhat similar lines, 1920 saw the publication in Munich of Klee's illustrations of Curt Corrinth's novella *Potsdamer Platz; or, The Nights of the New Messiah: Ecstatic Visions*—a persiflage of Expressionist messianism, playfully parodying the New Testament in the form of a tale of a wealthy young man from the provinces who leads a free-love revolution in Berlin before ascending to heaven—a commission that Klee took on without particular enthusiasm or reservations.[5]

Another picture will enter as well: Eberlein and Heinz Brüggemann have already suggested that Klee's watercolor riffs on the panel of Grünewald's 1515 Isenheim Altarpiece representing Christ's Resurrection and Ascension at once, pointing out the obvious, if not clinching, similarities between Klee's angel and Grünewald's Jesus: both glowing supernatural beings hover in *contrapposto*, hands outstretched, palms up (fig. 2.1).[6] Numerous details of Grünewald's Redeemer echo in Klee's funny little creature—the golden beard, the arrangement of fingers, the very pattern of the folds of the divinely illuminated drapery. The angel's huge head can be seen as referring to Grünewald's famous rainbow fireball around Christ's head, so radiant that it is hard to distinguish between head and halo. Quaytman's discovery makes this connection still more compelling. Now we can see that the representations with which the *Angelus* plays are of two of the historical watersheds most celebrated as such in nineteenth- and early twentieth-century Germany—Christ as dividing history into the eras of law and grace, and Luther's stand as initiating the modern era, *die Neuzeit*, which began with the Reformation in Hegel's periodization.[7] In the Protestant view of modernity that was dominant, though very much contested, in Imperial Germany, these were seen as moments that opened a gulf between a before and an after—for many, being fully modern entailed placing oneself fully after both these events. This was a crucial ideological support for the Prussian anti-Catholic policies of the 1870s called by their proponents the *Kulturkampf*—"attempts to subordinate the allegedly unmodern Catholic Church to the supposedly modern German state"—and likewise served as a means of excluding Judaism as unmodern.[8] Klee's work confounds the chronological logic of turning points that the images he compounds set forth. The array of dates on the multiple edges of Klee's picture is perplexing and prominent—1920, 1520-something in a print syntax that cannot be 1520-something, 1920—suggesting that chronology is a central concern here.[9] One of Quaytman's paintings responding to her discovery brings out this point beautifully (see fig. 1.13).

Klee's 1920 picture, intensely involved with images springing from around four hundred years earlier, must be seen as in dialogue with the art-historical writings of Klee's contemporaries. In Klee's own library was Wilhelm Worringer's 1908 book on Cranach.[10] The art historian Worringer, whose conception of

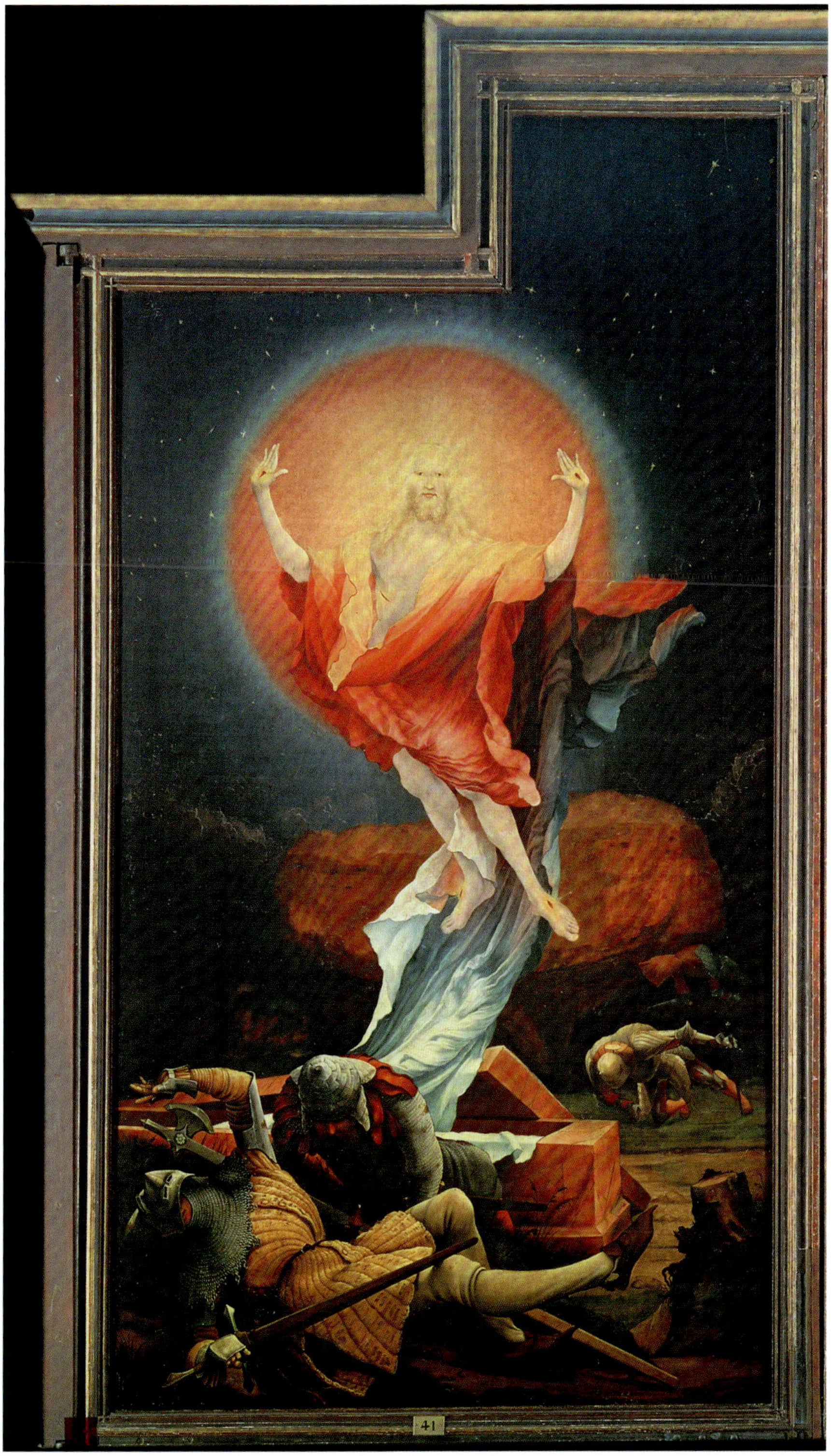

FIGURE 2.1 Mathis Grünewald, *Isenheim Altarpiece*, detail of *The Resurrection* (outer wing panel), 1515. Oil on panel, 2.49 × 0.92 m. Musée Unterlinden, Colmar. Photo Credit: Scala / Art Resource, NY.

abstraction was important for Klee and many Expressionists, lauded Cranach's pre-Reformation "Gothic" work at the expense of his later Lutheran work.[11] Worringer is at pains to point out that, unlike some who saw in the Gothic a union of the religious and the sensuous that was lost with the Reformation, he does not see Protestant art as a contradiction in terms: "Dürer's *Apostles*, Rembrandt's portraits, Beethoven's symphonies are for us truly Protestant works of art."[12] But he does see the consequences of the Reformation on Cranach's religious art as dire: "To grasp the contrast, one needs only to compare Cranach's religious work before and after the Reformation. There sensory vividness, fullness of expression, and pictorial cohesion—here a one-after-another succession of allegorical scenes that mocks any such cohesion and only attains vividness and coherence through rationalistic interpretation. We get theological treatises instead of pictures."[13]

Klee also owned the 1919 book on the Isenheim Altarpiece by the Munich Expressionist art critic Wilhelm Hausenstein, who played a pivotal role in bringing Klee's own work to public attention.[14] The *Angelus*, I argue, makes itself a space for the reconfiguration of images seen as marking important moments in conceptions of German art history and of world history that were contested when and where Klee made it, in Munich in the aftermath of the German revolution of 1918–1919. In that time and place, for modernist artists, critics, and art historians, among others, these images were active and contested, this past supercharged.

Munich—capital of predominantly Catholic, rural, and agrarian Bavaria, a city that became famous in the nineteenth century as a center of the fine arts (Klee moved there to study art after finishing high school in 1898) and of beery merrymaking—was the site of violent and especially protracted political struggle after the German Empire's defeat. In November 1918, King Ludwig III of Bavaria was the first of the German monarchs to be dethroned. An ultranationalist student assassinated Kurt Eisner, the journalist and Independent Social Democrat who was the first premier of the Bavarian Republic; afterward, conflict among Majority Socialists, anarchists, and communists resulted in a rapid succession of governments in Munich. The first group favored parliamentary democracy, the latter two a *Räterepublik* (a republic governed by *Räte*, councils of soldiers and workers, like the Russian soviets). Freikorps paramilitary units bloodily took the city at the beginning of May 1919, killing hundreds involved with or suspected of involvement with the *Räterepublik*.[15]

Religion was a powerful force in these events: the party that won the most votes in the Landtag election of January 1919 was the Bavarian People's Party (BVP), representing political Catholicism and campaigning against the revolutionaries as, among other things, church destroyers (fig. 2.2).[16] Many Bavarians, including the BVP, wanted to preserve the exceptional rights and

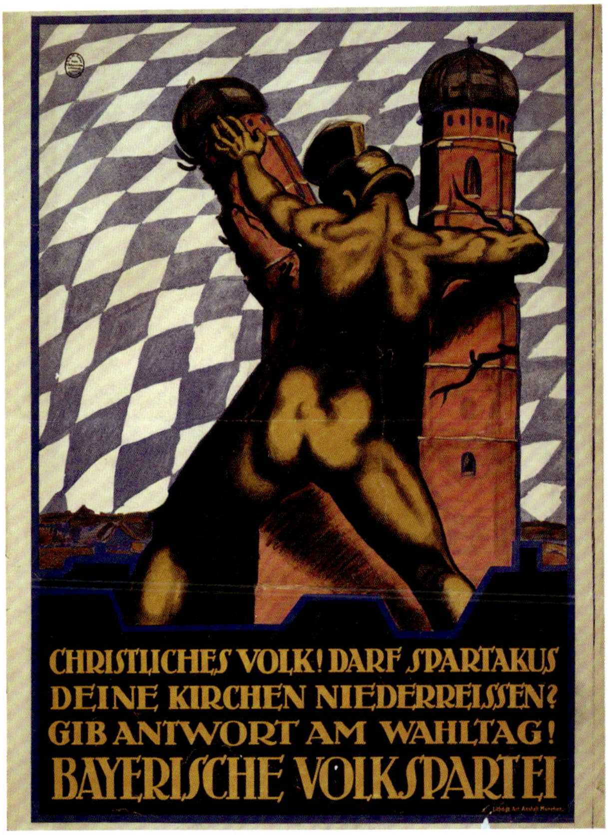

FIGURE 2.2 Hermann Keimel, *Christian People! Will You Let Spartacus Tear Down Your Churches? Answer on Election Day! Bavarian People's Party*, 1919. Lithograph, 100 × 75 cm. https://www.loc.gov/item/2004666128/.

privileges that the kingdom of Bavaria had enjoyed within the German Empire and feared that the new constitution that delegates were drawing up in Weimar would enshrine the domination of the Protestant north; this weakened the hand of the Majority Socialists, who supported the process unfolding in Weimar. It did not escape the notice of counterrevolutionaries that Jews were prominent among the revolutionary leaders in Munich; virulent antisemitism was widespread on the right, which saw its enemy as "Jewish-Bolshevist revolution."[17]

It may be more surprising that many of the revolutionaries and their supporters in Munich hoped that the November Revolution might create the historical conditions of possibility for a new religion. "May a religion come to us from the revolution, a religion of action, life, love, a religion that makes happy, redeems, and overcomes," wrote the German-Jewish communitarian anarchist socialist Gustav Landauer in a new foreword to his *Call to Socialism*, dated January 1919, during his involvement with Eisner's government; Landauer, who briefly served as the commissioner of enlightenment and public instruction for the *Räterepublik*, was beaten and killed in May 1919.[18] The history of hoping for a new religion is long, a project of Romanticism reformulated in the prewar years in Munich perhaps most prominently by the Blaue Reiter group. In Hausenstein's 1921 book on Klee, which I've mentioned, a central question was what to make of this hope after May 1919.[19]

Klee, who had never before engaged in politics, was not uninvolved. On what turned out to be the last day of the brief rule of the first short-lived *Räterepublik* led by Ernst Toller, in which the anarchist socialism of his associates Landauer and Erich Mühsam predominated, Klee wrote a letter pledging his support to Munich's Action Committee of Revolutionary Artists, which backed the *Räterepublik*, although he was, in the words of Joan Weinstein, its "least visible member."[20] Reflecting on the *Räterepublik* in a letter to the artist Alfred Kubin shortly after its suppression, Klee stressed what he saw as positive in it: while the "individualist art" they both make is, he admits, "a capitalist luxury" ill fitted "for collective consumption," he insists that they both "are nevertheless something more than curiosities for rich snobs. And what in us somehow aims beyond that, at eternal values, would be better supported in a communist community."[21]

At the University of Munich early in 1919, a little less than a month before Eisner's assassination, the sociologist Max Weber gave a lecture, "Politics as a Vocation," to the League of Free Students in which he deployed the famous Luther quotation inscribed on our engraving—"Here I stand, I can do no other."[22] He sets up an opposition between the "ethics of conviction"—which he associates with the politically active intellectuals of the November Revolution, which he calls "this carnival that is being flattered with the proud name of 'revolution'" (76)—and the "ethics of responsibility." Then he uses Luther's words to show how the two may come together: "I find it immeasurably moving when a *mature* human being . . . who feels the responsibility he bears for the consequences of his own actions with his entire soul and who acts in harmony with an ethics of responsibility reaches the point where he says, 'Here I stand, I can do no other.'" For Weber, this exemplifies "the authentic human being who *is capable* of having a 'vocation for politics.'"[23]

In 1921, after the "carnival" was violently put down and the BVP premier Gustav von Kahr had turned Bavaria into a "cell of order," a welcoming haven for extreme rightists from across Germany, Ernst Bloch published in Munich his *Thomas Münzer as Theologian of Revolution*, mentioned in the previous chapter, seeking a positive figure of the messianic revolutionary in the early Reformation, in this chiliastic preacher who at first followed Luther but sided with the peasants in the Peasants' War.[24] He was following a tradition on the left of seeing Luther as betraying what was best in his own work; Engels had written that, in his Bible translation, Luther had given the peasants "a powerful weapon," "the picture of another society which knew nothing of the ramified and artificial feudal hierarchy," which they used to attack the latter, but that "Luther turned the same weapon against the peasants, extracting from the Bible a veritable hymn to the authorities ordained by God. . . . Thus Luther repudiated not only the peasant insurrection but even his own revolt against religious and lay authority."[25]

The left-wing Munich critic Hausenstein linked the Isenheim Altarpiece—displayed in the city for almost a year after the signing of the armistice, through this period of revolution and counterrevolution—to the social radicalism, in part religiously inspired, that culminated in the Peasants' War, in implicit contrast to Luther.[26] The altarpiece was exhibited in the Alte Pinakothek (half an hour on foot from Klee's studio in the Schloss Suresnes in Schwabing) from November 22, 1918, shortly after the proclamation of the Bavarian Republic (until then, the possibility of air bombs precluded its display) until it was packed up for its return trip to Colmar on September 27, 1919, after the White Terror had put an end to the succession of revolutionary governments in Munich and Bavaria had become part of the Weimar Republic.[27] The display of the altarpiece was a major event (fig. 2.3): the museum staff, feeling it

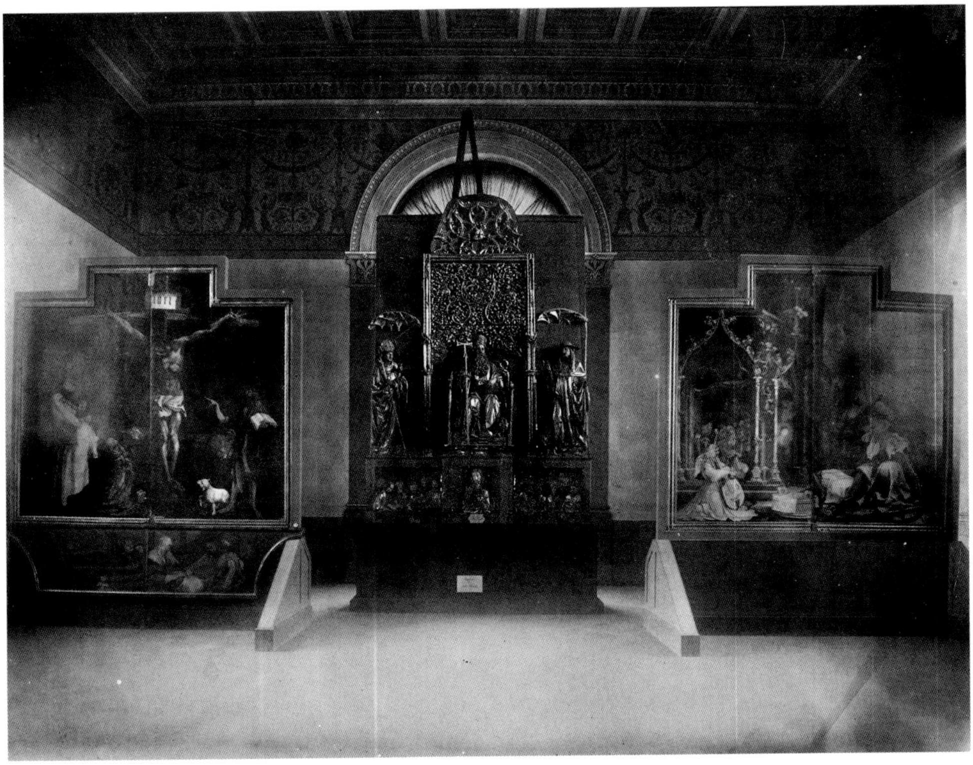

FIGURE 2.3 Walter Gräff, *Alte Pinakothek, Room II with Grünewald's Isenheim Altar*, 1918–19. Bayerisches Hauptstaatsarchiv.

important to broaden access to the treasure it temporarily housed, added new opening hours that stretched until dusk (the museum had no artificial lighting), with free admission.[28] After the altar left, the room that had housed it and its estimated hundred thousand visitors—an exceptional surge in foot traffic in the museum—needed to be refurbished.[29]

Before the altarpiece came to Munich, it was already a lodestone for artists and intellectuals; a reproduction of it was hanging in Benjamin's study in 1917.[30] The extraordinarily complex, double-winged *Schnitzaltar*, commissioned by the Antonite Order in the Alsatian village of Isenheim, was originally made to show one of three different configurations to suit different times in the church calendar. When closed, the altarpiece was dominated by the crucified Christ; the first opening revealed panels representing the Annunciation, Madonna and Child, and the Resurrection; and the second opening exposed Nikolaus Hagenauer's carved limewood figures, Saint Anthony at the center. The altarpiece's control of visibility, by means of its hinged wooden panels, folding and unfolding, was an essential part of its iconographic program: it is no accident that the Resurrection panel is the reverse side of the Crucifixion panel representing the dead body of Christ on the cross (similarly, the panel that, when the altarpiece was closed, showed Mary mourning is the reverse of the panel of the Annunciation when the altarpiece is open).The altarpiece's own modern vicissitudes overdetermined its reception; its history was sometimes seen as exemplifying the changes undergone by art in processes of secularization, both broadly and in the narrower sense of the transfer of property from religious to lay authority. In 1794, the French Republic confiscated the altarpiece's disassembled parts from the Isenheim convent for which it was made. Since 1853, the panels have been displayed simultaneously—impossible if the retable were intact—as one of the chief treasures of the Musée d'Unterlinden in Colmar, an institution housed in another secularized convent, about fifteen miles from Isenheim.

The altarpiece's location entwined its reception with competing French and German claims to the disputed border region of Alsace, annexed by the new *Reich* in 1871, after France's defeat in the Franco-Prussian War. The removal of the panels to Munich and the way this transfer was understood in Germany must be seen in this context. Colmar was not far from the Vosges Front during the First World War, and thus the Musée d'Unterlinden took the precaution of storing its most precious works, including the Isenheim Altarpiece, in the vault of the Colmar savings bank.[31] As the war dragged on, the administration in Colmar was urged to find a safer location, farther from the front; in 1916, the organizers of an exhibition in Berlin requested the work and touted the advantages of the relocation for the work's safety.[32] However, a small group successfully maneuvered for Munich against Berlin as the destination for Colmar's treasures: the Munich-based sculptor Theodor Georgii, who happened to be stationed in Colmar, took a great deal of initiative, with the support of Munich museum directors (Georg Habich and Friedrich Dörnhöffer) as well as Rupprecht, Crown Prince of Bavaria, and the panels were transported to Munich in February 1917.[33] After the war, the altarpiece figured in the German press as a sublime figure of German painting and of the Germanness of the region of Alsace. Responses to the altarpiece's departure from Munich in September 1919 bear vivid witness to this. In keeping with the 1917 agreement between the city of Colmar and the Staatliche Gemäldegalerie of Munich, the paintings were transported back to Colmar—which was returned to France under the terms of the Treaty of Versailles, signed just a few months earlier. There were rumors both that it would be exhibited in the Louvre as a trophy and that the city of Colmar was planning on selling the work to America.[34] Some who were pained that the altarpiece's home museum was again part of France consoled themselves by asserting that, wherever it might go, it would continue to testify to their own view of Alsace as "old German cultural land."[35]

During the period of the altarpiece's exhibition in Munich, there were frequent requests that a copy of the altarpiece be made that could stay in Germany after the return of the original.[36] Supporters of the making of a copy—envisioned as ideally life-size, made with materials as similar as possible to Grünewald's, and at once faithful yet "in a certain sense free spiritual recreation" rather than a "slavish imitation" of Grünewald's panels, to be placed in a church, such as perhaps Munich's Frauenkirche[37]—included the artist and restorer Max Doerner and the prominent art magazine *Der Kunstwart*, but the museum refused to allow it for reasons articulated by the art historian Rudolf Oldenbourg, an Alte Pinakothek staffer, in an exchange between Doerner and Oldenbourg in the pages of a major Munich daily in February 1919. The exchange explored broad questions—the value of copies in face of developments in mechanical reproduction, tourism, and art connoisseurship; the unequal social distribution of these developments; and the way the modern, disarticulated display of the altarpiece maximizes its visibility while contradicting its original use. But the grounds for the museum's refusal were narrow: Oldenbourg averred that, while the kind of copy envisioned and indeed perhaps to be carried out by Doerner might well be desirable, the copyist at work would literally obstruct the viewing of the altarpiece, especially regrettable given the relatively short period of the work's stay in Munich, and copies could of course be made once the panels were returned to Colmar.[38]

It was during its stay in Munich that the altarpiece reached the peak of its fame, widely reproduced as the embodiment of "the Gothic" and "the German," as the precursor of contemporary Expressionist art, and as the focal point of a quasi resacralization of art.[39] In the book in Klee's library, Hausenstein wrote: "Never before could people have made such a pilgrimage to an altarpiece;

it was like in the Middle Ages. . . . After the mechanisms of more than four years of war, the masses gathered together for the first time before the spirit of a German artist—probably the greatest we have ever had . . . in the midst of the shabby monotony . . . there remained a sanctuary. Not a church. Only the museum . . . the art of our time claimed the altarpiece for itself."[40]

The old images Klee compounded, in short, were neither obscure nor inert allusions in Munich in 1920.

In her essay, Quaytman insightfully connects her discovery to religious iconoclasm, speaking of "the injunction against graven images" in Jewish and Christian traditions and describing what Klee does with the engraving as an act of image breaking.[41] Now, there are a number of avant-garde works around 1920 that deface reproductions of Old Master paintings: we might put Klee's alongside Duchamp's work on Leonardo's *Mona Lisa* (1920; fig. 2.4), or Schwitters's (1921; fig. 2.5) on Raphael's Sistine *Madonna*. But the *Angelus*, exceptionally, can be said to put its quiet version of vanguard vandalism in relation to a longer history of iconoclasm.[42]

As a protagonist in sixteenth-century debates about iconoclasm, it is difficult for Luther to play its innocent victim.[43] His position was complex: while

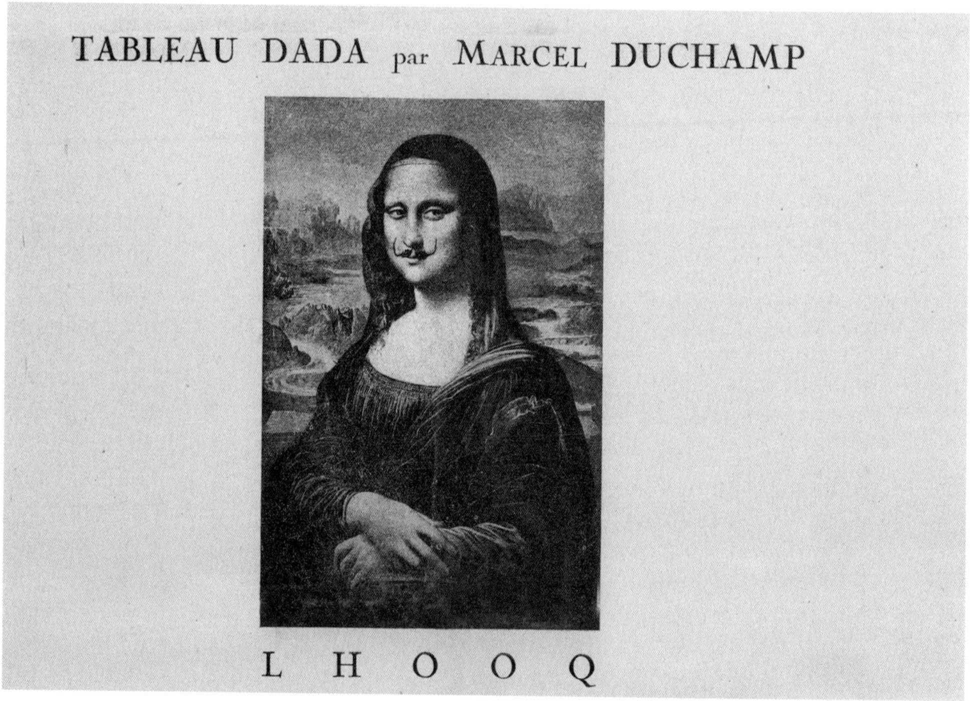

FIGURE 2.4 Marcel Duchamp, *Tableau Dada: L H O O Q*, cover of the journal *391*, no. 12, edited and published by Francis Picabia, March 1920, detail. Source gallica.bnf.fr / Bibliothèque nationale de France.

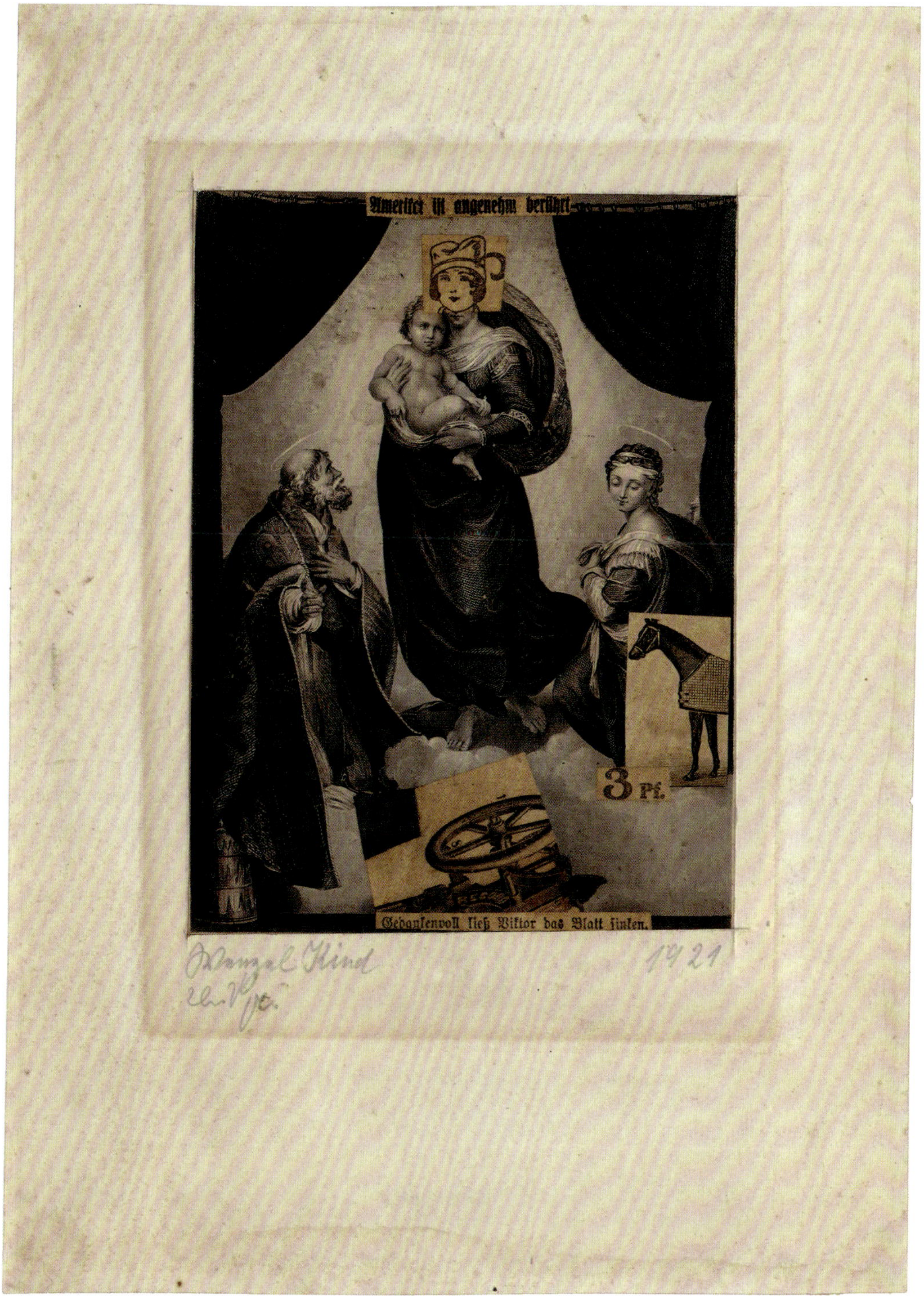

FIGURE 2.5 Kurt Schwitters, *Mz. 151 Wenzel Kind Madonna mit Pferd* [*Mz. 151 Knave Child Madonna with Horse*], 1921. Paper on paper, 17.2 × 12.9 cm (original mount opening); 29.8 × 21.4 cm (original mount); 19.3 × 14.9 cm (sheet). Oeuvre cat. Orchard/Schulz 0799. Inv. D 76. Collection of the NORD/LB in the Savings Bank Foundation of Lower Saxony, on loan since 1994. Sprengel Museum, Hannover, Germany. © 2021 Artists Rights Society (ARS), New York. Photo: Herling / Gwose bpk Bildagentur / Art Resource, NY.

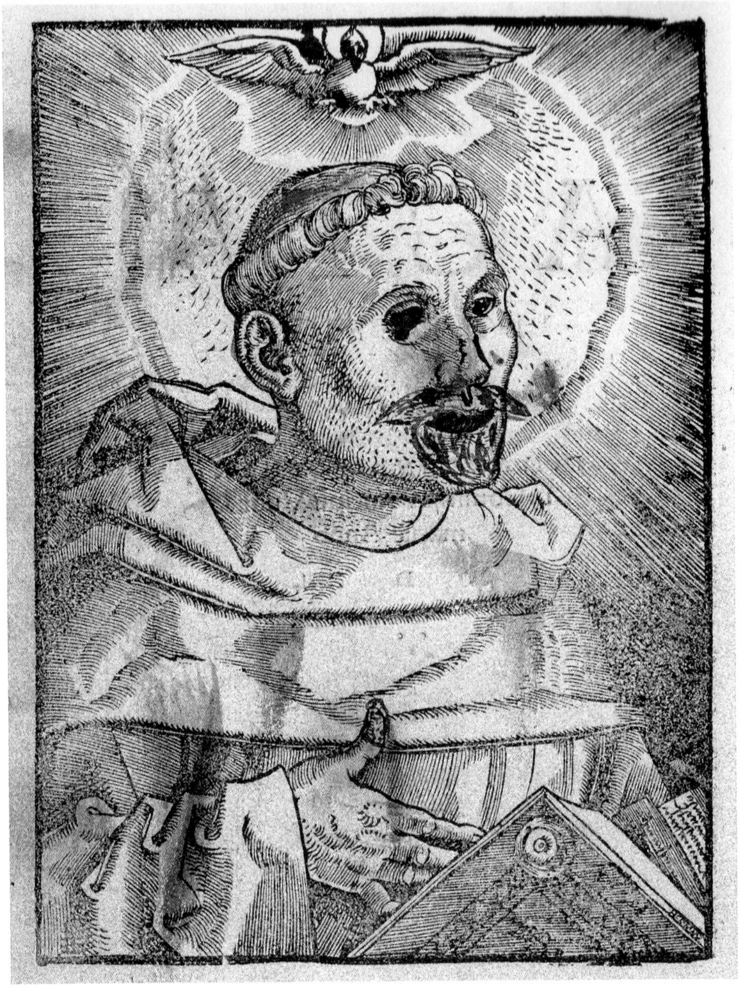

FIGURE 2.6 Hans Baldung Grien, *Martin Luther*, 1521. Woodcut defaced with pen and ink, date of defacement unknown. Universitätsbibliothek Marburg.

his opposition to what he saw as the church's idolatry encouraged some to purge images, he famously opposed iconoclasm.[44] According to Luther, the crux was the beholder's attitude, not the thing itself, and a completely imageless religion of the Word was in any case impossible, since the words of Scripture ineluctably make images in the believer's "heart."[45] If one sees the Reformation as an episode in the many long histories, theological and artistic, of contests of word and image, as brandishing the Hebrew Bible's critiques of the image against Christian usage, Calvin is the one who sharpened the conflict while Luther sought a compromise.[46] In fact, Luther portraits themselves were treated at times like *Heiligenbilder*, saints' pictures, as the papal nuncio at the Diet of Worms reported, noting how people carried and kissed them.[47] Such behavior prompted the Catholic controversialist Hieronymus Emser to ask in 1522, "For since Luther allows his own charming features to be painted and publicly displayed, why should the Church not treasure and venerate images of the beloved saints?"[48] There were even miracle stories about Luther portraits that were said to sweat or survive fires unsinged.[49] Accordingly, some of Luther's orthodox enemies turned iconoclasts: see, for instance, this defaced Luther woodcut, with moustache, beard, and gouged eyes (fig. 2.6).[50]

Here's another crucial difference: Leonardo's portrait and Raphael's Madonna were understood as supreme masterpieces. Luther portraits from the Cranach workshop, not so much. Now, Cranach's pre-Reformation work found admirers in the early twentieth century—and Ernst Ludwig Kirchner was not alone in paying homage to Cranach's female nudes.[51] But Klee's aforementioned praise in a 1902 letter of the Luther portrait in the Uffizi is rather unusual, for neither the aims nor the means of the Luther portraits fit most art historians' and critics' ideas about art.[52] As Worringer wrote: "For past generations, Cranach was above all the friend of the reformers, the painter of Lutheranism. His fame as an artist was based on his subject area. Today it is this side of his art that most discredits him."[53] This subject matter went hand in hand with a mode of production that Worringer describes as a "sad peripeteia," a falling away from the pre-Reformation work: Worringer stresses the economic logic, the role of operating capital and of the division of labor, in Cranach's workshop from the beginning of the Reformation onward.[54] In short, Müller's print after Cranach is an icon of Protestantism, not of art. One of a series of honorific portrait prints he made of reformers (Calvin, Hus, Melanchthon), it does not strain to deliver the peculiarities of Cranach's style.[55] Müller is one of many artists who supplied one of the chief demands of Protestants in terms of images—for portraits of reformers to hang in homes and educational institutions, to circulate as frontispieces in books.[56]

In line with what would seem to be a ground rule of art reproduction, you might think the print refers to a particular Cranach painting, but it does not. Neither the art connoisseur nor the stickler for historical accuracy could be satisfied with this print, which mixes and matches Luther representations with little regard for chronology. Now, the Cranach workshop developed a number of Luther "models"—the pious young monk, the disguised outlaw, the humanist, and so on.[57] The print is mostly based on the widespread "stout doctor" type, produced by the Cranach workshop from 1539 (fig. 2.7)[58]—an older Luther, untonsured and antimonastically jowly, in the academic gown in which he began preaching in 1524. It combines this type with the hands from the "young monk" line (fig. 2.8) and Luther's legendary words of 1521, which, it seems, determine the date on the printed image. This mixing and matching might be said to be more or less faithful not to any particular product but to Cranach's mode of production: the replication and recombination of standardized types, as facilitated in the Cranach workshop by the pouncing and tracing of linear faces and figures.[59]

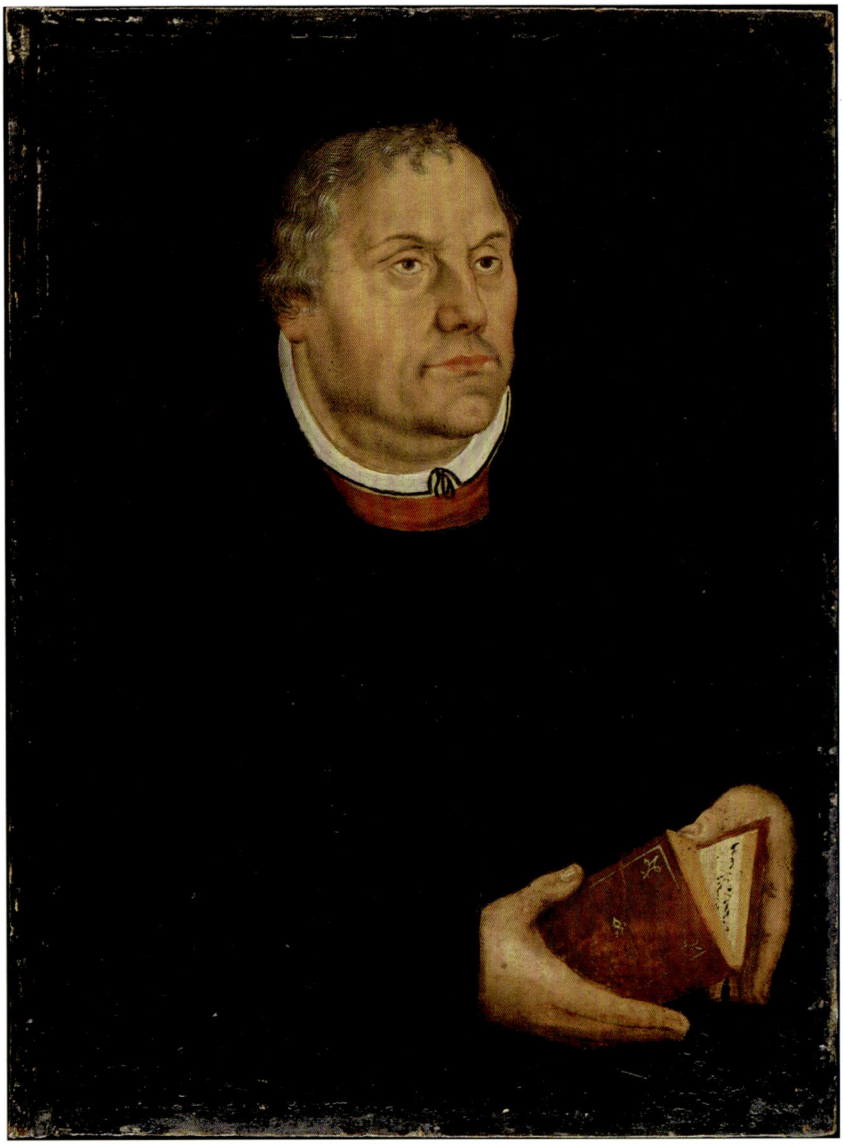

FIGURE 2.7 *Martin Luther*, copy after Lucas Cranach the Younger, ca. 1570–80. Oil on panel, 22.4 × 16.9 cm. Kunsthistorisches Museum Wien, Gemäldegalerie. Photo: KHM-Museumsverband.

The icon of Protestantism Klee defaces can be seen, then, as inimical to the art values that viewers saw in Raphael and Leonardo: since German Romanticism, there has been a narrative of the Protestant Reformation as the death of art.[60] The story told usually went something like this: the achievements of Dürer and Grünewald, who established themselves on the eve of the Reformation, could not be built upon, for the Reformation—even when it stopped well short of iconoclasm—undermined the religious uses of art on which these artists ultimately depended. According to Hegel, the "need for inner spirituality" drove the Reformation to pry "religious ideas . . . from their wrapping in the element of sense," returning them to "the inwardness of heart

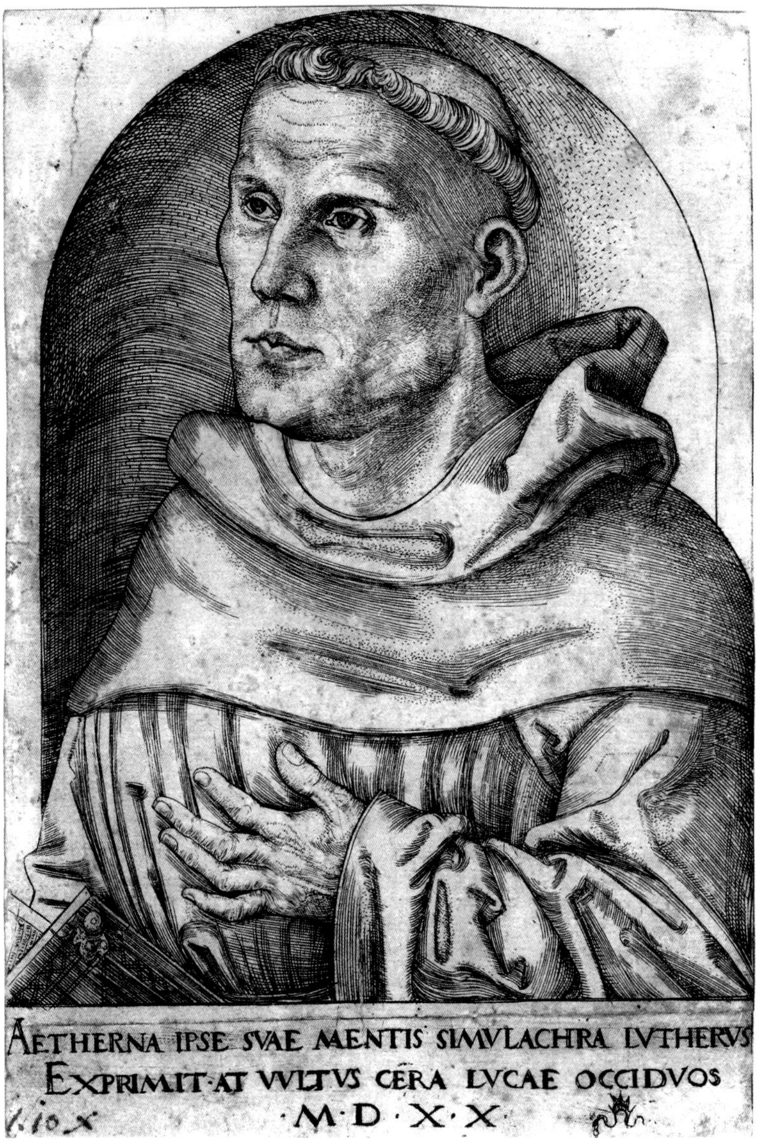

FIGURE 2.8 Lucas Cranach the Elder, *Portrait of Martin Luther as an Augustinian friar*, 1520. Engraving, 16.9 × 11.6 cm. The British Museum.

and thinking."[61] Therefore, notoriously, Hegel claimed that "art, considered in its highest vocation, is and remains for us a thing of the past."[62] Despite all Hegel's praise for Dutch seventeenth-century painting, which he sees as caused precisely by "movement away from the Catholic Church"—in that particular historical situation, "to joy in the world as such, to natural objects and their detailed appearance, to domestic life in its decency," for Hegel, thinking's gain was art's loss.[63] The Luther portrait Klee used might be seen not only as referring to this putative death of art but also as exemplifying what religious images are like afterwards—instrumentalized, dull, and dry. It follows that Klee's defacement may be far indeed from an antiart gesture.

Within the terms of art discourse in Munich around 1920, putting a picture recalling Grünewald's resurrected Christ over a printed portrait of Luther bearing Cranach's monogram would seem to announce pretty clearly something like the resurrection of art from the tomb in which Protestantism had laid it.

In Worringer's book on Cranach, which I've mentioned Klee owned, we find the following comparison, in strongly Christian language, between Grünewald and Cranach: "It requires only the name of one Matthias Grünwald to put the 'painter' Cranach back in the place he deserves. One utters Grünwald's name and a memory, strong as a revelation, rises up. . . . A storm of living color. Life, life it cries out of the dark ardors; the great deed of liberation was done, the awakening of dead color by the spirit, the spirit of space-forming light."[64] Klee layers Grünewald over Cranach—or better, the modern artist's reinterpretation of the otherworldly image of Christ's transfigured body over the pedestrian reproductive print of Luther, an image that could be seen as representing both the historical circumstances that sundered the religious and the sensuous as well as the ensuing degradation of the image.[65] The *Angelus novus* seems like a cryptic version of a frequent Expressionist theme, a triumphant announcement of modern art as reenchantment.[66]

Of the Isenheim Altarpiece, Hausenstein wrote, "For almost the last time, Grünewald once again mustered the courage for an altarpiece in the grandest style."[67] Similarly, the art historian Wilhelm Niemeyer called Grünewald "the last altarpiece painter, in the profound sense of the altarpiece as work of art, the last one for whom the painted panel was entirely a part of the larger structure of the altarpiece and a consequence of the idea of the altar."[68] For Hausenstein and many others, the pathos of the Isenheim Altarpiece lay not only in the suffering it represented with such vivid corporeality, distortions of scale, and otherworldly color but also in its timing, its location at the end of an art-historical narrative—in their own knowledge that, in a few short years, the Reformation would initiate such changes in practice, doctrine, and patronage that this altarpiece would stand as not only one of the most impressive, but one of the last, of its particular kind.[69] Of course, altarpieces continued to play vital roles in Lutheran as well as Catholic churches, but they differed in form and function from pre-Reformation altarpieces.[70] But many art historians felt that, although, for instance, Cranach's altarpieces and other pictures in the service of the Reformation might accompany what was arguably a spiritual advance beyond the Isenheim Altarpiece, they did not hold a candle to the earlier work *as* art: in Hausenstein's words, "So many emancipations from the old church, so many new restrictions for art."[71]

The prewar writings of Klee's associates in Der Blaue Reiter in Munich testify to their sense of a possibility of reversing, in a new or renewed religion, this putative decline of the powers of art; to a degree, they may be seen as pursuing a project of reenchantment echoing that of Romantics such as Novalis and Ludwig Tieck.[72] Lisa Florman has demonstrated how Kandinsky's *On the Spiritual in Art* takes issue with Hegel's notorious end-of-art thesis while remaining in some respects quite close to the philosopher's presuppositions.[73] Franz Marc, writing in *The Blue Rider* almanac, felt that a return to the inseparability of the religious and the sensuous was immanent, and he claimed that the German avant-garde groups' aim was to create "symbols . . . that belong on the altars of the coming spiritual religion and behind which the technical producer disappears."[74]

In this reading, the engraving acts as a foil, emphasizing by contrast the newness of Klee's new angel, which presents itself at the same time as a return to a pre-Reformation regime of the image. To function as foil, the engraving's visible edge is sufficient: that is enough to see its dot-and-lozenge syntax (made all the more rotely mechanical by Müller's apparent use of a "ruling machine"), which would have looked supremely fuddy-duddy in 1920.

Similarities allow the contrast to register. Every visible element of the print might be compared with some element of Klee's watercolor: the sitter's drapery with the angel's, the tone of the background as rendered by the mesh of printed lines with Klee's watercolor wash, the date with the date, the monogram with Klee's signature.[75] Despite differences in scale and proportions, we can guess from the margin alone that the engraved figure's head more or less lines up with the angel's—as Quaytman explored in some of the paintings she exhibited in New York in 2015 (fig. 1.14).

Many connections can be made between these two layers. Klee's angel is, as discussed in the previous chapter, an oil-transfer drawing, a process Klee often used to copy a drawing, or a tracing of a drawing, onto another surface, using a sheet of paper covered with oil paint or greasy ink as transfer paper. Tamara Trodd has drawn attention to how Klee's oil transfers are "visibly *reproduced*," "*visibly imprinted*, as opposed to drawn."[76] This process of transferring linear images—evidenced by the surrounding blotches, marking the pressure of Klee's hand against the transfer paper, as well as by the very quality of the line—might be compared with those used in the print: the tracing or pouncing used by the Cranach workshop to make recognizable Luther portraits in huge quantities as well as, much more distantly, engraving itself.[77] The *Angelus novus* as a whole loosely resembles what Trodd describes as Klee's "temporary apparatus" for oil-transfer drawing, the putting together of "interleaved pages, stored, and retrieved, and reprocessed"—the portrait engraving seems to become a component of Klee's artisanal procedure of reproduction.[78]

Iconographic links can also be made: Reformation texts and images, from Johann Bugenhagen's funeral sermon for Luther to a broadsheet showing a black-robed, winged, trumpet-blowing Luther flying above the pope, sometimes compared the reformer to an angel.[79] Furthermore, the head of Klee's angel seems to respond to certain significant features of Luther's in the underlying engraving—the plump jowls and untonsured curls that signal the ex-monk's opposition to asceticism, the eyes looking off to the right. The angel can be seen as combining features of the engraving's Luther and Grünewald's Jesus—aspects of the occluded engraving, we might say, are reproduced on the opaque paper with which Klee covers it.

Alternatively, you could link the images by comparing the angel not to Luther but to the Bible he holds. In the Abrahamic religions, an angel is a divine messenger (the word derives from the Persian military mounted messenger service).[80] Klee's angel, facing the beholder, mouth open, seems to be in the act of delivering his message. But as Scholem remarked in "Walter Benjamin and His Angel" (1972), Klee's angel might also be seen as figuring a message written rather than spoken; he noted that its head may be surrounded not by hair but by "scrolls of writing (*Schriftrollen*) on which his message may have been inscribed."[81] Elaborating on Scholem's words, Geoffrey H. Hartman has written of the hairdo as made of "curlers that it is tempting to see as unfolding scrolls, possibly Torah scrolls," and the figure as a whole as "a grotesque being . . . helplessly reading itself."[82] Indeed, the translucent scroll-like forms that unroll out of the angel's head make his fingers and feet resemble furled rolls; taking Scholem's observation further, one might say that much of the body might be seen as made up of surfaces for writing, a combination of rolls and codex, the latter suggested by the V shape of the angel's upheld arm-wings, the way his hands seem to be made of overlapping identical units, and the notched yellow shape just to the left of the orange shape at the center of the torso, resembling a bookmark. The angel-messenger's body might be seen as composed of blank Scripture; turning back to the engraving, one might say that there the book plays the angel's role as deliverer of God's word, which Luther, mouth closed, has received.

In this reading, the point of all these similarities is to bring out the differences, the distance between the modernist artist's angel and the nineteenth-century reproductive engraving of a mash-up of an Old Master's portraits. The print's visible margins are all that is needed to see that the logic of bodies differs strikingly between the two layers, to register the contrast between the new angel's flattened transparency, emphasized by the splayed outwardness of its orans gesture, and the involutions of Luther's dark drapery along the bottom edge. The fact that Luther was widely understood as a paragon of "inwardness" reinforces the contrast still further.[83] The cut-off inscription on the engraving emphasizes again that Luther is an earthbound figure: here *he* stands while the angel hovers.[84] Similarly, there is a sharp contrast between the linework of the two layers, between the engraving's elaborate hatching emulating the tonal range of oil painting, on the one hand, and the doodled quality of the oil-transfer drawing, on the other hand.

Related to these differences is, of course, the sharp contrast between how the two layers were made. There's a host of angels in Klee's work. Most, but not all, were made long after the *Angelus novus*; the previous chapter mentioned Klee's related small watercolored drawing *Angelus descendens* (fig. 1.11), which Eberlein sees as also referencing Grünewald's resurrected Christ in particular.[85] In general, Klee's angels might well be seen as a riposte to Courbet's famous remark—"Show me an angel, and I'll paint one."[86] They are an ideal motif for Klee's understanding of art as that which "does not reproduce the visible, but rather makes visible," as he wrote in an important essay on graphic art published in 1920.[87] The Luther engraving's relationship to Lucas Cranach's portraits of Luther is, it seems, quite complex and indirect, but it could be said to use Cranach's name primarily as that of, in Worringer's words, the "friend of the reformers," as someone close to the great man who could make a good likeness of his fleshly sitter.[88] This scenario is visualized in, for instance, the Munich artist Heinrich Stelzner's historical genre painting *Cranach Painting Luther at the Wartburg*, circa 1890, in the collection of the Neue Pinakothek in Munich since 1912 (fig. 2.9). In his 1924 lecture "On Modern Art," Klee contrasted portraiture's traditional concern with likeness to a modernist emphasis on relations among formal elements.[89]

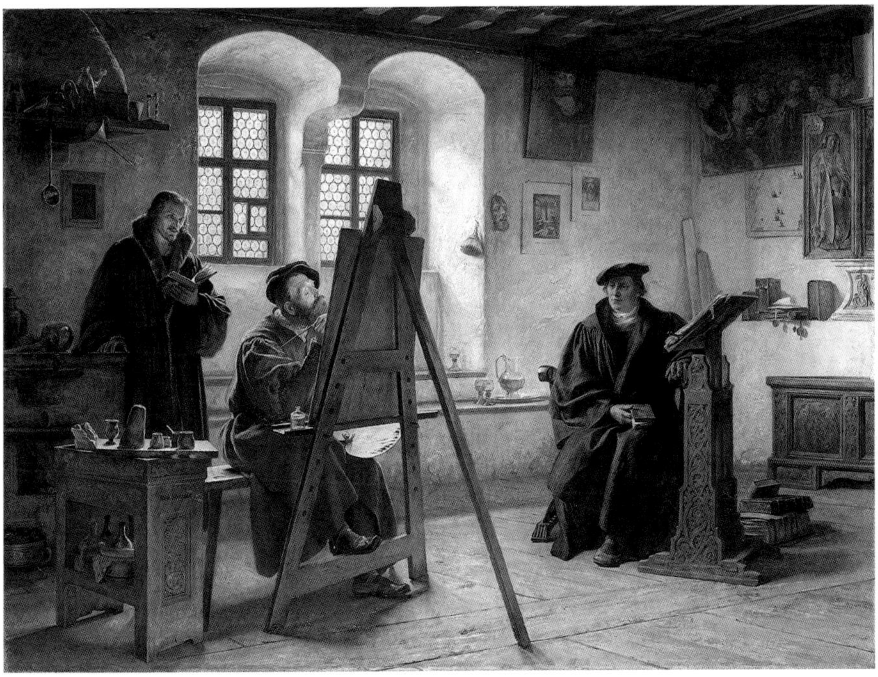

FIGURE 2.9 Heinrich Stelzner, *Cranach Painting Luther*, ca. 1890. Oil on canvas, 138 × 187 cm. Bayerische Staatsgemäldesammlungen, Neue Pinakothek, Munich. Inv. 8682. Photo: bpk Bildagentur / Bayerische Staatsgemäldesammlungen / Art Resource, NY.

So the "modern" and the "new" are set off here against the old-fashioned portrait engraving. Again, Schwitters's collage *Knave Child* (fig. 2.5) is an illuminating comparison. To borrow from Brigid Doherty's analysis of it in relation to Benjamin's writings about Dada and technological reproducibility, it updates the Sistine *Madonna*, giving the Virgin a chic new hat and matching face, and almost obliterating Raphael's famous cherubs with a technical illustration of a machine that might be seen as mimicking a cherub's tilted head as he gazes up.[90] Parts of the montage can be seen as "mock[ing] . . . the kind of contemplative immersion associated with the reception of pictures in devotional contexts," writes Doherty.[91] Widely shared links among modernity, fashion, mechanization, and disenchantment reinforce *Knave Child*'s mockery—the bits of paper Schwitters pastes over the reproduction of Raphael's masterpiece are more products of "reproductive technologies for printing words and images for a mass market."[92]

In contrast to Schwitters's collage, the single piece of paper with which Klee covers over the Cranach reproduction—the *Angelus*, *novus* as it is—also gestures toward a more distant past. Its use of the Latin word for new stands in pointed contrast to Luther's association with translation into the vernacular. Given what lies beneath the angel, Klee's work seems to seek to reanimate a pre-Lutheran dispensation of communication. While the cut-off Luther quotation under the portrait represents Luther's speech at the Diet of Worms, his mouth is closed, and such direct angelic oral communication as the uppermost layer pictures is displaced by the mediacy of the Scripture Luther holds. The idea that the Reformation marked the beginning of an era of the

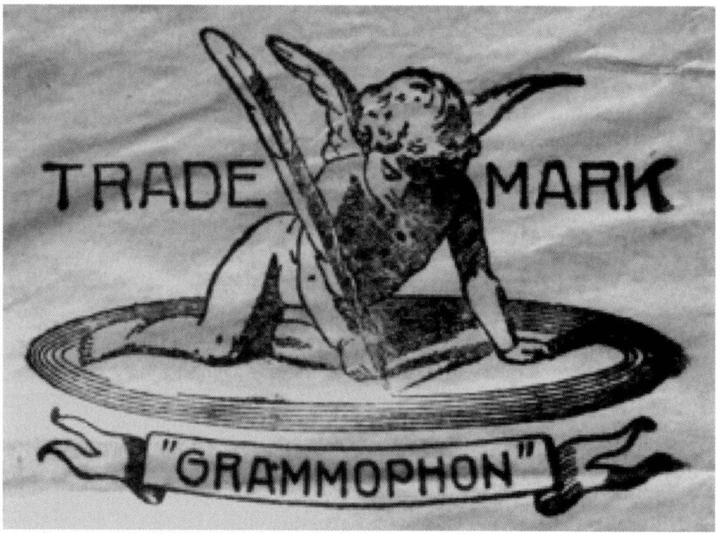

FIGURE 2.10 Deutsche Grammophon trademark of the "Recording Angel" inscribing a disc, introduced around 1900

dominance of the printed book, inaugurated by the enormous success of Luther's Bible and the Protestant doctrine *sola scriptura*, "by Scripture alone," was widespread and vivid circa 1920, precisely because many saw newer media technologies as marking its end. Among others, Benjamin saw his present in this light, writing the following later in the 1920s: "Just as this era is the antithesis of the Renaissance in general, it contrasts in particular with the situation in which the art of printing was discovered . . . when the book in the most eminent sense of the word—the Book of Books—had, through Luther's translation, become the people's property. Now everything indicates that the book in this traditional form is nearing its end."[93] Angels were sometimes used to figure the capacities of newer media technologies: take the old Deutsche Grammophon trademark of the "Recording Angel" inscribing a disc, introduced around 1900 (fig. 2.10).

In the *Angelus*, the mediate textuality of the old book, it seems, contrasts with the direct orality of the new and yet still older angel—and the angel comes out on top.

There's a lot of contextual evidence for the reading I just presented, of the new angel as the new art as the resurrection of art, reenchanted and immediate. Art discourse after the November Revolution would seem to make this highly plausible; many saw Expressionism as leading toward a "new religious art."[94] Klee might seem to take up Hausenstein's words of the previous year, in the book Klee owned, about the relation between the Isenheim Altarpiece and contemporary art: "The abstractness of our art is only meaningful if it is the precursor of a new objectivity in the picture. Our speculative graphic art will only be fruitful if it is a prolegomenon to future altarpieces. In Grünewald's hand, art became once again complete: altar. . . . Then there was the great divide. But did not a demand of similar dimensions arise on this side of that divide?"[95] It seems that Hausenstein is aiming these words directly, though not solely, at Klee—Hausenstein was writing elsewhere, around the same time, about Klee as the most important contemporary practitioner of what he calls here "speculative graphic art," which culminated in his 1921 book on the artist.[96] Is Klee affirming here that his art is "fruitful" in Hausenstein's terms, "a prolegomenon to future altarpieces"? As mentioned earlier, it was in Hausenstein's Klee book that the *Angelus* was first reproduced—just three pages after the critic speaks of "the aura of ascension" in Grünewald's altarpiece, and, incidentally, cropped to the edge of the watercolor paper.[97] But the tone of Klee's work doesn't quite fit; the small-scale work, the snaggletoothed homunculus of an angel, gestures toward and undermines such an aspiration. There were artists who tried, in various and complex ways, to fulfill versions of it. For Hausenstein, Hans von Marées is the prime example; one might also think of artists, such as Beckmann or Dix, who, in various ways and to divergent ends, cited the Isenheim Altarpiece and made multipanel works that allude to pre-Reformation polyptychs, often monumental in scale (fig. 2.11). Or the carved, painted, and hinged *Small Altarpiece* made in 1920 by Alfred Partikel and Gerhard Marcks, the latter one of the first Bauhaus masters (fig. 2.12). Or Gropius's 1919 "Program of the State Bauhaus in Weimar," illustrated by Feininger's woodcut of a cathedral, which ends with the vision of a new communal art reunified with architecture creating the "new building of the future . . . which, from the million hands of craftsmen, will one day rise toward heaven as the crystalline symbol of a new and coming faith" (fig. 2.13).[98] But even though Klee would begin teaching at the Bauhaus the next year, I don't think Klee's *Angelus* fits in here.

Klee's picture takes up one figure from one panel of the altarpiece, rather than aiming for the completion Hausenstein saw in the Isenheim Altarpiece; its allusion to the monumentally scaled altarpiece might be seen as emphasizing its difference from such an object made for the use of a religious community, its own smallness, keyed, as Klee's art consistently is, to the scale of a private room. One might well explore the *Angelus* in relation to another art-historical concept: that of the *Andachtsbild*, or devotional picture. The term, while used

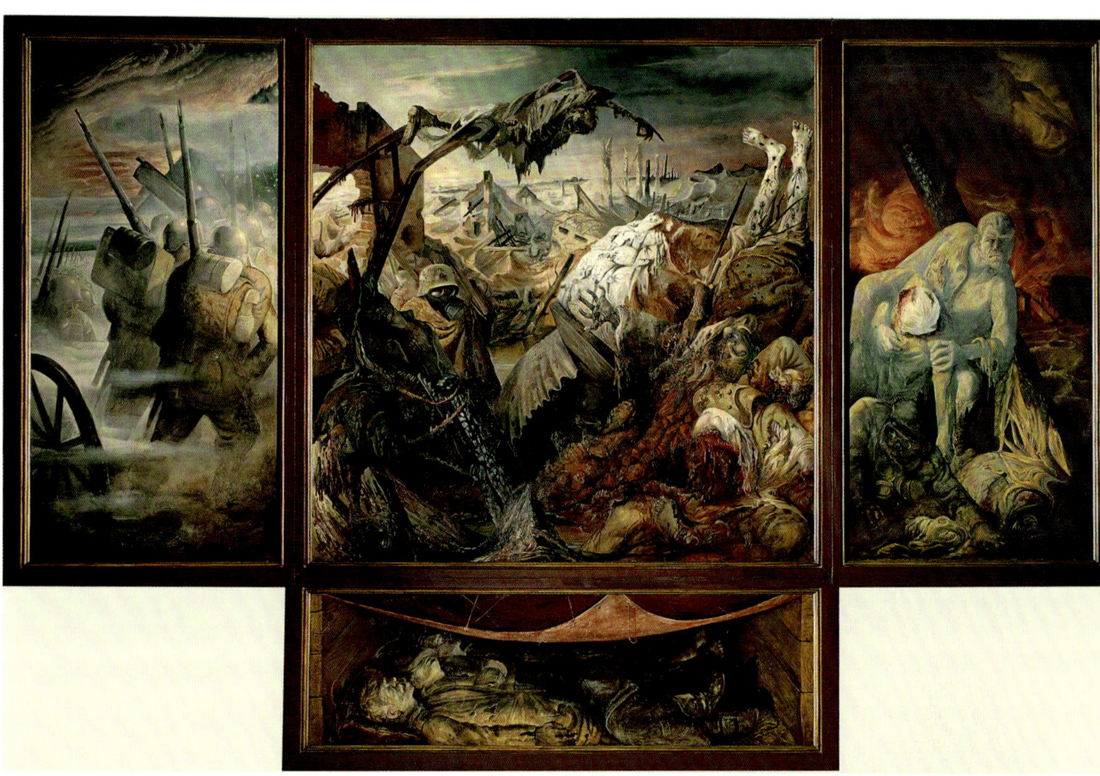

FIGURE 2.11 Otto Dix, *The War*, 1929–32. Triptych, oil on wood, middle panel 204 × 204 cm; left and right wings 204 × 102 cm each; predella 60 × 204 cm. Staatliche Kunstsammlungen, Dresden. © 2021 Artists Rights Society (ARS), New York / VG Bild-Kunst, Bonn. Photo: Erich Lessing / Art Resource, NY.

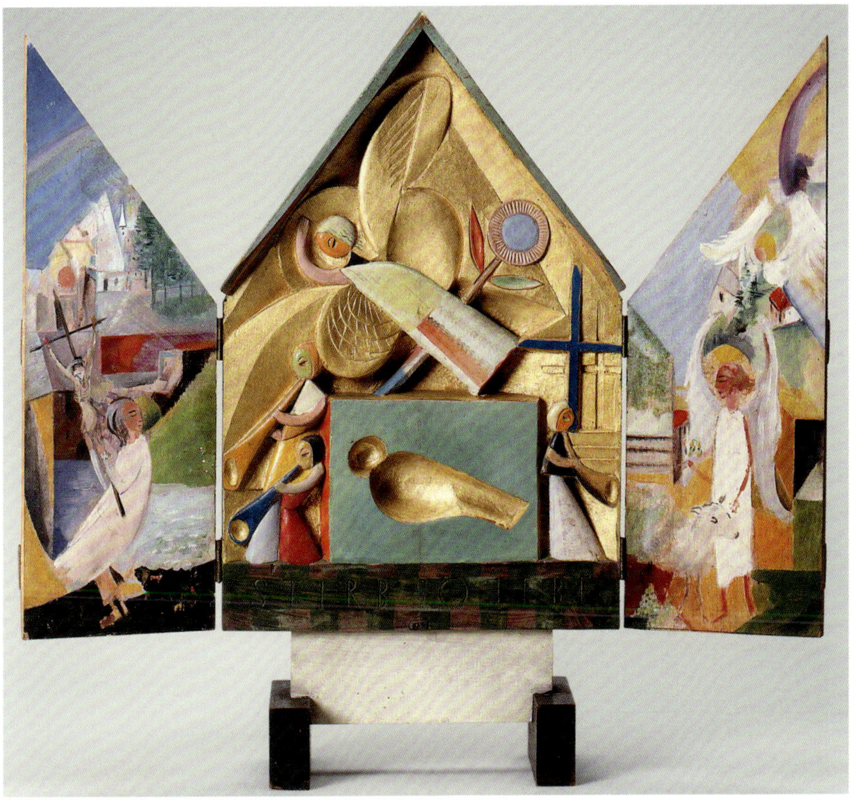

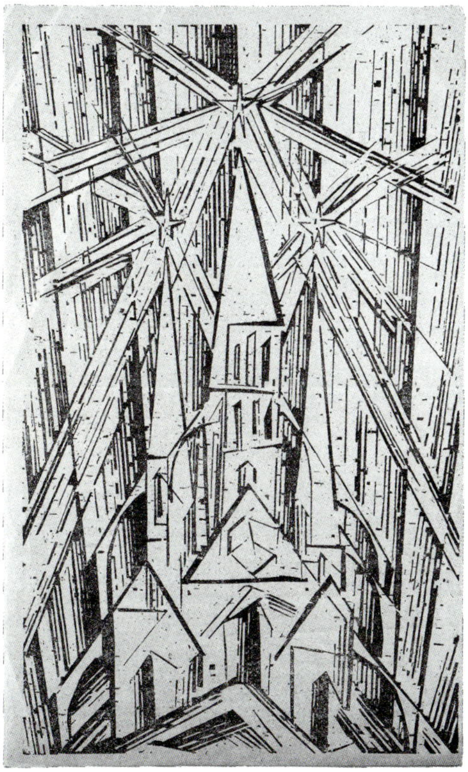

FIGURE 2.12 Gerhard Marcks and Alfred Partikel, *Small Altarpiece (Altärchen)*, 1920. Painted wood, 41 × 44 cm. Gerhard-Marcks-Haus, Bremen. © 2021 Artists Rights Society (ARS), New York / VG Bild-Kunst, Bonn.

FIGURE 2.13 Lyonel Feininger, cover illustration for Walter Gropius, *Program of the State Bauhaus in Weimar*, April 1919. Woodcut on green paper. Yale University Library.

already in the nineteenth century, effloresced in German art-historical scholarship after the First World War, in the writings of Georg Dehio, Wilhelm Pinder, and Erwin Panofsky.[99] The term was used for a new type of image developed in the late Middle Ages to serve new practices of affective, private contemplation in contrast to liturgy; it was strongly linked with devotion in the home rather than the church, and thereby both with objects small in scale and with use characterized as private, subjective, personal.[100] As discussed in the previous chapter, Benjamin, in a 1931 letter, self-mockingly referred to the *Angelus* as among his *Heiligenbilder*, saints' pictures, a frequent synonym for *Andachtsbilder*, but, unlike the former, often rather pejorative.[101] In what seems almost like a riff on Benjamin's letter, to which he does not refer, O. K. Werckmeister has criticized the way that Benjamin's own later description of the "angel of history" became, as it were, "an *Andachtsbild*" in the late twentieth century "for a dissident mentality vacillating between historical abstraction and political projection."[102] Panofsky's influential 1927 definition of the pictorial type emphasizes that it affords the individual beholder "the possibility of *contemplative immersion*" in the picture, often by isolating out of a larger narrative a single figure or group of figures, bringing the action to a "standstill."[103] The concept of the late medieval *Andachtsbild*, as conceived in interwar art history, has some loose similarities with Klee's *Angelus*—singling out a single, hovering figure from both the complex scenography and the elaborate narrative construction that is Grünewald's altarpiece for liturgical use to create a picture scaled for an individual viewer-owner. But if most of the favored motifs for *Andachtsbilder*—for instance, the Man of Sorrows or the Pietà—invite the beholder's compassion for the suffering they depict as part of their devotional purpose, it would be, to say the least, difficult for the pious beholder imagined in the literature on *Andachtsbilder* to know what to do with the *Angelus*.

If Klee's angel mimics Grünewald's Christ, he seems to do so rather mockingly, rendering the blinding radiance of the halo around Jesus's head as the oversized noggin of a caricature. In fact, the *Angelus novus* may not be Klee's only send-up of the altarpiece's hovering Redeemer. His oil-transfer drawing *Mister Sol* (1919, 78) (fig. 2.14), or as Klee additionally titles it, *Das Haupt am Himmel*—made in May 1919 and therefore either during or shortly after the White Terror in Munich—may also be seen as riffing on the Resurrection panel of the Isenheim Altarpiece, then still on display in the Alte Pinakothek: the two contourless, frontal faces are radiant, solar.[104] Taking this as a parody of Grünewald, the title would seem to blaspheme against "the spirit of space-forming light" (to borrow Worringer's words) in Grünewald, chiming with Klee's rendering of Grünewald's effulgence as a linear sign for radiance, black lines spoking out from a disc between the figure's two eyes, a laconic abbreviation that says "light" without mimicking its effects. The *Mister* of the title—it is *Mister Sol*, not *Herr Sol*, in the original—might even resonate with the rumors that some American moneybags was going to buy the altarpiece.[105] This modest drawing might be connected in still other ways to both the famous altarpiece and the *Angelus*: Marie Kakinuma has discussed *Mister Sol* as one of Klee's double-sided recto-verso pictures, a group that provides an important context for the related yet distinct layering of images in the *Angelus*.[106] The oil-transfer drawing *Mister Sol* relates meaningfully to a face concealed behind it (in this case, a pencil drawing of a face on the verso of its support), although it was only an ill-judged remounting of the work decades later that revealed the pencil drawing and thereby the play Kakinuma discusses between the two sides as a double-sided reflection on the position and persona of the artist, related to his own meditations, in writings and pictures, on masks. *Mister Sol* might be seen as taking up the altarpiece's own extensive elaboration of significant relations between recto and verso (the double-sided panels of the double-winged *Schnitzaltar* originally allowed it to be reconfigured for different times in the liturgical calendar); in Munich, as in Colmar, its disarticulated presentation allowed visitors to walk around to see both sides. The oil-transfer *Angelus* might be seen as a variation on the play on the part of *Mister Sol* with the double-sided panels of the retable, with their capacity to relate what they show with what they conceal.

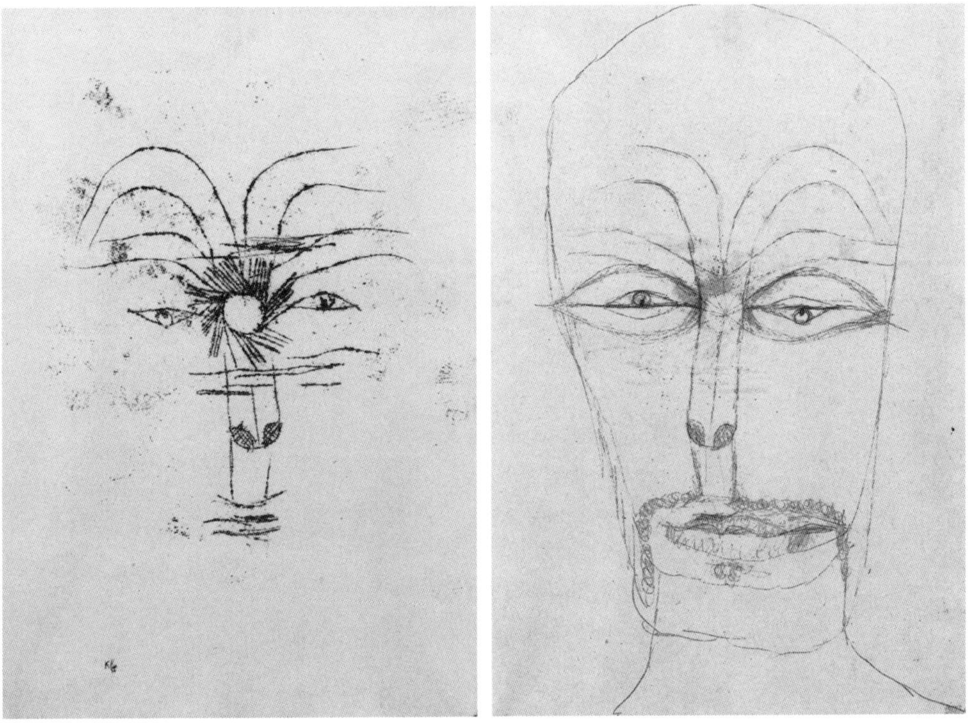

FIGURE 2.14 Left: Paul Klee, *Mister Sol*, 1919, 78. Oil-transfer drawing on paper, 27.2 × 19.6 cm. Private collection. Right: Paul Klee, back of *Mister Sol*, 1919. Pencil on paper.

Klee's use of color in the *Angelus* should also be considered. Since Grünewald became well known in the nineteenth century, he has been widely considered one of the greatest colorists of the Northern Renaissance; I cited earlier Worringer's passage on Grünewald as inspiriting color. His handling of light and color in the Resurrection panel in particular has attracted much attention—out of the black night bursts the glory of Christ as prismatic color, illuminating the atmosphere and the shroud unfurling around him. In the *Angelus novus*, however, just as in Klee's other watercolored oil transfers, the

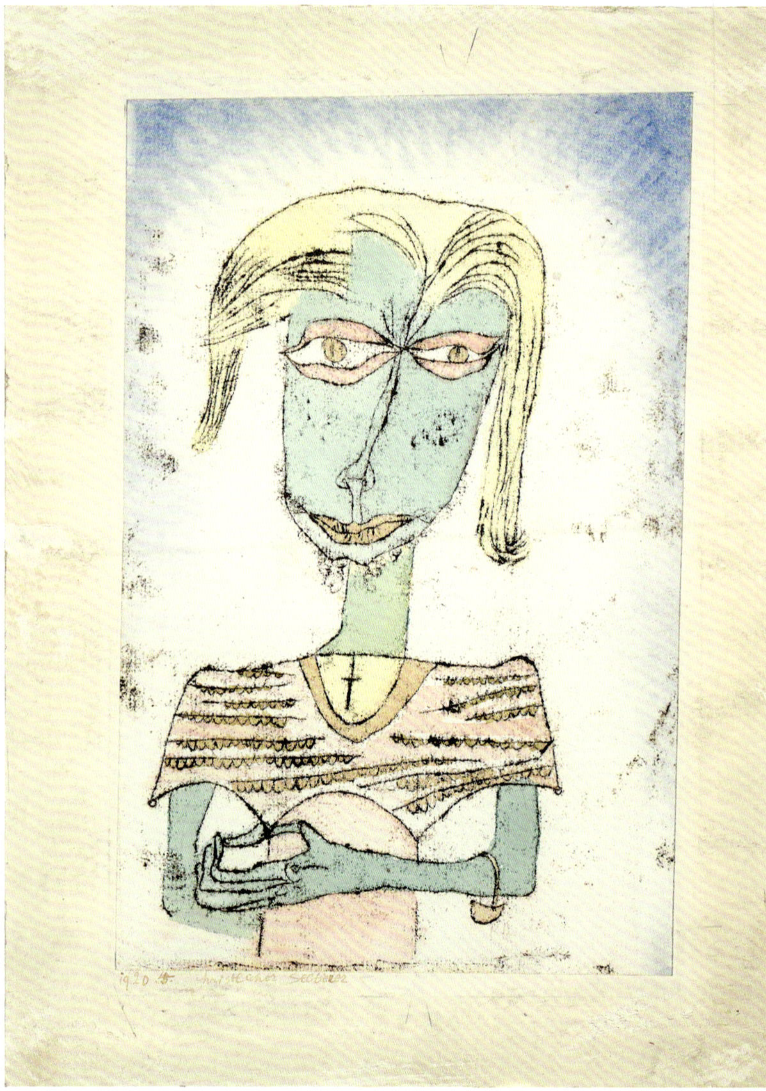

FIGURE 2.15 Paul Klee, *Christian Sectarian*, 1920. Oil-transfer drawing and watercolor on paper on board, 31.5 × 23.2 cm. Museum of Modern Art, New York. James Thrall Soby Fund. Digital Image © The Museum of Modern Art, New York / Licensed by SCALA / Art Resource, NY.

traced lines dominate.[107] While many of Klee's oil transfers are garishly, kitschily colorful, such as the pinks and greens of the 1920 *Christian Sectarian* (fig. 2.15), the *Angelus* is mostly brown, with tints of red and yellow, suggesting an artificial aging of the picture.[108] Charles W. Haxthausen has written about a number of works, mostly made in the 1920s, in which Klee conjures paradoxical temporalities by combining simulated traces of age with stylistic markers of the new and modern; for instance, in *Inscription* (1926) (fig. 2.16), writes Haxthausen, Klee "has simulated the effect of aged paper, complete with fox-

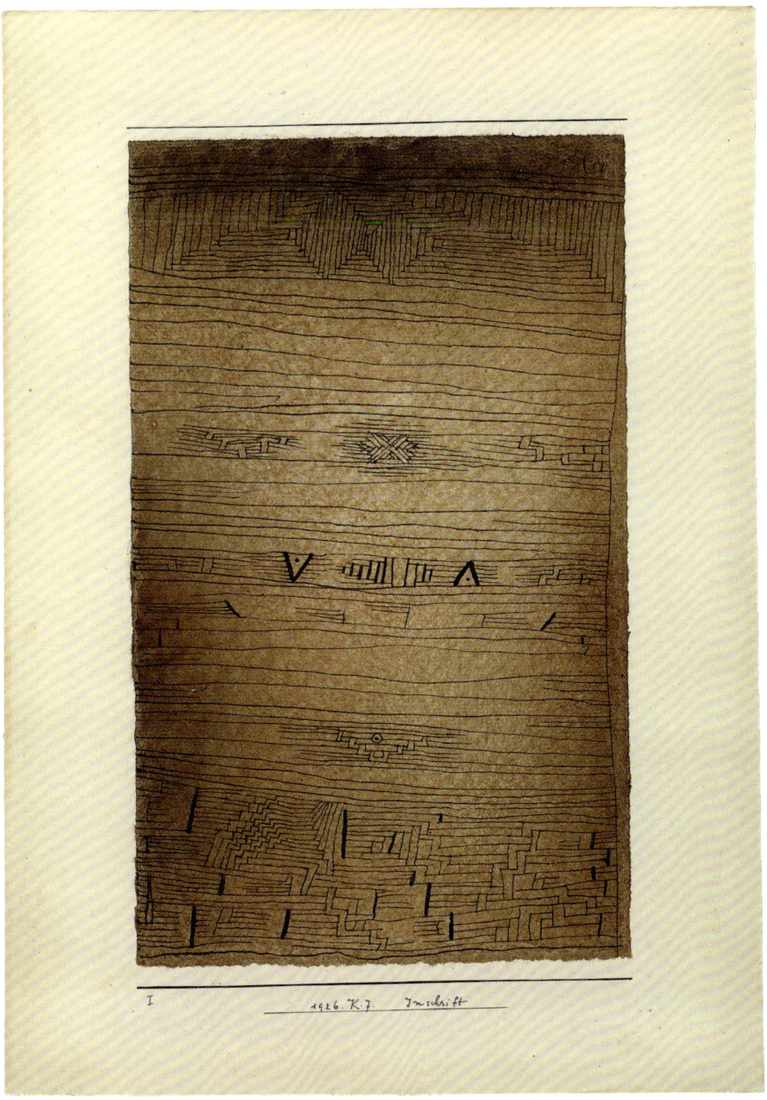

FIGURE 2.16 Paul Klee, *Inscription*, 1926. Watercolor and ink on paper, mounted on board, 31.1 × 22.2 cm. Solomon R. Guggenheim Museum, New York, Solomon R. Guggenheim Founding Collection, By gift. Photo: The Solomon R. Guggenheim Foundation / Art Resource, NY.

ing that speckles its surface," so that our attention is drawn less to the "what the inscription signifies" than to "the sheet's afterlife, its survival through history. . . . All of this, of course, is a fiction, for the watercolor has no such history and the viewer knows it."[109] The *Angelus*, with its watercolor faux foxing applied in the area between the chin and shoulders, may be counted among these works.

To understand the ambivalence suggested by Klee's little age-spotted caricature of Grünewald's Christ, it may be useful to examine a reference to Luther in Klee's previously mentioned essay on graphic art, published the same year that he made his angel. Klee's essay is an idiosyncratic modernist theory of abstraction, centered not on painting but on "graphic art"—drawing, above all. Disputing any notion of an essential division between the temporal verbal arts and the spatial plastic arts, Klee emphasizes the similarities between writing and graphic art in particular, using Luther to celebrate the primacy of the idea in graphic art: "In the beginning is the deed, perhaps, but the idea lies above it. And since infinity, like a circle, has no definite beginning, the idea may be seen as primary. In the beginning was the word, Luther translates."[110]

Klee's Luther reference is wrapped in an allusion to Goethe's *Faust*, to the scene in which the scholar Faust translates the beginning of the Gospel of John into German. The media theorist Friedrich Kittler has glossed the scene as Faust's entry into the Romantic hermeneutics of "free translation," leaving behind the humanists' word-for-word practice.[111] Faust begins, like Luther, with "In the beginning was the word," but unsatisfied by his own bookish labors, he tries out alternatives, finally settling on "Deed." Klee reverses Faust's trajectory, making a tactical alliance with Luther, against Faust, to shore up the claims of the idea as word in graphic art. In Klee's 1916 diary, he opposes himself to the "Faustian" ("Everything Faustian is alien to me"), contrasting himself with what he sees as the "Faustian element" in his friend Marc.[112]

Hence, perhaps, some of the ambivalence. Much of Klee's art at this time took on modernist ideas to parody them; the *Angelus* may be seen as such a parody of the Expressionist vision of modernism as the resurrection of "the Gothic."[113]

So, Klee's *Angelus novus* both gestures toward and undermines a vision of the new art, including his own, as a new angel announcing a resurrection of art that would make it no longer, to return to Hegel's phrase, "a thing of the past." An ambivalent icon, it hovers, rather than taking a stand like Luther, both enacting and deflating hopes such as Marc's or Hausenstein's of a turning point ahead. While before the war, Marc wrote in *The Blue Rider* almanac of his present as at the end of the artistic-*cum*-religious epoch of Christianity and the beginning of a new one—"we believe that today we stand at the turning point between two long epochs"—Klee's angel calls into question the logic of turning points shaping the millenarian anticipations of Expressionists who believed strongly that art indexes such epochal transformations.[114]

The images of Christ and Luther it compounds are of celebrated watersheds, understood, in ideologies dominant in early twentieth-century Germany, to have cleaved history irrevocably into before and after. But each of these images is in Klee's work marked by an emphatic temporal dispersal, disjunctions of style, motif, date, and apparent condition—the reformer as he looked in portraits of 1539 onward in a print of 1838 dated 1521, and the age-browned angel, called new in a dead language, dated 1920 mimicking a figure painted in 1515 that was understood as having reached the zenith of its contemporaneity in 1918–1919. Layered together, we have a paradoxical compound that at once makes much of and confounds chronology, neither timeless nor aligned neatly with a moment of fabrication. In this respect, it is perhaps fitting that Klee's picture has not at all become best known along the lines I have proposed in this chapter's attempt to excavate what this image would have meant when it was made in 1920.

CHAPTER 3

1922

In the early 1920s, probably 1920 or 1921, Walter Benjamin wrote a page of notes revolving around objects as symbols and in particular the problems of certain "objects of the highest order" that "*point* to God." There is one explicit question among them: under a numbered list of what appear to be different concepts for thinking about objects in relation to what they are not but what they point toward (symbol, meaning, sign, representation), Benjamin writes: "How do works of art relate to these (e.g., Klee)?"[1] These notes, relating to his early writings about intentionality, identity, and the philosophy of language, announce themselves as part of the preliminary stages of planning a *Habilitation* thesis, the "second dissertation" required to teach in the German university system.[2] Benjamin gives two examples of such symbols, both taken from Christian worship: the cross and the Eucharist. Benjamin briefly cites Luther ("Luther: The bread *is* the body of Christ"), referring, it seems, to the arguments between Luther and the Swiss reformer Huldrych Zwingli about Christ's presence in the Eucharist, and he implies that Luther's view of the union of bread and body is erroneous but better than Zwingli's ("To say 'means' instead of 'is' would be even more false").[3]

We cannot be certain whether Benjamin's question relates to his acquisition of Klee's *The Presentation of the Miracle* in 1920 or of the *Angelus novus* in 1921; his interest in Klee's art began earlier, during the war. Both the Klee pictures he owned could be said to raise the question of how works of art might relate to, while remaining distinct from, theological symbols, most obviously in their inscribed title's references to theological concepts (miracles, angels) and in their distance from religious uses, a distance Benjamin would make reference to by pretending to collapse when he termed his Klees *Heiligenbilder*.[4] The *Habilitation* thesis Benjamin submitted in 1925, the *Origin of the German Trauerspiel*, dealt with Luther, and with Dürer's engraving *Melencolia I*, but never mentions Klee.

This chapter argues that Benjamin's writings about the angel have more to do with Klee's picture than has often been suspected. My argument is not that Benjamin saw the work along the lines proposed in the preceding chapter.

Rather, some of Benjamin's writings may be seen as an acute response to Klee's work, to features of the latter that escaped most later commentators, while turning that response toward some concerns of his that Klee did not share. I argue that Benjamin did catch Klee's reference to the panel of Grünewald's 1515 Isenheim Altarpiece representing Christ's Resurrection and Ascension (see fig. 2.1). In his memoir, Scholem speaks of Benjamin's intense involvement with the *Schnitzaltar* during the 1910s, of the reproduction of it that "hung on the wall of his study, where it would remain for many years to come," the "special trip" he made to Colmar to see the panels in person, and the frequent references he made to them.[5] I argue further that Klee's game of triangulating and superimposing images in tension with one another did not escape him.

The focus of this chapter is on rereading the first major role that the *Angelus novus* played in Benjamin's writings, in the period directly following his purchase, when Benjamin attempted, in response to a publisher's invitation, to launch a new journal that he called *Angelus Novus* (fig. 3.1).[6] In a letter to Scholem, Benjamin refers to the picture as the "primal image" (*Urbild*) and to the journal as its "copy" (*Abbild*).[7] Benjamin devoted serious effort to the journal in 1921–1922, but it was never published. His 1922 announcement of its

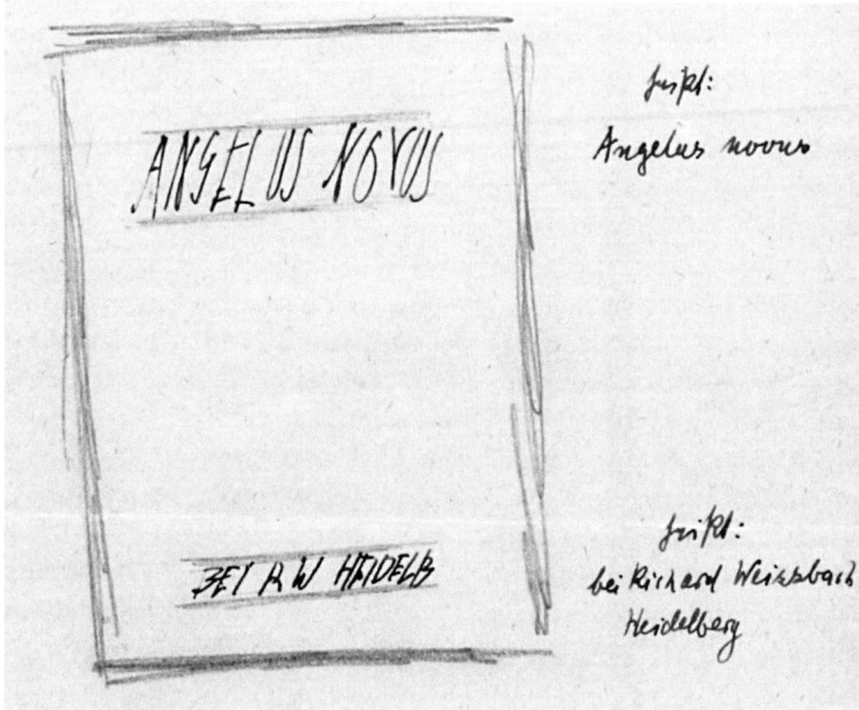

FIGURE 3.1 Walter Benjamin, sketch of cover layout for the journal *Angelus Novus* enclosed in a letter to the publisher Richard Weissbach, December 3, 1921, detail. Deutsches Literaturarchiv Marbach.

program mentions neither Klee nor the picture directly but ends with a paragraph that glosses the title as pointing to the journal's hoped-for ephemerality and contemporaneity (*Aktualität*) as follows: "According to a legend in the Talmud, the angels—who are born anew every instant in countless numbers—are created in order to perish and to vanish into the void, once they have sung their hymn in the presence of God."[8]

Now we are in a position to see that Benjamin decided to join Klee's game of superimposing conflicting images by superimposing a textual image of his own, of ephemeral Talmudic angels, as it were atop Klee's caricature of Grünewald's risen Christ, doubling Klee's gesture of layering one contradictory image over another. Klee's reference to this specifically Christian devotional image—and one that was often seen as the most "German" of paintings—was part of the point of Benjamin's rewriting of it in his essay announcing the *Angelus Novus* journal in terms of specifically Jewish angelology, about which Scholem had informed him.[9]

A little sketch Benjamin sent to Scholem in a 1921 letter in which he updated his friend on his work on the journal suggests that the way Klee's picture refigures Jesus as an angel was of interest to Benjamin as he developed the journal project (fig. 3.2). Benjamin inscribed his drawing "ECCE ANGELUS IN ITINERE"—"Behold the angel en route," echoing Pontius Pilate's words in

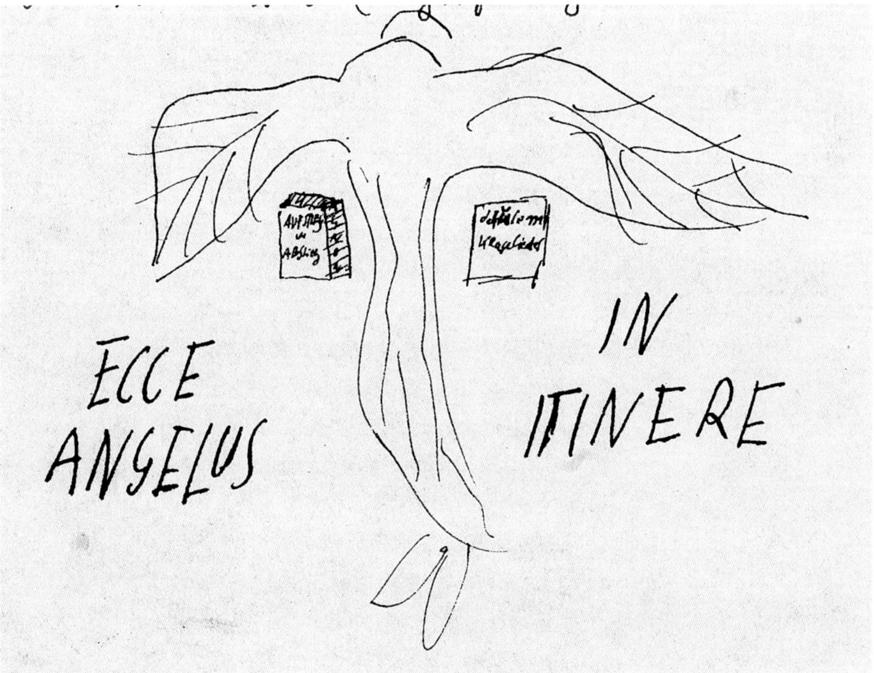

FIGURE 3.2 Walter Benjamin, letter to Gershom Scholem, October 27, 1921, detail. Archives Department, the National Library of Israel.

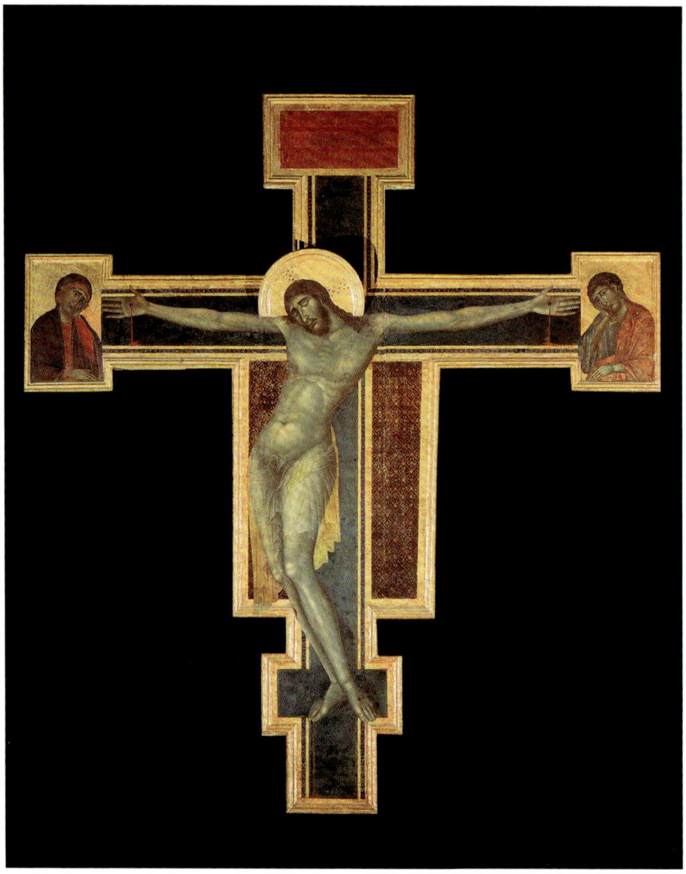

FIGURE 3.3 Cimabue, *Crucifix*. Tempera and gold on wood, 448 × 390 cm. Museo dell'Opera di Santa Croce, Florence.

the Gospel of John, "Ecce homo," "Behold the man," as he presents the thorn-crowned Jesus to a hostile crowd of "Jews" who demand his death (a frequent occasion for anti-Jewish caricature in Christian art).[10] Benjamin's sketch shows what appears to be a leaf-winged angel (which looks nothing like Klee's) crucified and haloed, roughly following the iconographic conventions of *Christus patiens* (fig. 3.3). (Given Benjamin's fascination with the Isenheim Altarpiece, it is worth mentioning that his sketch does not much resemble its Crucifixion.) The leaf wings in Benjamin's sketch pun—in German, *Blätter* is the usual word for either the leaves of a plant or the pages of a publication—making the crucified angel into a personification of the journal as well as a revision of Klee's angel.

Moreover, Benjamin, I suggest, was interested in the picture in part as a locus for a particular kind of Jewish-Christian exchange, as I explore by examining the 1922 essay Benjamin wrote setting forth the "governing principles" of the journal, and his correspondence with those who were to contribute to it, in the context of a contemporary efflorescence of attempts at interreligious dialogue.[11]

Howard Eiland and Michael W. Jennings, the authors of the magisterial Benjamin biography, call Benjamin "a central figure in the religious revival that swept Germany in the years following World War I"; they note that his "increasing politicization" was bound up with his "fascination with the attempts . . . to work toward a new German society conceived as a . . . commingling of religious faiths" undertaken by the Jewish philosophers Martin Buber and Franz Rosenzweig and Benjamin's close friend Florens Christian Rang, a Protestant theologian.[12] The 1910s and 1920s in Germany saw a number of efforts toward interreligious, and especially Jewish-Christian, exchange undertaken by some of those active in religious socialism and/or what Martin Buber called the "Jewish Renaissance"; exemplary is the journal *Die Kreatur* (*The Creature*), put together, following Rang's conception, by one editor from each of what were often understood as the three main confessions in Germany: Judaism, Protestantism, and Catholicism.[13] Benjamin also attended to some extent to the religio-political events in Munich in spring 1919; he wrote a letter to Scholem in June 1919 attempting to pump him for information on the situation in the wake of the White Terror, and his 1921 sketch "Capitalism as Religion," which argued that the apparently profane practices of capitalism must be seen as relentlessly cultic ("not merely, as Weber believes . . . a formation conditioned by religion, but . . . an essentially religious phenomenon"), cited the *Call to Socialism* of the German-Jewish communitarian anarchist-socialist Gustav Landauer, mentioned in the previous chapter.[14]

A survey of attempts at interreligious exchange in these years is far beyond my scope, and the difficulties of this territory are daunting. German Jews conceptualized their differences from and relations to other groups in Germany in manifold ways, in terms of religion, ethnicity, race, culture, and experience, and the different conceptualizations crossed and interfered with each other in complex ways. For instance, in the German-Jewish neo-Kantian philosopher Hermann Cohen's "Germanness and Jewishness" of 1915, Cohen writes that German Jews must "convince all our fellow Jews throughout the world of the religious significance of Germanness" as part of the larger project of uniting "the people of the world . . . in the consciousness of a messianic humanity."[15] The 1910s saw major shifts in these discussions, as Michael Brenner has explained. In the nineteenth century, emancipation was usually joined to a conceptualization of Judaism as "a private religious faith of individual German citizens," but Buber and others saw this process of confessionalization as leaving German Jews (divided, moreover, among Liberals, Orthodox, and nonbelievers) without a *Gemeinschaft* (community).[16] At the beginning of the First World War, as Brenner writes, some German Jews, such as Cohen, had high hopes that the war would bring about "the full integration of Jews" into "a German *Volksgemeinschaft* [people's community]," as German Jews fought and died for Germany. There were hopes as well that a victorious German Empire would be the instrument freeing Russian Jews from tsarist oppression. But they ended in bitter disappointment, especially as antisemitism intensified during the war and especially in its counterrevolutionary aftermath.[17] Understanding Buber's attempts in these years to construct new relations between Jews and Christians—often involving the figure of Jesus—and the responses they provoked, will require keeping this larger context in mind.

I look here in some detail at what I argue is one such attempt by Buber, a small-scale one in the form of an essay on Grünewald's Isenheim Altarpiece. A related effort undertaken by Ernst Bloch in portions of the first edition of his messianic-Marxist-Expressionist *Spirit of Utopia* (1918) will also enter the discussion. Both Benjamin and Scholem were at times harshly critical of Bloch, and even more so of Buber. Examining both their targets and their criticism will aid in making visible the interreligious dimension of Benjamin's engagement with the *Angelus* in the early 1920s.

This dimension has been difficult to see in part because Benjamin began to reorient his work toward Marxism in the following years. Although Scholem's indispensable writings argue for the importance of the theological in Benjamin's writing, they have also played some part in deflecting attention from the particular connections I follow in this chapter. In his "Walter Benjamin and His Angel," Scholem devotes less than a paragraph to discussion of the *Angelus Novus* journal project.[18] From the start, Scholem kept his distance from this project, while Benjamin urged his collaboration, straining their friendship; as Scholem wrote in his 1975 memoir, *Walter Benjamin: The Story of a Friendship*, "The high expectations which Benjamin had for my collaboration were rather embarrassing to me. After all, I could not conceal from him the fact that I did not feel impelled to collaborate on a German periodical in what seemed to me like an especially visible manner while my mind was on quite different things and goals—something that Benjamin certainly must have been aware of."[19]

In Scholem's scathing attack of 1964 on the "myth of German-Jewish dialogue," he wrote that this so-called dialogue "consisted . . . only of a chorus of Jewish voices and was, on the level of historical reality, never anything else but a fiction."[20] Scholem sometimes wanted to see in Benjamin's writing an exclusive relation to Jewish traditions—particularly when he summarizes. A short, seemingly matter-of-fact, passage from Scholem's 1965 essay "Walter Benjamin" exemplifies both how and why "Benjamin's 'theological thinking'" could at times strain Scholem's presentation of it: it "took its bearings (instinctively, I almost added) from Jewish concepts. Christian ideas never held any attraction for him. Indeed, he had an undisguised distaste for the type of neo-Catholicism which, at the time, was much in vogue among Jewish intellectuals in Germany and France."[21] Scholem parenthetically signals his own reservations, stemming from what he describes as Benjamin's "factual ignorance" of

Judaism, which coexisted with his interest in it, follows this with a sentence ("Christian ideas never held any attraction for him") that is unequivocal and falsifiable, and he presents the next sentence as if it provided strong evidence for the claim it follows, when in fact—as Scholem himself later wrote in his *Story of a Friendship*—it had much to do with Benjamin's reading of the liberal Lutheran theologian and historian Adolf von Harnack's monumental *History of Dogma* (1886–89) in its "entire three fat volumes."[22] In a March 1918 letter to Scholem, Benjamin reported that Harnack's book had helped him see "how ignorance . . . is a strong source of the contemporary neo-Catholic trend, particularly as it has affected intelligent Jews."[23]

The remarks of Scholem's former student and fierce critic Jacob Taubes on Harnack and the cultural Protestantism (*Kulturprotestantismus*) of which he was a leading representative can illuminate why Scholem sometimes preferred not to dwell on Benjamin's reading of Harnack. Taubes speaks of the First World War as causing the disintegration of "the synthesis of cultural Protestantism" and of German-Jewish participation in it, which Taubes characterizes as that of "a minor partner who took himself to be a partner while the other one didn't take him to be a partner at all."[24] While Harnack's earlier *History of Dogma* traced the elaboration of Christian doctrine as a husk of Hellenistic philosophy from which the teachings of Jesus should be freed by historical criticism such as his own, completing the work of the Reformation, his 1921 book *Marcion: The Gospel of the Alien God* not only discusses, as the *History of Dogma* did, the important early Christian heretic who proposed that the God of the Hebrew Bible was an evil demiurge but also asserts that Protestantism should take up Marcion's proposal and discard the Hebrew Bible.[25]

When Scholem probes Benjamin's writings in more detail, he necessarily takes account of how they draw on both Jewish and Christian elements (although this phrase is too symmetrical and tidy to do justice to the vexed historical entanglements in play).[26] For instance, in "Walter Benjamin and His Angel," Scholem discusses a diverse array of concepts—Jewish, Christian, both, and occasionally neither—as informing Benjamin's idiosyncratic and shifting conception of the *Angelus*: Christian Baroque allegory (as discussed in Benjamin's *Trauerspiel* book), Jewish angelology (about which Scholem himself was Benjamin's main source of knowledge), Satan ("not directly from the Jewish tradition" but as refigured by Baudelaire), the "claws of Satan" of "Christian tradition," and the "kabbalistic concept of *tikkun*."[27] The fact of combination is plain to see; more difficult to analyze is its modality. As Michael W. Jennings argues, one of the limits against which Benjamin defined his theological thinking was syncretism. Rather, Jennings proposes, Benjamin attempts "an embrace of a theological position that juxtaposes, rather than mixes, elements from different faiths . . . remain[ing] aware of the differences and tensions among its elements," a "theology as montage practice."[28]

But more broadly, the invisibility of the interreligious aspect of Benjamin's engagement with Klee's picture is a consequence not of Scholem's interpretation of his friend's work, but of the fact (to which Scholem's interpretation might itself be seen as in part responding) that the mode of interreligious discussion for which it seems Benjamin's journal was to make a place did not happen. As we will see, Benjamin envisioned writing undergirded not by tolerance, or by experience, but rather by the hoped-for coming of a new form of religion—in Benjamin's words in the 1922 *Angelus Novus* journal announcement, "future religious orders."[29] In Benjamin's use of this image, I am tracing the faint contours of what did not take place.

When Benjamin, in his journal announcement, describes the publication as striving for true contemporaneity, one might initially assume that it is devoted to the literary and cultural life of a presumably secular modernity, despite Benjamin's use of the singing and vanishing angels of the Talmud as figuring such contemporaneity. But according to the announcement, contemporaneity must be linked to religious becoming: Benjamin writes that the journal will demonstrate its contemporaneity by its "philosophical universality" and that, from the journal's perspective, "the universal validity of spiritual [*geistig*] utterances must be bound up with the question of whether they can lay claim to a place within future religious orders." Benjamin does not use the ecstatic language with which Expressionists sometimes spoke of a future religion, nor does he speak with their prophetic certainty; as mentioned in the previous chapter, in *The Blue Rider* almanac, which Benjamin owned, Marc asserted that the present was "the turning point between two long epochs," the end of the Christian epoch and the beginning of a new one.[30] Benjamin insists on soberly articulating the need for "future religious orders" rather than speaking as if they already existed:

> Not as if such orders were already visible on the horizon. What is visible is the fact that without them, none of the things that are struggling for life can make their appearance and mark these days as the first of a new epoch. For that very reason, it would seem to be the right time to lend an ear not to those who imagine that they have already discovered the arcanum but to those who objectively, dispassionately, and unobtrusively give expression to hardship and need. . . . [S]piritualist occultism, political obscurantism, and Catholic expressionism will be encountered in these pages only as the targets of unsparing criticism.[31]

My first task is to give some sense of the context of Benjamin's articulation of this "need."

Clearly, Benjamin sought to set his project apart from other tendencies then prevailing in the postwar religious revival. Looking back later, Benjamin would write about how, in the years right after the war, an "oppressive wealth of ideas . . . swamped" the Germans: "the revival of astrology and the wisdom of yoga, Christian Science and chiromancy, vegetarianism and gnosis, scholasticism and spiritualism."[32] It seems that, in 1922, Benjamin was anxious to set apart his journal's project from such a range of beliefs and practices, dismissed as "spiritual occultism." He implies that their proponents are self-deluded, whereas, he writes, "we shall aspire to rationality." He envisions a broad discussion of religion: "Because none but free spirits are to discuss religion, the journal will feel free to go beyond the frontiers of our language, indeed of the West, and move to a consideration of other religions."[33] Benjamin's particular condemnation here of "Catholic expressionism" should be noted especially when considering Benjamin's response to Klee's *Angelus*, which can be seen as both gesturing toward and mocking Expressionist visions of modernism as resurrecting "the Gothic," a Romantic myth of art's integral social role before the Reformation. In the previous chapter, I mentioned the currency of these ideas among intellectuals supporting the November Revolution. One version of such a vision of the Gothic that Benjamin had read a couple of years earlier may be found in the art-historical section of Bloch's *Spirit of Utopia*, which celebrates a homology between Gothic ornament and Christianity.[34]

Benjamin first presented his journal project in a 1921 letter to Scholem as "structured entirely and unconditionally in keeping with my conception of the journal when I first thought of it many years ago"—"to be exact," he writes, in a proud gesture of underlining the consistency of his conception in the face of the profound changes brought about by the war, "in July 1914."[35] While no simple continuity should be assumed between Benjamin's youthful prewar writings and his later writings pertaining to the *Angelus Novus* journal project, some of the former, animated by the hope for a new religion do shed some light on Benjamin's joining of ephemeral contemporaneity with the coming of a new form of religion in the *Angelus Novus* announcement a decade later.

Benjamin's 1912 "Dialogue on the Religiosity of the Present" takes place between an enlightened critic of religion and an "I" who in fact seems to represent many of Benjamin's views at that time.[36] This "I," mocked by the interlocutor as "reactionary," announces that a new religion will come—"The dualism of social morality and personality will be acknowledged. From this need a religion will be born"—and with it an "honest socialism."[37] The "I" sees contemporary cultural life as the place where this process will unfold—indeed, he makes a claim that might initially seem bizarre, asserting that it is the literati (as he makes clear, in the rather derogatory sense of idle, café-frequenting intellectuals) who, as the "oppressed," will produce a new spiritual ground for daily life.[38]

In the "Dialogue," there is no explicit mention of Jewishness or Judaism. However, in Benjamin's contemporaneous letters to Ludwig Strauss—provoked in part by Moritz Goldstein's 1912 essay "German-Jewish Parnassus" and the ensuing debate about the role of Jews in German cultural life, and in part by Benjamin's first encounter with Zionism—Benjamin speaks of Jews in particular, in their participation in European cultural life, as the dualists and as the literati characterized in the "Dialogue" (which Benjamin mentions in the letters) as these bearers of the new religion.[39] Benjamin was not alone in posing the question of the *religious* position of the café, that metropolitan space of intellectual sociability and the nexus of avant-garde movements, and of the "literati" who frequented it—often, and not unrelatedly, Jewish, outside the university, and short on cash. Benjamin, in his "The Life of Students" (1915), disputes a comment made by a "celebrated German university professor" on the "coffeehouse literati according to whom Christianity is finished"; in contrast, Max Brod, writing in 1916–1917 in Buber's *Der Jude*, central organ of the postassimilatory "Jewish Renaissance," criticized in two articles a turn among "our young Jewish literati" toward "a new gnosis or a neo-Christianity."[40]

The Jewish engagement in culture of which Benjamin speaks does not take the form of involvement with Jewish culture in particular. At the time, Benjamin was a leading activist in that small part of the German Youth Movement propounding the educational reforms developed by Gustav Wyneken, and Benjamin tells Strauss he discovered his own "Jewishness" through his deep involvement in the Youth Movement and with many other Jewish adherents of the "German" Wyneken.[41] This engagement appears to provide Benjamin with his model of an internationalist "*Kultur*-Zionism that sees Jewish values *everywhere* and works for them" unfolding in European culture, which he opposes to "Palestine-Zionism."[42] In an earlier letter to Strauss, it is precisely in the context of speaking of this "Jewish cultural work [*Kulturarbeit*]" that Benjamin expands on his idea that the literati are, while despised by most (and therefore, he claims, occupying a place parallel to that of "the poor in spirit, the oppressed, and the meek" for early Christianity), carrying on a crucial and religiously significant process of taking on new ways or forms of life (*die neuen Lebensarten*) first discovered in art: "This is their serious mission: to win from art, which they themselves cannot make, spirit for contemporary life."[43] Similarly, in the next letter, Benjamin speaks of the "rigorously dualistic conception of life"—related, it seems, to the "dualism of social morality and personality" in the "Dialogue"—as something he finds both in himself and in the other most ardent, mostly Jewish, supporters of Wyneken's program; he underlines the connection of Jewishness and dualism with a reference to Buber.[44]

Benjamin concludes his argument for "*Kultur*-Zionism" with a sentence—"Here I want to stand and, I believe, you must also stand here"—that echoes

Luther's famous words at Worms.[45] As Brian Britt comments, by "citing Luther in defense of his Jewish self-understanding," Benjamin presents his Jewish and German identifications as inextricably intertwined.[46] Notably, Benjamin marks his identification with Jewishness, Germanness, and at the same time with a broader transnational Europeanness using terms and references—Luther, *Kultur*—central to liberal, Protestant German nationalism from the *Kulturkampf* through the First World War. References to Luther of various kinds were common in German-Jewish articulations of Jewishness, and not only among those who shared Benjamin's allegiance to "*Kultur*-Zionism": take, for instance, the "95 Theses on Judaism and Zionism" that Scholem wrote in 1918 for Benjamin's birthday (but did not give him).[47] The reference to Luther in the form and title of a piece of writing that takes "Judaism and Zionism" as its subject is not quite as strange as it might first seem. Not only was Luther simply an unavoidably central figure in Wilhelmine Germany, but those translating from the Hebrew Bible into German—one of Scholem's main activities at the time—had somehow to grapple, often phrase by phrase, with the way their target language was itself understood as having been formed by Luther's translations of Hebrew.[48] Rosenzweig's articulations of the difficulties of translating Hebrew into German in light of the importance of the Luther Bible suggest the complexities potentially in play here. In 1921, Rosenzweig replied to Scholem's criticism of his translation of the grace after meals as relying on "the language of the church" as follows: "Only someone who is inwardly convinced of its impossibility can be a translator. . . . The *specific* impossibility is in every case different. In my case its name is Luther. . . . He who translates into German must in one way or another translate into a Christian language."[49] Later, the Luther Bible was a constant, inevitable, point of reference in the making and the reception of the Buber-Rosenzweig German translation of the Hebrew Bible.[50] Rosenzweig explained that Luther's translation of the Hebrew Bible, in the main domesticating, is foreignizing, closest to the Hebrew, at precisely those points that Luther sees the "Old Testament" speaking most directly to him *as a Christian*.[51]

Benjamin's own essay "The Task of the Translator" was originally to be published in the first issue of the *Angelus Novus* journal; in it, he cites Luther as among those whose fulfillment of that task "extended the boundaries of the German language." Benjamin conceived of translation as a crucial aspect of the journal's project, as "the strict and irreplaceable school of language-in-the-making" from which German writing must learn.[52] Translations and commentaries on translation dominate the planned table of contents of the first issue: besides his own "Task of the Translator," he wanted to see Scholem's "On Lamentation" (an essay relating to Scholem's translation of the Hebrew Bible's book of Lamentations) and translations of S. Y. Agnon's stories "The Old Synagogue" and "Rise and Fall" from Hebrew into German.[53] (Rang's essay on the "Historical Psychology of Carnival" is the odd one out.)

Benjamin's planned journal can be usefully located in relation to others by tracing where contributions considered for its first issue were in fact published. Agnon's story "Rise and Fall," in Scholem's translation, found a place in Buber's *Der Jude*.[54] The quarterly *Die Kreatur* published Rang's essay "The Historical Psychology of Carnival."[55] Rang's essay on Goethe's poem "Blessed Longing," from his *West-Eastern Divan*, which came out of Goethe's study of Persian poetry—which Rang offered for the first issue but Benjamin rejected—was published in Hugo von Hofmannsthal's journal *Neue Deutsche Beiträge* (*New German Contributions*).[56] Benjamin's own contribution to the first issue was published in his 1923 book of Baudelaire translations, but he also published later in *Die Kreatur*, and some of his most important writings ("Goethe's Elective Affinities" and a section of the *Trauerspiel* book) were published in *Neue Deutsche Beiträge*.[57] Benjamin, though, declined Buber's invitation to contribute to *Der Jude*.[58] The *Angelus Novus* journal might be understood as occupying a position between these three journals—perhaps an impossible one.

Buber edited both *Der Jude* and *Die Kreatur*; in the case of the latter journal, he served, following Rang's idea, alongside a Protestant and a Catholic editor. Victor von Weizsäcker, the Protestant editor, wrote that it "should be neither trans- nor inter- nor non-confessional. But faith went into exile for all of us, and everyone spoke to the others from his exile."[59] Rosenzweig, who has been called one of the "leading spirits" of the journal, wrote as follows in a 1924 letter to Buber about the possibilities of postliberal Jewish-Christian dialogue.[60] Under the regime of liberal tolerance, wrote Rosenzweig, "The Christian ignores the Jew to be able to tolerate him, the Jew ignores the Christian in order to be tolerated. . . . Now . . . we have already entered a new era of persecutions. Nothing can be done about this, neither by us nor by well-meaning Christians. What can be done, however, is that this era of persecution should also become an era of religious dialogue, as in medieval times, and that the silence of the last centuries be ended."[61] Both *Der Jude* and *Die Kreatur* were central to interlinked projects of conversation among confessions in the Weimar Republic. How the *Neue Deutsche Beiträge* might relate to these projects is more elusive; moreover, Benjamin rejected Rang's Goethe essay for publication in *Angelus Novus* (because of, among other things, its "gnostic metaphysics") before Hofmannsthal accepted it. However, Hofmannsthal's journal is in some ways a telling comparison to Benjamin's, as a 1922 letter from Benjamin to Rang suggests: immediately after telling Rang that he has given up on pursuing the publication of the *Angelus Novus* journal for the time being, Benjamin writes: "Occasional work with Hofmannsthal, by the way, would certainly be agreeable."[62] The sequence implies that Benjamin saw contributing to Hofmannsthal's little magazine, the first issue of which had just come out that year, as in some measure substituting for the journal project that he felt he had to give up. This was more or less how Rang presented the matter to Hofmannsthal.[63]

While Hofmannsthal's religious and political views contrasted sharply with Benjamin's in many respects—in the years after the dismemberment of the Habsburg Empire, Hofmannsthal saw himself as recreating the values of Catholic Austria in cultural projects such as the Salzburg Festival—there are striking similarities between the *Angelus Novus* project and Hofmannsthal's, as Bernd Witte has pointed out.[64] While Witte describes Hofmannsthal's journal as "extremely exclusive," with its "bibliophile format and private circulation," Benjamin wanted his journal to be an order of magnitude more so.[65] While Hofmannsthal intended the costs of the journal to be borne by 1,500 to 1,800 paying subscribers, Benjamin intended to offer his as a numbered limited edition of 100 (he envisioned the subscribers as patrons backing the journal on behalf, it seems, of the even smaller number of its true readers).[66] This exclusivity was important for how each intended his magazine to function: Hofmannsthal writes that he will think of the subscribers as a "closed circle," Benjamin stresses the "very narrow closed circle" of contributors.[67] Animating both endeavors is a conviction of the centrality of language and of translation. Benjamin wrote to Hofmannsthal in a letter of 1924 venturing that they both share what Benjamin calls "the conviction guiding me in my literary endeavors": "That every truth has its home, its ancestral palace, in language; and that this palace is constructed out of the oldest logoi."[68] In the first paragraph of Hofmannsthal's announcement for his journal, he defines the *Beiträge* (contributions) of the title as contributions *to* language, which he equates with the "spiritual life of the nation": "language is all."[69] Roughly parallel to Benjamin's assertion in his announcement that the *Angelus* will move beyond the boundaries of the "West" ("des Abendlandes") to consider "other religions," Hofmannsthal wrote about his journal's aim of "transcending the sacrosanct old boundary of classical-Christian culture" by means, for instance, of commentaries on Buddhist and Sufi texts by scholars and translators such as Karl Eugen Neumann and Hans Heinrich Schaeder.[70] Yet the very cosmopolitanism of his *Neue Deutsche Beiträge*—the "concept of world literature" achieved by means of "sensitive and discrete juxtaposition" that Hofmannsthal had written about in his notes planning his journal—was framed by what Michael P. Steinberg has termed Hofmannsthal's "nationalist cosmopolitanism," his assertions of Austria as the special site of transcultural exchange and of German as the language of translation par excellence: "We are Germans and . . . our language, which is indeed our spiritual and intellectual destiny, has been given the characteristic that in it, as in no other language, the spiritual and intellectual creations of other peoples, even of those foreign to us, can rise again in their magnificence and reveal their distinctive essence."[71] Citing Luther, Stefan George, and above all Goethe's theory of translation in the

West-Eastern Divan—also touchstones in Benjamin's essay on the "Task of the Translator"—Hofmannsthal positions German as translation and translation as German. Alongside *Der Jude* and *Die Kreatur*, Hofmannsthal's conservative postwar project of regrounding culture in his journal by focusing above all on language and translation also provides context for the *Angelus Novus*—a journal that, as Benjamin wrote, aimed to offer, in light of a contemporary "crisis" of German poetry and language, a "form that has always had a beneficial effect on it in its periods of great crisis: translation," and that connected this offering with "future religious orders."[72]

Unlike Hofmannsthal's journal, *Der Jude* and *Die Kreatur* were both especially concerned with creating a new mode of conversation between Judaism and Christianity in Germany.[73] For both Rang and Buber, the utopian, international, and multireligious Forte-Circle of intellectuals, founded in 1914 as a "refuge for eminent minds," including Rang, Buber, and Landauer, appears to have been an important starting point.[74] In 1923, Benjamin "attended the first meeting of the 'Frankfurt Circle,' an interfaith group drawn together by Rang and . . . Buber that included Jews, Catholics, and a range of Protestants" to discuss "the possibility, under current conditions, of a political revival informed by religious principles."[75]

Like Rang, Buber was heavily involved in these projects—but unlike Rang, *not* in the *Angelus Novus* journal. Benjamin was a determined opponent of Buber's mysticism of experience (*Erlebnismystik*) in part because Buber's cult of experience drove his outspoken enthusiasm for the First World War. According to Scholem, Benjamin "said derisively that if Buber had his way, first of all one would have to ask every Jew, 'Have you experienced Jewishness yet?'"[76] I focus my discussion of the way Benjamin wanted to differentiate his *Angelus Novus* journal project from the kind of interreligious dialogue Buber propounded by contrasting Buber's and Benjamin's dealings with Grünewald's Isenheim Altarpiece.

Buber's short essay on the Isenheim Altarpiece, "The Altar," was published in the January 1914 issue of the Expressionist monthly *Die weissen Blätter* and again in his 1917 collection of essays *Events and Encounters*.[77] When the latter came out, Scholem wrote some vituperative pages in his diary on Buber's book, which Scholem describes as "in *every* respect . . . of an unprecedented loathsomeness."[78] It seems likely that he shared his criticism with Benjamin; the two frequently discussed their shared critique of Buber's *Erlebnismystik*.[79]

Events and Encounters collected a series of short essays on various topics, most of them, like "The Altar," published in *Die weissen Blätter* in 1914. They take up a variety of aesthetic-*cum*-religious topics, none out of place in such a journal: in Scholem's derisive words, "God, the world, Frank Wedekind, the body, Grünewald's altarpiece and whatever else swam in the sauce."[80] As discussed in the previous chapter, Grünewald's 1515 altarpiece was a frequent topic in artistic and especially in Expressionist circles in Germany.

The first three paragraphs of Buber's essay show in broad strokes how he places the Isenheim Altarpiece. Like many commentators who saw in Grünewald the last great gasp of the Gothic, Buber stresses the continuity between Grünewald's vision and the piety of the Middle Ages.[81] Buber's essay does so by insisting on the kinship between Grünewald and the Dominican theologian and mystic Meister Eckhart "who preached two centuries before in Alsatian cloisters."[82] Buber was steeped in German Romantic thought and the writings of Christian mystics—he had written his 1904 dissertation on Nicholas of Cusa (influenced by Eckhart) and Jakob Böhme (revived, like Eckhart, by the Catholic Romantic Franz von Baader). Buber stresses at the outset of his essay a contrast between the purported integrity of the culture of the Middle Ages and the fragmentation of modernity: "As it did with all great old works, our epoch (in its very first days) has had the altar dismantled."[83]

As Paul Mendes-Flohr explains, Buber's essay on the altarpiece rehearses again the Nietzschean "doctrine of unity" that appears in Buber's early writing so often and in so many different contexts, the "Heraclitean" embrace of flux in which the apparent separation and individuation of things dissolve that Buber saw in the mystical aspects of many different religious traditions.[84] This doctrine was fundamental to Buber's *Erlebnis* mysticism, which Scholem and Benjamin found so objectionable. As Mendes-Flohr writes: "Buber's pre-dialogical thought is dominated by an interest in mysticism, particularly in the unitive *Erlebnis*. This interest was . . . a correlate of his concern with the putative decline of man's spiritual and aesthetic sensibilities attendant to the rise of bourgeois *Zivilisation*. Buber attributed this decline to the contemporary acceptance of the individuated, phenomenal world as the single and ultimate reality."[85] As Buber explains in the introduction to his 1909 collection of *Ecstatic Confessions*, he understands mystical experience as "transcending individuation," experiencing the oneness of the I as "God-experience," and he sees the myths of many different traditions, those "proclaimed by the Vedas and the Upanishads, Midrash and Kabbala, Plato and Jesus" as offering, in various forms, the "symbol (*Sinnbild*) of what the ecstatic experienced (*erlebt*)."[86] The very unitive transcending of phenomenal differences that defines, according to Buber, the experience of ecstatics across a whole range of religions might be seen as something that Buber echoes on another level in his own project of revealing those commonalities, sometimes through the aesthetic. The closing sentences of Buber's essay on the altarpiece—"We cannot penetrate behind the plurality to find living unity. We can, out of plurality, enact living unity"—reads both as the "teaching" of Eckhart and Grünewald and as speaking of Buber's own project.[87] For the readers of this literary journal in 1914, Buber was the best-known representative of the "Jewish Renaissance," in Scholem's words, a "spokesman for Judaism"[88]—his very well-received books of Hasidic stories, *The Tales of Rabbi Nachman* (1906) and *The Legend of the Baal-Shem* (1908), presented the lore of the *Ostjuden* as spiritual treasures for the educated German-speaking public, Jewish and Gentile.[89] The running header printed, in line with the journal's usual practice, at the top of each page of Buber's essay on the Isenheim Altarpiece—"Martin Buber, Events and Encounters"—already sufficed to present the essay as an encounter between the famous Christian altarpiece and the famous Jewish writer, and the sentences cited earlier would also read as Buber's essay gesturing toward itself as a transreligious attempt to enact "living unity" "out of plurality."

Buber's reading of the polyptych is highly selective, focusing on three figures from two of its many panels: the Virgin Mary and Mary Magdalene mourning beneath the cross on the altarpiece's closed wings (fig. 3.4), and the resurrected Christ rising from his tomb on one of the panels of the first opening (fig. 2.1). The fact that but one sentence of Buber's essay is devoted to the central

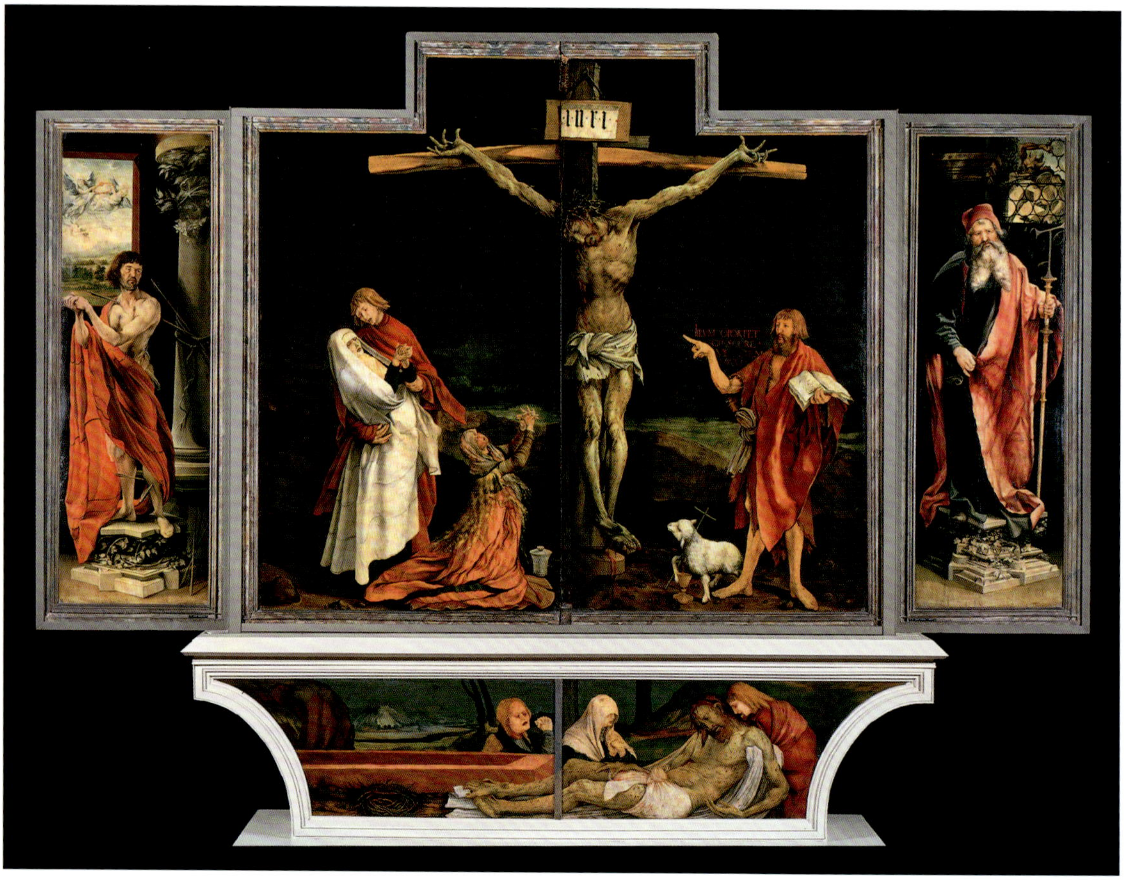

FIGURE 3.4 Mathis Grünewald, *Isenheim Altarpiece* (closed position), 1515. Oil and tempera on limewood panels, 376 × 534 cm. Musée Unterlinden, Colmar.

figure of Jesus on the cross ("a Christ with frail martyr's body and outstretched fingers of nailed hands"[90])—which commands so much attention from so many commentators—suggests how unusual Buber's reading is.[91] He explicates what he understands as Grünewald's teaching by contrasting how each of these three figures relates to color: the Virgin's absence of color; Mary Magdalene's disorderly abundance of color in her flesh, hair, and garments; and the resurrected Christ's spectral display of prismatic color. The way that each of the mourning women relates to color is found lacking: the Magdalene "is vowed to manifold color as Mary is to the unified absence of it; but her wealth of color is not bound by sense, and Mary's whiteness is cut off from life."[92]

In the panels of the first opening of the altarpiece, Buber calls attention to the angels emanating from the glory of heaven painted as streaming down from the clouds above Mary holding the baby Jesus, which he sees as taking on color as they descend (fig. 3.5): this, he writes, "is the miracle of the becoming of color, the emanation of the many out of the one."[93] But what interests Buber

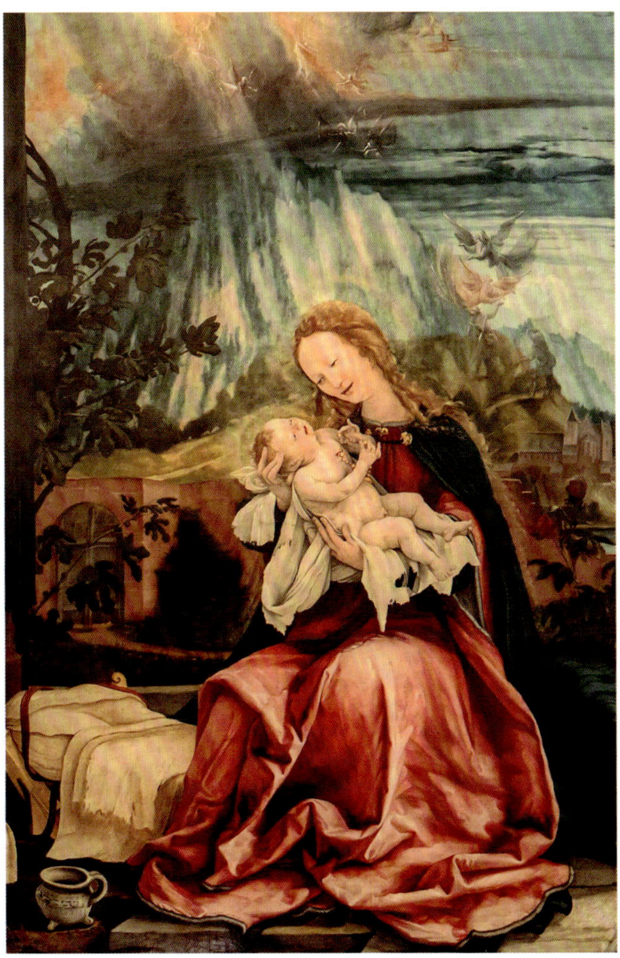

FIGURE 3.5 Mathis Grünewald, *Virgin and Child* (panel of *Isenheim Altarpiece*), 1515, detail. Oil on panel. Musée Unterlinden, Colmar.

more is “the other mystery,” moving in the opposite direction—“the becoming of one out of the many,” represented by the rising apparition of the resurrected one: “He loves the world, he rejects none of its colors, but he can receive none of them before it is pure and intensified. He loves the world, but he fights for his unconditionality against all that is conditioned. He loves the world in a way nearing the unconditional, he bears the world upward to its Self.”[94] In Buber’s gloss, the colors of Grünewald’s altarpiece teach Buber’s favored solution to the problem of individuation that occupied so much of his early work, the embracing and intensification of the individuated and manifold as part of the act of “shap[ing] the world to unity.”[95] “The rising one” trumps the two inadequate relations to the multiplicity of the world represented by the two mourning women: “How can Magdalene’s variegated color compare with his world spectrum? What is Mary’s white unity before his all-embracing one? He includes all hues of being.”[96]

In the Isenheim Altarpiece, Buber finds, it seems, another “symbol” of the kind he wrote about in his 1909 *Ecstatic Confessions* collection, another demonstration of how the ecstatic *Erlebnis* of oneness transcends the multiplicity of the individuated world, in this instance encoded in the very disposition of colors in the altarpiece’s panels. The colors of painting might themselves be seen as differences among the multiplicity of things in the individuated, phenomenal world given by vision—making the altarpiece itself, to extrapolate from the terms of Buber’s reading, potentially something like the varicolored Magdalene—but instead the altarpiece, in Buber’s reading, uses the very language of color to speak of the unitive act of the “rising one.”

In general, Buber refers to the panels’ figures by their conventional names, but he emphasizes his own refusal of any simple label for “the rising one.” The essay’s task of itself performing a kind of transreligious enacting of “living unity” “out of plurality” becomes especially difficult in the section of Buber’s essay on this ascending figure, for here Buber must negotiate a central conflict between Jews and Christians. In a long descriptive passage on the colors of the Resurrection panel, the figure is not called “Jesus” or “Christ,” but rather “the rising one” and “the person who ties the world together”; in the next paragraph, Buber refuses and then accepts identifications, then generalizes out from there: “This is not the Jew Jeshua, treading the soil of Galilee and teaching in his day; it is also Jeshua. This is not the incarnate Logos, descending from timeless preexistence into time; it is also the Logos. This is the man, the man of all times and of all places, the man of the here and now, who perfects himself to the I of the world. This is the man who embraces the world but does not become manifold in its manifoldness; rather, out of the strength of his world-embracing, he has himself become unified.”[97] At this juncture, we need to understand something of the prominent place of Jesus as the Jew that Christians take as Christ in Buber’s publications of the 1910s, texts that played important roles in the making of assertive "postassimilatory" Jewish identities.[98]

Buber's positioning of Jesus as an exemplary Jewish figure is prominent in the *Three Addresses on Judaism* that Buber gave at the Bar Kochba Association in Prague in 1909–1910 and published in 1911, and that exercised an enormous influence on many young German Jews at the time: Scholem wrote later, "I would be unable to mention any other book about Judaism of these years, which even came close to having such an effect—not among the men of learning . . . but among a youth that heard the summons to a new departure that many of them took seriously enough to act on it."[99]

Similarly, Buber's close friend Landauer (who shared Buber's interest in Christian mysticism and indeed was especially interested in Meister Eckhart, who, Landauer wrote, "must be raised from the dead") and Ernst Bloch attempted to revalue Jesus as a great Jewish prophet while refusing the Christian assertion of Jesus as messiah and redemption accomplished. Counterpunching the then-influential anti-Jewish "pan-Babylonian" school of thought led by the Orientalist Friedrich Delitzsch, Bloch saw Christian understandings of Jesus's death and resurrection ("vicarious reparation by means of cross- and sacrifice-magic," in Bloch's phrase) as a step backward, reassimilating him to what Bloch presents as ancient Near Eastern astral idolatry, religions of dying-and-rising sun gods.[100] For many of Buber's readers, however, the vision of Jewishness that he presented in the *Three Addresses* became strange in the following years; as Scholem wrote, "I am among those who in their youth, when these speeches appeared, was deeply moved by them and who—even as happened to the author himself—many years later can now read these pages only with a feeling of deep estrangement."[101] The profound changes mentioned earlier in German-Jewish conceptions of German Jews and their relations to non-Jewish Germans over the course of the war and its counterrevolutionary aftermath must be taken into account here.

In the *Three Addresses*, Buber presents Jesus as one of the greatest Jews, one of the most exemplary of the unitive act as springing from the acute awareness of duality that Buber sees as the ground of Jewish religiosity (to which, as mentioned earlier, Benjamin referred in one of his 1912 letters to Strauss), and as the major figure of one of the three main movements renewing Jewish religiosity—"the prophetic, the Essenic-early Christian, and the kabbalistic-hasidic."[102]

Unavoidable in Buber's and others' refigurations of Jesus as exemplar of Jewishness are the relations between Jewish and Christian messianisms, both very much in play in Expressionist discourse.[103] The word "Christ" is derived from the Greek word for "anointed," translating the Hebrew word *mashiah* that is roughly transliterated as Messiah.[104] A pithy and apposite introduction to them may be found in Scholem's later essay "Toward an Understanding of the Messianic Idea in Judaism" (1959), which aims to analyze "tensions in the Messianic idea and their understanding in rabbinic Judaism."[105] As Scholem writes, doing so requires some consideration of Christian messianism, for, in Jewish messianism, "even where it is not stated explicitly, we shall often enough find as well a polemical side-glance, or an allusion, albeit concealed, to the claims of Christian Messianism."[106] While Scholem's essay never mentions the revisions of Jesus put forward by Buber and others, much of its first paragraph could be usefully cited here:

> Any discussion of the problems relating to Messianism is a delicate matter, for it is here that the essential conflict between Judaism and Christianity has developed and continues to exist. . . . A totally different concept of redemption determines the attitude to Messianism in Judaism and in Christianity; what appears to the one as a proud indication of its understanding and a positive achievement of its message is most unequivocally belittled and disputed by the other. Judaism . . . has always maintained a concept of redemption as an event which takes place publicly, on the stage of history and within the community. It is an occurrence which takes place in the visible world and which cannot be conceived apart from such a visible appearance. In contrast, Christianity conceives of redemption as an event in the spiritual and unseen realm, an event which is reflected in the soul, in the private world of each individual, and which effects an inner transformation which need not correspond to anything outside. . . . What for the one stood unconditionally at the end of history as its most distant aim was for the other the true center of the historical process, even if that process was henceforth peculiarly decked out as *Heilsgeschichte*.[107]

The Christian "reinterpretation of the prophetic promises of the Bible to refer to a realm of inwardness" seemed to Christians to be "a deeper apprehension of the external realm" but to Jews to be "its liquidation and . . . a flight which sought to escape verification of the Messianic claim."[108]

Despite the basic polarization of Jewish and Christian messianisms that Scholem lays out—an essential part of the story of mutual differentiation and othering—there have been moments, writes Scholem, when Jewish and Christian messianisms have borrowed each other's attributes: "Judaism has again and again furnished Christianity with political chiliastic Messianism. . . . Christianity, for its part, has bequeathed to Judaism or aroused within it the tendency to discover a mystical aspect of the interiorization of the Messianic idea."[109]

One might well call Ernst Bloch's first major work, *The Spirit of Utopia* (1918), an explicit attempt to spark—borrowing Scholem's much later language—“messianic activism . . . on that peculiar double line of mutual influence between Judaism and Christianity.” We know that Benjamin spent a good deal of time with Bloch’s book—his review of it, which he tried but failed to publish, is now lost, but appears to have been a major effort.[110] Benjamin had serious reservations about the book; his “Theological-Political Fragment” may be seen as a determined and far-reaching riposte to it. When Benjamin writes in the latter that “to have repudiated with utmost vehemence the political significance of theocracy is the cardinal merit of Bloch’s *Spirit of Utopia*,” it must be understood that this was the opposite of Bloch’s intent.[111]

Benjamin’s and Scholem’s rejection of one section of Bloch’s book in particular, “Symbol: The Jews,” is especially illuminating to consider in this context. This section—mostly, it seems, written before the war, in 1912–1913—was dropped from the second edition of *Spirit of Utopia*, published in 1923.[112] Roughly along the lines of Buber’s use of the figure of Jesus in his articulations of modern Jewish identity, Bloch asserts that a younger generation of Jews, proudly embracing their Jewishness as their elders did not (“Pride in being Jewish awakens anew”), was at the same time embracing Jesus.[113] Bloch acknowledges the use that Christians have made of Jesus in persecuting Jews, discussing, for instance, how Luther’s reading of Paul’s expectation of the conversion of “all Israel” in Romans 11 turned it into violent anti-Jewish diatribe.[114] Nevertheless, Bloch asserts that the Jewish reappropriation of Jesus that he believes he perceives is not spurred by a desire to assimilate but is rather a laying claim to Jesus on the basis of Jewish identity: “Almost all the Jews of the younger generation have no trouble saying the name of Jesus . . . the superstitious reserve regarding the Nazarene event in their spiritual history is disappearing, Jesus returns at last to his people. . . . They [younger Jews] feel and understand that only they and no one else, just as they witnessed Joseph’s story and the psalms, so too they could make the early Christian community and the gospels. It would seem as if Jews had come to a place where they must again regard as their own most intimate business what took place as Christianity and in the escaping substance of Christianity, after the other, foreign peoples have worked on Christianity, to fatigue and perhaps to the end.”[115] In the section’s concluding paragraph, Bloch envisions “Jews” and “Germans” together turning to a third messiah yet to come, in terms religious, political, and aesthetic: “The last, unknown Christ sleeps within us, in the deepest, still nameless place . . . anticipated by Moses, surrounded by Jesus, who himself announced a Paraclete still to come. . . . So it is still thinkable and understandable from the curve of history so far—or it must become thinkable again . . . that through the thousandfold energies, through the eons-wide perspective of a new proclamation, Jewishness with Germanness again means something last, gothic, baroque, so as—united with Russia, this third recipient of waiting, of the bearing of god and messianism—to prepare the absolute time.”[116]

Bloch's assertion of a widespread German-Jewish reappropriation of Jesus and his reading of this as preparing the way for a new messianism provoked attacks from many quarters. Two were published in *Das Ziel* in 1919, both written by German-Jewish writers active in Expressionist circles in Berlin. Salomo Friedlaender's lengthy review of the book began "The third empire, the third testament, the spirit of utopia. Is there enough insecticide for such *Kreuzspinnen*?"[117] (The pun here hinges on the double meaning of *Kreuzspinnen*, which can mean either cross spiders—a kind of orb weaver with a distinctive cross on its abdomen—or cross insanity.) For Friedlaender, Bloch's book is self-important, cloudy-headed "otherworldliness (*Jenseiterei*)," and much of Nietzsche's criticism of Christianity can be leveled once again against this voguish new version of the same old world denial.[118] Friedlaender implores Bloch: "Put aside this priestliness! Become sober and profane!"[119] Kurt Hiller, in an afterword to Friedlaender's review, sought to nuance Friedlaender's attack on Christianity; he tried to keep, as he presents it, the baby Jesus from getting thrown out with the Pauline bathwater, and proposed, echoing Bloch's vision of a new Jewish-German union, that "Christ and Nietzsche (curious—a Jew and a not un-Slavic German!)" are the two poles of a sphere that "we" must create.[120] This differentiation aside, Hiller affirms Friedlaender's criticism of Bloch, writing that Bloch gives justification to those who use the "damned term of abuse and mockery 'literati'" and concluding his essay by describing Bloch as "not a Christian, but rather an emetic."[121]

In a 1920 letter to Benjamin, Scholem's response to Bloch's book is similarly vituperative, but more focused, especially on the aforementioned section "Symbol: The Jews": "I have the impression that here Bloch encroaches, in the worst fashion and with inappropriate means, upon an area whose boundaries the book might at best define. . . . [H]e makes statements about the stories of the Jews, history, and Judaism, which clearly bear the terrible stigma of Prague." (By Prague, Scholem means Buber, who had given his *Three Addresses* in that city.) Scholem goes on to say that the "Jewish generation" of which Bloch writes—the proud young Jews out to reclaim Jesus—"does not exist."[122] For Scholem, much of the problem lies in Bloch's use of "testimonies that derive from the German-Jewish or Jewish-German sphere and thus prove nothing but this original sphere," thinking that "it is all right for him to intermingle testimonies indiscriminately." Scholem says that, for his part, he sees no "credible evidence bespeaking a decline of the 'traditional reserve' before the founder of Christianity among the Jews—if I (presumably with justification) disregard evidence from the hermaphrodite spheres (*Zwittersphären*)," by which, it seems, Scholem means the aforementioned "German-Jewish or Jewish-German" discourses.[123] Scholem sees the *Spirit of Utopia* as foisting a "central Christology" on Jews and this leading to a sloppily indiscriminate handling of sources, disregarding the philological principle of the separation of sources: "*Quellenscheidung*!!!" writes Scholem, using a term associated with the "higher criticism" of the Bible.

Benjamin replies that he agrees with Scholem's assessment of the chapter "The Jews" and says that the book's "axiomatic Christology" and "epistemology" must be contested.[124] The elevating synthesis of Jewish, Christian, and socialist messianisms in Bloch's book—a synthesis that makes its "central Christology" predictable, picking up as it does on well-worn themes of supersessionism in Christianity as well as in utopian socialisms—repelled both Scholem and Benjamin. Perhaps Benjamin saw Bloch's book as speaking as one of "those who imagine that they have already discovered the arcanum," in the words of his *Angelus Novus* journal announcement, which says that it will seek to listen instead "to those who objectively, dispassionately, and unobtrusively give expression to hardship and need."[125]

These responses to Bloch allow us to see something of the fraught territory that Buber attempted to negotiate by both denying and affirming the identification of Grünewald's resurrected Christ with the historical Jesus and with the Logos of Johannine Christology, and then rereading him as a figure "of all times and of all places." The position and importance of the altarpiece for Buber may be further elaborated by connecting Buber's Grünewald essay with his essentializing binary anthropology of "Occident" and "Orient," as developed, for instance, in his *Three Addresses* and even more in his essay on "The Spirit of the Orient and Judaism" (an address of 1912–1914 published in 1916).[126] Buber's characterization of the altarpiece in these terms is emphatic. His essay opens with the phrase "This is the altar of the spirit in the western world (*im Abendland*)," a phrase that Buber repeats in the first sentence of the second paragraph: "This is the altar of the spirit in the western world, and Colmar is as great as Benares."[127]

Buber's opposition of "Occident" and "Orient" may be seen as responding to anti-Jewish orientalism "by idealizing and romanticizing the Orient."[128] The importance of the Isenheim Altarpiece for Buber might be seen as implicitly bound up with its status as, in Buber's terms, a site of translation of "Oriental" teaching into "Occidental" language.

In "The Spirit of the Orient and Judaism," Buber characterizes the "Occidental" and the "Oriental" "human type" as having opposing relations to the outside world. While Buber begins his essay by championing the view of the "Orient" held by Herder, Goethe, Novalis, and Görres while criticizing contemporary "racial theory" and the application of the methods of the natural sciences to psychology and history, he terms these two opposing relations "sensory" and "motoric," referring, it appears, to the sensory and motor neurons discussed in nineteenth-century physiology: for Buber, the motoric is dominant in the "Oriental" (including Jews as a special category), the sensory in the "Occidental."[129] Buber elaborates: in contrast to the "Oriental" "motor-type man," in whom "sight is not sovereign" and for whom "the world appears as limitless motion, flowing through him," the "Occidental" "sensory man" is "guided by the most objective sense, sight," and therefore perceives the world around him as "objectified, as a multiplicity of things which is spread before his eyes."[130] Buber comments as follows on the development of Christianity in the "West" as Europe's adaptation of "the teaching of the Orient":

> Judaism won the Occident for the teaching of the Orient. By means of this teaching Judaism became the representative of the Orient at its best. . . . None of the great religious teachings originated in the Occident. The Occident received and spiritually reworked what the Orient had to offer, assimilating it to its own forms of thought and sensibility . . . it has religious geniuses of the greatest authenticity, but none of them has, by himself alone, raised the mystery out of the abyss and set it down in the world of man . . . even the greatest of them, Eckhart, is but a late emissary of the Oriental master.[131]

Extrapolating from Buber's double insistence on calling Grünewald's retable "the altar of the spirit in the western world (*im Abendland*)" and his joining of the painter and Eckhart as "brothers" in light of this essay, it seems that for Buber the altarpiece is an exemplary site where one can see the Occident's receiving of the teaching of the "Oriental master" Jesus, exemplary because of its faithful translation of that teaching into a quintessentially visual form ("The language in which Grünewald teaches . . . is that of the miracle of color"[132]) especially well suited, one surmises from this essay, to the capacities of the "Occidental." Indeed, read in relation to this essay, Buber's passing reference to Grünewald as a German, which seems at first to contrast with the great emphasis placed on Grünewald's Germanness by many of the altarpiece's enthusiasts at the time, seems more significant. In its original 1916 publication, "The Spirit of the Orient and Judaism" posited a world-historical role for Germany as leading a spiritual renewal by bridging Occident and Orient, thereby salvaging, in Buber's view, the spirit of the Orient from the threats of colonization and Europeanization.[133] Reading the Grünewald essay in relation to the 1916 publication, it seems likely that, at the time that Buber wrote "The Altar," the retable was for him, as for so many at the time, an exemplar of the German spirit, which, more unusually, Buber sees as characterized by a special gift for absorbing and mediating "Oriental" and especially Jewish culture.[134] In the 1916 essay, Buber adduces Luther's Bible translation, the influence of Spinoza, and the currency of Marx and Lassalle as instances of this gift; "The Altar" implies that Grünewald's retable could belong on this list as well.[135]

One might perhaps venture that Buber's 1916 vision of Germany as quintessentially transcultural may have been a kind of wishful projection onto Germany as a whole of Landauer's and Buber's shared prewar sense, which Mendes-Flohr explores in his *German Jews: A Dual Identity*, of the importance of affirming "cultural admixture" and multiplicity as part of modern German-Jewish identity (in Landauer's words, "I accept my complexity and hope to be even more many-sided than I am now aware of"), over against versions of German nationalism that denied or denigrated the "foreign."[136] In "The Spirit of the Orient and Judaism," Buber explicitly valorizes cross-cultural borrowing as such, with reference to historical criticism of the Bible (again, Delitzsch's school seems to be the clear target): Babylonia and Egypt "culturally enriched the young Jewish nation. A group of scholars thought it could be deduced from this fact that the Jewish mind is unoriginal and unproductive. But all their efforts were founded on a basically false premise: that it is inherent in the nature of an individual's or a people's substantive productivity not to take over from others any matter for their creations. The opposite is true . . . Not where one finds a 'motif' but what one does with it is historically decisive."[137] As Mendes-Flohr has demonstrated, Buber's vision of Germany as having a unique world-historical role to play as the preeminent spiritual crossing of Orient and Occident—a vision whose politics in 1916 could not be called ambiguous—appeared grotesquely misguided to Buber's close friend Landauer, who wrote Buber a letter criticizing his German nationalist position (however differently structured from other available varieties of German nationalism), which led Buber both to rethink his emphasis on *Erlebnis* and to oppose the war; in the second edition of Buber's book, published in 1919, as Buber wrote in a brief note, "passages were deleted in which the German nation is called upon to lead the return and to establish a new era of concord with the Orient. The German nation did not assume the function referred to in these passages and is now no longer capable of doing such."[138]

Buber's essay on Grünewald's altarpiece, written before this shift in thinking both on the place of *Erlebnis* and the role of Germany, explicitly finds in the altarpiece a mystical experience of unity—figured by the blinding coming together of colors in Grünewald's painting of the luminous, ascending body of Jesus. Read in relation to Buber's contemporaneous writings, the essay implicitly positions the retable as an exemplary translation of this mystical experience of unity from "Oriental" Jewish religiosity into the "Occidental" language of painting—and itself, in its own work of elaborating, from the perspective of a representative of the "Jewish Renaissance," this same mystical experience of unity bodied forth in Grünewald's colors, as enacting another unity, on the terrain of the multiple religious traditions in Germany.

Benjamin also wrote about Grünewald's halos in the 1910s, with, it seems, those of the Isenheim Altarpiece in mind, in the "The Rainbow: A Conversation about Imagination" (ca. 1915) and "Socrates" (1916)—after Buber first published his essay in 1914 but before its 1917 republication.[139] The rainbow halo of the Resurrection panel that is the crux of Buber's essay seems also to be the focus of some of Benjamin's hermetic sentences. Of course, Buber and Benjamin are hardly alone in remarking on it. Neither Buber nor Benjamin mentions the sources that likely informed the altarpiece's prismatic luminosity (the rainbow as God's covenant with Noah, the Virgin as rainbow in the *Revelations* of the Swedish mystic Saint Bridget.)[140]

As Scholem notes, what particularly fascinated Benjamin in the panels of the Isenheim Altarpiece was "what he called *das Ausdruckslose*, their quality of expressionlessness." Benjamin, it seems, set his esteem for the panels against the usual praise for Grünewald among his contemporaries, from Expressionist painters to the art historian Wölfflin, for whom Grünewald exemplified the art of expression (*Ausdruckskunst*) in the German Renaissance.[141] In Benjamin's "The Rainbow," a dialogue about perception, art, nature, and "the color of imagination [*Phantasie*]," one of the two speakers, a painter, speaks of the rainbow as "the purest manifestation of this color that spiritualizes and animates nature throughout, that . . . makes of nature the mute, apperceived primal image of art" and notes that "Grünewald painted the halos of angels on his altar with the colors of the rainbow, so that the soul as imagination [*Phantasie*] shines through the sacred figures [*die heiligen Gestalten*]."[142] In "Socrates"—about gender and spirit, eros and knowledge, with reference to the *Symposium*—Grünewald is cited halfway through: "Grünewald painted the saints [*die Heiligen*] with such grandeur that their halo emerged from the greenest black. The radiant is true only where it is refracted in the nocturnal; only there is it great, only there is it expressionless, only there is it asexual and yet of supramundane sexuality [*Geschlechte*]. The one who radiates in this manner is the genius, the witness to every truly spiritual creation."[143] In both, the halos of Benjamin's writing are elusive and cannot be simply pinned onto a particular bit of Grünewald's altarpiece—one can't be sure whether, at any given moment, he is speaking of the most prominent of the altarpiece's glories, that around Jesus ascending in the night (which would best fit Benjamin's "greenest black"), of those of Mary and the small angels of the enigmatic "Angels' Concert" panel and/or the fainter ones of the Madonna and Child. In "Socrates," the strange shift within a short sentence between the plural "saints" and their singular "halo" is especially difficult to grasp. Benjamin would seem to share with Buber a desire to avoid referring to the rising figure with the biggest halo as Jesus, but Benjamin, in sharp contrast to Buber, does not call attention to this very desire, which Buber does in the course of making his transreligious revision of Jesus, as "the man of all times and of all places, the man of the here and now, who perfects himself to the I of the world," the crux of his interpretation of the altarpiece. Rather, in both passages, Benjamin appears to assimilate the various haloed figures—given highly differentiated roles in the panels celebrating the Incarnation and Resurrection—into a larger, more general category of the holy (angels, saints, holy figures).

Perhaps there is some connection between Benjamin's odd move in "The Rainbow" of including the hovering figure in the Resurrection panel in a larger category of "angels" and the panel's own apparent condensation of the figure of the risen Jesus with the radiant "angel of the Lord" frightening the guards. Grünewald's panel combines different moments in the Gospels that narrate miraculous demonstrations of Jesus's divinity, including the Transfiguration (see Matthew 17, in which Jesus's "face shone like the sun"); Panofsky calls attention to the complexity of its condensation in "On the Problem of Describing and Interpreting Works of the Visual Arts" (1932), in which it serves as his central example of that problem:

> In order to establish a textual source, we flip through the passages in the Gospels that are chronologically relevant—only to find that there is nothing which fully corresponds to the iconography. The Gospels only narrate how the women close to the Redeemer (whose number may be one, two, or three, or are not mentioned at all) open the tomb and find it empty, and how one angel (or two) tells them that the Lord rose from the dead. Indeed we do not find the process of rising from the dead itself depicted before the twelfth century. Only a detailed study of further textual sources, and especially the history of types, will tell us that what we call *The Resurrection of Christ* by Grünewald is in fact a highly complex combination of the actual rising-from-the-dead, the Ascension, and the Transfiguration.[144]

While the identity of Grünewald's rising figure, with his radiant wounds, is in no way in question, one might connect the awestruck guards of the painting with those frightened by an "angel of the Lord" who comes to roll back the stone (see Matthew 28: "For fear of [the angel] the guards shook and became like dead men").[145] These guards, not mentioned in the other Gospels, appear in passages in Matthew with a clear polemical job in "the conflict between emerging Rabbinic Judaism and the smaller Jewish Christian minority": the "chief priests and the Pharisees" request them from Pilate to ensure that Jesus's followers do not "go and steal him away, and tell the people, 'He has been raised from the dead'" (Matthew 27).[146] The narrative continues with the guards telling the priests what they saw and the priests bribing them to say instead that Jesus's disciples took his body: "And this story is still told among the Jews to this day," concludes this section. In "The Rainbow," perhaps Benjamin was responding to the angel implied by the guards; perhaps he wanted to prize apart the altarpiece from the centrality of Jesus not only in Christianity but in Buber's refiguring of Judaism. In any case, it seems that he subsumes the most prominent haloed figure on the altarpiece into a holy plurality of "angels," "sacred figures."

Benjamin was ideally positioned to pick up on Klee's play on Grünewald's Resurrection panel, discussed in detail in the previous chapter: like Grünewald's Christ, Klee's angel glows and hovers, holding out its hands. Its huge head might be seen as a scurrilous take on the radiance of Grünewald's Christ, reimagined as caricatural disproportion. As mentioned earlier, Scholem wrote in his memoir of a reproduction of the Isenheim Altarpiece that hung for a long time in Benjamin's study.[147] The couple of sentences that Scholem devotes to his friend's interest in the Isenheim Altarpiece appear in his narrative of the events of early 1917, so it would seem Scholem is attesting to this reproduction's presence in Benjamin's room at that time; Scholem says it hung for a

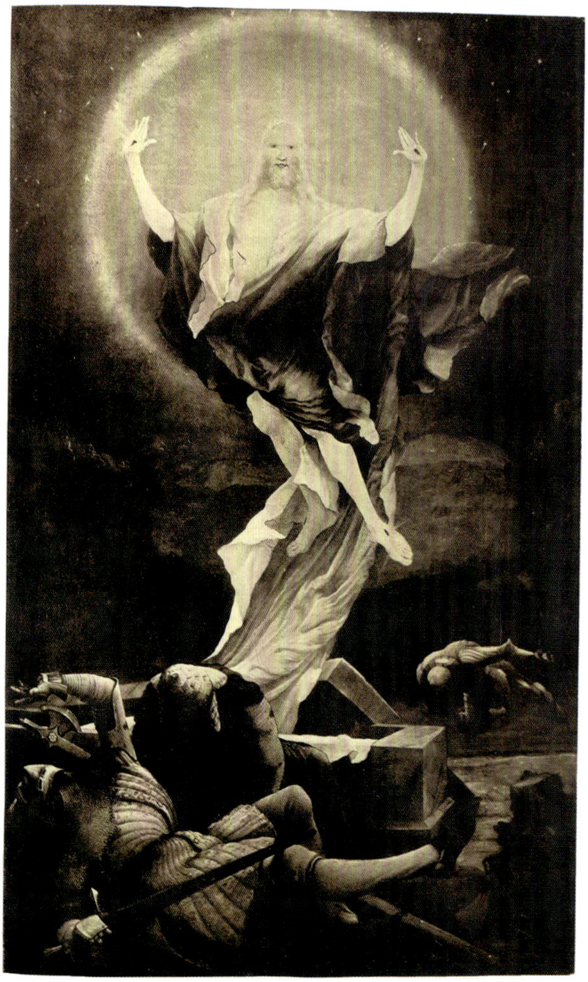

FIGURE 3.6 *Grünewald-Portfolio*, published by the Kunstwart (Munich: G. D. W. Callwey, 1907)

long time. We do not know if it was still there when the *Angelus* arrived at Benjamin's Berlin residence in November 1921, if the Klee and the Grünewald hung on his walls simultaneously, or if instead the Klee supplanted the Grünewald, with more or less time between the Klee going up and the Grünewald coming down.[148] Nor do we know which reproduction hung in Benjamin's room, of which panel or panels of the complex polyptych. Because Benjamin's written allusions seem to center on the famous Resurrection panel, it seems likely that the reproduction Scholem mentions includes that panel. There are many possibilities: readily available at the time were at least two different portfolios of good-quality photomechanical reproductions of Grünewald's Isenheim Altarpiece for use as room décor, the *Grünewald-Portfolio* published by the Kunstwart in 1907 including monochrome reproductions of six different panels of the altarpiece, and the color portfolio published by E. A. Seemann a few years later.[149] It is notable how especially striking is the resemblance between the *Angelus* and the Kunstwart's Resurrection, for the latter crops the panel down to a rectangle and is printed in a warm monochrome (fig. 3.6).

Klee's laconic figure alluding to Grünewald's resurrected Jesus Christ, this grotesque little so-called angel that lacks any obvious angelic attributes (the chimerical creature seems to have gotten bird feet instead of wings), also lacks the wounds by which Grünewald's hovering figure marks its identity as specifically the crucified Jesus of Nazareth as eschatological Messiah. Klee's inscription ("Angelus novus") together with the watercolor's allusion to the Resurrection panel builds in an instability between angel and Jesus that might have interested Benjamin, given his depiction of a crucified winged figure in the sketch he sent Scholem and labeled "ECCE ANGELUS" with reference to the journal project, as well as his apparent inclusion of the hovering figure in the altarpiece among the "angels" in "The Rainbow," years before Klee made the watercolor.

Klee's watercolor figure, caricaturing a famous Christ while labeled "angel," does not present itself as purged of the dross of particularity or as a finding of common ground among figures of holiness. On the contrary, the figure is one of combination and juxtaposition in which differences are emphasized rather than neutralized—not only in the border that shows that the picture superimposes the very unlike but also in the awkwardly combinatory appearance of the body itself. Contrast it with the delicate schematic figure of Klee's 1918 *Angelus descendens* (fig. 1.11), so comparable to the *Angelus novus* in pose and construction but bound together by continuous lines linking the parts of its body, creating a winsome angel without the *Angelus novus*'s admixture of the chimerical and monstrous. The latter might indeed seem to chime with Benjamin's theological thinking of the early 1920s as Jennings has described it, as "an embrace of a theological position that juxtaposes, rather than mixes, elements from different faiths . . . remain[ing] aware of the differences and tensions among its elements."[150]

What Benjamin did with the *Angelus* may be contrasted with what Buber sought to do with the altarpiece that Klee's watercolor excerpts and revises. Buber writes a description of the work of art that presents itself as an unfolding of a transreligious spiritual content that the work makes perceptible—the unitive act celebrated in various mystical traditions—in this case localized in Buber's reading of the figure of Jesus transfigured and resurrected. In contrast, Benjamin, in the announcement's sole gesture toward the *Angelus* of its title—the last paragraph of the journal announcement, on "the ephemeral aspect of this journal"—superimposes, so to speak, on top of Klee's own ironizing play with the Grünewald a new textual image, joining a Talmudic theme to the Latin title of his journal: "according to a legend in the Talmud, the angels are created—new every instant in countless numbers—in order, once they have sung their hymn before God, to cease and to vanish into nothingness."[151]

Benjamin references a passage from the Talmud that elaborates on a verse from the book of Lamentations—a response, traditionally attributed to Jeremiah, to the Babylonians' destruction of Jerusalem—which Scholem translated from Hebrew into German in 1917. Benjamin wanted to include Scholem's essay reflecting on this translation in the first issue of the journal.[152] The passage of Aggadah in question runs as follows: "Samuel said to R. Hiyya b. Rab: 'O son of a great man, come, I will tell thee something from those excellent things which thy father has said. Every day ministering angels are created from the fiery stream, and utter song, and cease to be, for it is said: They are new every morning.'"[153] Samuel quotes from Lamentations ("But this do I call to mind, Therefore I have hope: / The kindness of the Lord has not ended, His mercies are not spent. / They are renewed every morning—Ample is your grace!")[154] As Scholem writes, "Everlasting angels like, say, the archangels or Satan, seen as the fallen angel of the Jewish and Christian tradition, were evidently less important for Benjamin than the talmudic theme of the formation and disappearance of angels before God, of whom it is said in a kabbalistic book that they 'pass away as the spark on the coals.'"[155] The vision, linked to this verse of Lamentations, of ever-new, ephemeral angels made from a stream of fire to praise God and vanish again—a continuous flow of single-use beings, inexhaustible like divine mercy and fidelity—is specific to the Talmudic legend and its elaborations.[156]

Now, we need to appreciate how tense Benjamin's superimposition is. Benjamin connects the *Angelus*'s own rather paradoxical invocation of the "new"—using the old Latin word for "new," in pointed contrast, as I argued in the previous chapter, to Luther's work of translating into the vernacular—with the actuality (*Aktualität*) he hoped to see in his journal. In a move very roughly parallel to Klee's in the Latin title, Benjamin figures his *Angelus Novus* journal as the new, the ephemerally up to date by means of the old and traditional—connecting the ever-new angels of the Babylonian Talmud with the name of the journal, after the Klee picture that the announcement does not mention but that his friends knew: "May the journal's name mean it is granted such *Aktualität*"—that of the Talmudic angels—"the only true sort."[157] Klee's picture gestures toward and undermines understandings of the new, vanguard art, including his own, as a new angel announcing a resurrection of art that would make it no longer, *pace* Hegel, "in its highest vocation . . . a thing of the past"—linking to a Hegelian history of Christian art that then structured much art discourse. Nothing suggests that Klee intended his angel to be seen as one of these ephemeral Talmudic angels; its form juxtaposes features of Grünewald's resurrected Christ and of the Cranach workshop's portraits of Martin Luther.[158] Unlike what might be read as Buber's programmatic statement about the possibilities of transreligious encounter by means of art, such as the one he stages with Grünewald's altarpiece—"We can, out of plurality, enact living unity"—Benjamin's textual image, his rewriting of the *Angelus* with reference to the Talmud, comes after a paragraph in which he stresses the importance of "resist[ing] . . . dishonest attempts of the contributors to . . . create an atmosphere of mutual understanding and community . . . even the purest will and the most patient labor among the different collaborators will prove unable to create any unity." Rather, continues Benjamin, "the journal should proclaim through the mutual alienness [*wechselseitigen Fremdheit*] of their contributions how impossible it is in our age to give a voice to any communality [*Gemeinsamkeit*]."[159]

Many scholars have shown the extent to which the idea of a general Jewish aniconism as following from the Second Commandment is a modern construction that has little to do with how premodern Jews dealt with images.[160] This modern construction had, it should be emphasized, great currency in German-Jewish writing of the early twentieth century: Buber, for instance, characterized the ancient Jew as an "ear-man" (*Ohrenmensch*) rather than an "eye-man" (*Augenmensch*).[161] It enters into Scholem's contributions to his discussion with Benjamin in 1917 about contemporary art—"the new painters," in Benjamin's phrase, including Klee, whose name appears for the first time in Benjamin's writing in this exchange with Scholem and whose breakthrough exhibition took place at the Sturm gallery in Berlin that year. The interest Scholem then took in Picasso's Cubism hinges on his idea that it might potentially "become a new 'symbolism' that would, like mathematics and Judaism, obey the 'ban on the "image."'"[162] In rabbinic Judaism, the making of images of angels in particular has been at times subject to special restrictions, though many have been made nevertheless.[163] They were, not unrelatedly, very popular motifs in the visual culture of early Zionism, above all in the *Jugendstil* graphic work of Buber's friend Ephraim Moses Lilien (fig. 3.7); while Scholem, it seems, hoped he might see in the work of Picasso and Klee, non-Jewish artists, the potential

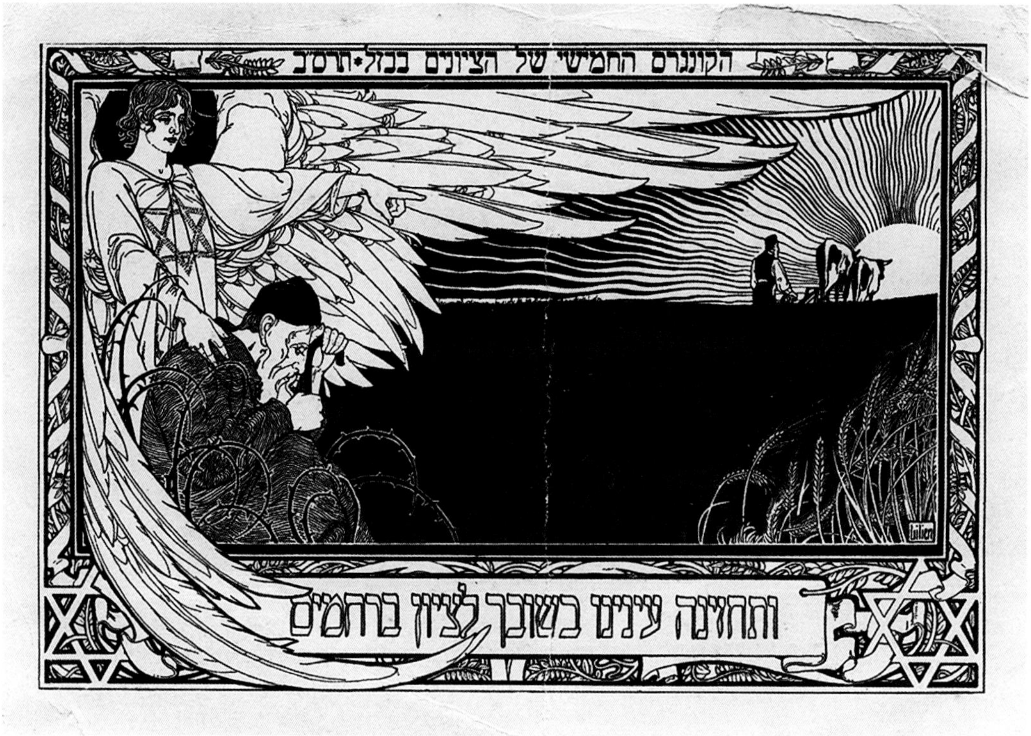

FIGURE 3.7 Ephraim Moses Lilien, *From Ghetto to Zion*, postcard for the Fifth Zionist Congress in Basel, Switzerland, 1901

for an aniconism he also saw in Judaism, Buber celebrated what he saw as a flourishing of image making by Jewish artists that he believed was not possible earlier, in, among other manifestations, Lilien's work with its large population of angels.[164] It must also be emphasized that, although I have been speaking of Benjamin's sentence on the angels of the Talmud as an "image," it emphasizes vanishing at least as much as appearance.[165] I suggest that Benjamin saw as a model Klee's own overlay of one image over another with which it is in contentious conversation—that, far from being oblivious to the visual features of Klee's work, he saw in it a model for juxtaposing by layering conflicting images. This can be seen as an acute response to Klee's work, not a blind imposition on it: in 1922, the "mutual alienness (*wechselseitigen Fremdheit*)" Benjamin thus created between his textual reinscription of Klee's image in terms of Talmudic angelology and Klee's own play with the image of Christ was part of the *point* of Benjamin's reinscription.

By the early autumn of 1922, it was becoming clear that the *Angelus Novus* journal was not going to be published: in a letter to Scholem and Elsa Burchhardt, Benjamin wrote that "the Angelus announced his own departure just as yesterday came to an end, as if he wanted to prove one last time what a good Jew he is. He has moved into his old house in the clay-colored sky (*am kleefarbenen Himmel*)."[166] Most immediately, the economic situation and worsening hyperinflation militated against it in two ways: on the one hand, the publisher delayed printing on account, he claimed, of the rising price of paper and the large advance the typesetter demanded, and, on the other hand, Benjamin feared that pursuing the journal project would come at the expense of his *Habilitation*, which he believed would put him in a better position in negotiating with his parents for financial support at a time when they were pressing him to get a job.[167] But Benjamin also had serious difficulties with his collaborators: Rang saw himself as central (when he told Hofmannsthal about the failed journal, he said that he, Benjamin, and Benjamin's dead friend Fritz Heinle composed its nucleus) and offered contributions (on Goethe's "Blessed Longing" and on Shakespeare) that Benjamin rejected.[168] Conversely, while Benjamin saw Scholem as a crucial part of the project, Scholem himself did not wish to contribute to it.[169] Scholem writes that Benjamin complained that the first issue of the journal "would contain thirty blank pages with this heading: 'Gerhard Scholem: The Empty Promises.'"[170] The correspondence between Benjamin and his would-be contributors suggests that the place that the *Angelus Novus* journal might have occupied in relation to other little magazines, between *Neue Deutsche Beiträge*, *Die Kreatur*, and *Der Jude*, might not have been possible.

Compelling evidence of Benjamin's estimation of the prospects for exchange between Jews and Christians in Germany, for which his journal might have been a venue of sorts, may be found in his letters to Rang of November 1923. The immediate context is Rang's request that Benjamin contribute a response to a book Rang had written calling on Germans to volunteer to work to rebuild the regions of Belgium and France that the German military had devastated. Benjamin was reluctant. He prodded Rang to think of the danger in which a public statement on a topic as controversial as reparation on the part of a Jew could put Rang's cause and Benjamin personally. In a letter to Rang dated November 26, 1923, Benjamin speaks of his uneasiness with the prospect of the publication of his response in Rang's book and of his concerns about how faculty members in Frankfurt, where he was pursuing his *Habilitation*, might respond to his involvement; Benjamin mentions that his "particular sponsor"—Franz Schultz—"is on the *far* right." Benjamin also urges Rang to consider whether including responses in the publication might undermine Rang's polemic, recommending that Rang not publish any if he receives fewer than seven, and adding, "of this number, how many may be Jews? Not more than one quarter! This is my firm conviction."[171] In the end, however, Benjamin did contribute.[172] While Rang's foreword positions the responses at the end of his book as indicating that a small community of like-minded men supported the basic position he articulates there—"This group of people already constitute a community, as is necessary for the building of the body of the people. . . . I speak from the strength of this community"—Benjamin's response in fact signals distance.[173] Although Rang met Benjamin's recommended minimum of seven responses from a range of positions (for instance, one respondent states at the outset that he is Catholic, another that he is a worker), his solicitation and inclusion of responses from both Benjamin and Buber put him just over Benjamin's quota.[174]

While Benjamin spoke of "religions" and "languages" in the 1922 journal announcement, he speaks of "peoples" and "nationalities" in a letter to Rang of November 18, 1923: "Let me begin with the current situation of Germanness. . . . [Y]ou represent genuine Germanness (indeed, at the risk of annoying you, I would almost like to say that . . . you are the only one who does). . . . Jews today endanger even the best German cause for which they stand up *publicly*. . . . Secret relationships between Germans and Jews can be maintained with an entirely different kind of legitimacy . . . nowadays everything having to do with German-Jewish relationships that has a *visible impact* does so to their detriment; furthermore, nowadays a salutary complicity obligates those individuals of noble character among both peoples to keep silent about their ties."[175] Benjamin speaks of the murders of Landauer and foreign minister Walther Rathenau as Jews who *had* stood up publicly—both politically active Forte-Circle associates, both killed by right-wing groups.

Benjamin's journal never came out; its announcement was published only posthumously. Rang, the Christian most invested in Jewish-Christian exchange among Benjamin's friends, died in 1924. Benjamin continued to refer to Klee's picture in terms of Jewish angelology: at the end of the 1931 essay on Karl Kraus, in which Klee's *Angelus* is adduced alongside Loos and Scheerbart as an aid to understanding "a humanity that proves itself by destruction," Benjamin recasts the connection between the *Angelus* and the vanishing Talmudic angels at the end of the journal announcement nine years earlier, counterposing to the figure of the "new man" that of "a monster, a new angel": "Perhaps one of those who, according to the Talmud, are at each moment created anew in countless throngs, and who, once they have raised their voices before God, cease and pass into nothingness. Lamenting, chastising, or rejoicing?"[176] But like the layered complexity of Klee's picture, which made it possible for me to articulate this dimension of Benjamin's writing, the complexity of Benjamin's contentious layering of vanishing Talmudic angels over Klee's ironizing refiguration of Grünewald's resurrected Christ has been practically invisible. For it never took place in any public or realized sense. My very attempt to illuminate what did not happen has the frailty of an explication of something that, as Scholem wrote of the broader context to which it belonged in his 1964 "Against the Myth of the German-Jewish Dialogue," did not exist "in any genuine sense whatsoever, i.e. *as a historical phenomenon*."[177] In 1921–1922, however, it seems that Benjamin, unlike Scholem, pursued the hope that it might happen in his journal project and palimpsestic rewriting of Klee's image as an angel of the Talmud. As Benjamin wrote in a letter telling Rang that he had ceased to work on it, "this unwritten journal could not be any more important or dear to me if it existed."[178]

EPILOGUE

In 1940, twenty years after Klee made the picture, Benjamin wrote a short text citing it, "On the Concept of History." The ninth of its numbered sections is quoted in full in the introduction to this book. It begins with an epigraph—four rhyming lines from "Greetings from the Angelus," the poem in the angel's voice that Scholem wrote for Benjamin's birthday in 1921—with one line emphasized by Benjamin: "*I would like to turn back*." The three sentences following are devoted to the "picture by Klee." The rest, the main part of the thesis, is an elaborate, longer but still highly compressed description of another angel, "the angel of history." The "thesis" presents Klee's *Angelus novus* as a kind of model for its own figure of the "angel of history": "This is how the angel of history must look," writes Benjamin after the sentences describing the angel drawn by Klee. The text goes on to speak of what the angel of history wishes to do—"stay, awaken the dead, and make whole what has been smashed"—and of what prevents him from doing it—"a storm . . . blowing from Paradise . . . has got caught in his wings." Locating him in a complex quasi-biblical topography of spatialized time—the angel faces the past, but a storm "from Paradise" blows him ceaselessly "into the future, to which his back is turned"—the thesis opposes what "we" see when we look at the past ("a chain of events") to what the angel sees ("one single catastrophe"). The last line asserts that the storm caught in his wings is what "we" term "progress."

This section of Benjamin's text is far from a thesis in the usual sense of a proposition or assertion, as in the numbered theses of a scholastic disputation, like Luther's, or even the "95 Theses on Judaism and Zionism" that Scholem wrote for Benjamin.[1] Rather, it is a *Denkbild*, a short, highly structured piece of prose that mimes emulating certain qualities of pictures.[2] Sigrid Weigel, borrowing a phrase from Benjamin, reads the ninth thesis as a "dialectical image" dealing with "the position of theological tradition, from which the figure of the angel comes, towards and in history."[3]

"On the Concept of History" attacks the conception of history as progress and the "homogenous, empty time" it presupposes, criticizing in particular its role in the Social Democratic Party of Germany.[4] It pursues how history is thought in historicism, in historical materialism, and in theology, asserting that this is crucial for responding to the dominance of fascism and the inability of socialists to counter it; the Hitler-Stalin Pact of 1939 is obliquely mentioned as defining the moment of its writing, "a moment when the politicians in whom the opponents of fascism had placed their hopes are prostrate, and confirm their defeat by betraying their own cause."[5] Its opening set piece tells of an apparatus including a chess-playing puppet made to look like an automaton and the dwarf chess master hidden within it who controls the puppet: "The puppet called 'historical materialism' is to win all the time. It can easily be a match for anyone if it enlists the services of theology, which today, as we know, is wizened and has to keep out of sight." Quaytman cites these sentences in the last paragraph of her essay on her discovery.[6]

This book depends on the connection between the *Angelus novus* and "On the Concept of History": otherwise it would not have been possible to hope that a book about the former could find more than a handful of readers. But this book has also depended on setting the 1940 theses aside, using the Luther portrait the *Angelus novus* had hidden within it all along to estrange the picture from its usual discursive roles since the Benjamin boom, to take it away from Benjamin's lines on "the angel of history," to explore what connections it made and what hopes it responded to in the early 1920s. After attempting this in the preceding chapters, at this juncture it is meet to return to the thesis of 1940. I would like to make two modest suggestions about how the *Angelus novus*, in its additional complexity that we are now in a position to grasp, might have been generative for Benjamin's writing of "On the Concept of History."

This epilogue is speculative—no direct lines can be drawn here. But even the thesis's stress on the angel as having a face ("turned toward the past") and a back ("the future, toward which his back is turned") might be newly striking in relation to the layering of time-stamped faces in Klee's picture. Quaytman's long inquiry was driven in part by her sense that the discovery of the old engraving embedded in the *Angelus* reveals that Benjamin's *Denkbild* relates chiastically to Klee's picture—Klee's angel, facing us, turns his back on the sixteenth century.[7] Given the concerns of "On the Concept of History" with messianism, historical citation, and the relation between theology and history, its citation of the *Angelus novus* may look less idiosyncratic than perhaps it used to.

My first suggestion begins with a detour through an excerpt from Bloch's *Spirit of Utopia*, this time not from the first edition, written during the war and published shortly before its end—the one Benjamin read—but the significantly different second edition of 1923. The first edition was published before the revolution; the second had to grapple with its failures. In this second edition, toward the beginning of the last section of the book, Bloch presents the situation in Germany as follows:

> We repeat again: And of course, as though one had not been burned badly enough, this is how it remains even today. The War ended, the Revolution began and with it, seemingly, the open doors. But correct, these soon closed again. The black-marketeer moved, sat back down, and everything obsolete drifted back into place. The profiteering farmer, the mighty *grand bourgeois* truly put out the fire in places, and the panicked *petit bourgeois* helps to enfeeble and encrust, as always. Nonproletarian youth is more coarse and stupid, has its head thrown further back than any youth before; the universities have become true burial mounds of the spirit, hotbeds of "Germany, awaken!" and filled with the stink of rigidity, corruption and gloom. So those who have apparently been restored completely reenact what the reaction of a century ago auditioned . . . They reenact that Restoration's recuperation, when the cloddish slogans, the corporative state were recalled; when the traditionalism of *Vaterland* was rampant against the truly Christian, indeed even quite properly medieval idea of humanity; when that insensible Romanticism appeared that forgot Münzer yet revered the junk of heraldry, that ignored the true German popular tradition, the Peasants' War, and saw only knights' castles rising into enchanted, moonlit nights.[8]

Bloch's 1923 *Spirit of Utopia* presents the period of reaction that followed hard upon the November Revolution as reenacting, in a "doubly imitative Romanticism," that of the repressive years between the Congress of Vienna and the revolutions of 1848 that recuperated only the princes' sixteenth century. The sense of reenactment is reinforced—"We repeat again"—by the fact that this very passage late in the book repeats almost word for word a passage from its opening pages.[9] I don't assume that Bloch, despite his apparent involvement in Benjamin's purchase of the *Angelus novus*, knew anything of its interleaved Luther print of the Restoration period that might well be seen as the Luther who wrote "Against the Murderous, Thieving Hordes of Peasants." But Klee's picture and these parts of Bloch's book might perhaps be said to share a sense of the recursive structure of reaction in Germany after the November Revolution as appealing to the authority of a past that itself appealed to the authority of a past—of the way the counterrevolution repeated the gestures of the *Deutschtümelei* of the post-Napoleonic period, which in turn presented itself as modeled after feudal authority in the Reformation era as if it had never been challenged. Klee's picture—pressing together a Luther portrait whose sixteenth-century date refers to no particular Luther portrait and is rendered in the syntax of nineteenth-century reproductive engraving, and a drawn angel that echoes aspects of the underlying Luther's appearance—might be seen as sharing something of Bloch's sense of repeating again.

That movements of political reaction cite past citations of the past in a highly selective manner is not surprising, pungent as it might have been in counterrevolutionary Germany in the early 1920s. Much stranger is Benjamin's idea of a revolutionary mode of citing the past, as in his fourteenth thesis: "History is the subject of a construction whose site is not homogeneous, empty time, but time filled full by now-time. Thus, to Robespierre ancient Rome was a past charged with now-time, a past which he blasted out of the continuum of history. The French Revolution viewed itself as Rome reincarnate. It cited ancient Rome in exactly the way fashion cites a bygone mode of dress."[10]

In the *Arcades Project*, Benjamin's attempt to "carry over the principle of montage into history,"[11] to construct both a history of metropolitan capitalism and a new kind of history writing by means of citation, Benjamin writes of the "dialectical image": "It's not that what is past casts its light on what is present, or what is present its light on what is past; rather, image is that wherein what has been comes together in a flash with the now to form a constellation. In other words, image is dialectics at a standstill. For while the relation of the present to the past is a purely temporal, continuous one, the relation of what-has-been to the now is dialectical: is not progression but image, suddenly emergent."[12]

We might be tempted to see in the unobtrusive montage of Klee's *Angelus* "the relation of what-has-been to the now." But the relation of the two upper layers of the *Angelus* does not fit Benjamin's "image" as "that wherein what has been comes together in a flash with the now to form a constellation." Not only does each layer have its own chronological perplexity that relates more closely to the very different mode of historical citation described by Bloch, but Benjamin goes on to write that "the place where one encounters" such dialectical images "is language."[13] Klee's *Angelus* is not a "dialectical image"—an intricate concept that belongs inside Benjamin's writing, to imagine a certain kind of textual "image" to which he aspired in his writing of history—but perhaps part of its importance for Benjamin might have had to do how it might appear to be a material figuring of "image" as "that wherein what has been comes together in a flash with the now" as the superimposition and gluing together of sheets of paper. Perhaps Klee's picture provided a crude model of the "dialectical image" that it is not, something that Benjamin might have used as a rough mock-up of a textual construction, of the "dialectical image" he aimed to write: Benjamin's citation of Klee's picture in the ninth thesis, which can be seen as such a dialectical image, might be seen to suggest as much.

Heinz Brüggemann has insightfully suggested that Benjamin's ninth thesis might be seen as a "superimposition of two pictures: Grünewald's resurrection and Klee's new angel."[14] He also suggests that Klee's *Angelus* itself might be seen as a "distorting, disfiguring, at once destroying and constructing disputation with Grünewald's *Resurrection*"—implying then that Benjamin's famous *Denkbild* is, among many other things, an elaboration on an allusion in Klee's picture.[15] Some of the features of "the angel of history," Brüggemann contends, might be seen as indirectly suggested by Klee's watercolored drawing by way of the altarpiece panel that it recalls and that Benjamin knew so well. Benjamin's description, writes Brüggemann, "enters the force field of redemption and resurrection, closer to that of the messiah than of an angel, and also closer to the pictorial world of Grünewald, in which the soldiers lie like wreckage piled up before the open grave, and the rainbow colors of the halo of light proclaim redemption, reconciliation between God and humanity."[16]

Brüggemann connects his argument with Scholem's reading of the ninth thesis in "Walter Benjamin and His Angel" (1972). In "On the Concept of History," says Scholem, "Benjamin divided up the function of the Messiah as crystallized by the view of history of Judaism: into that of the angel who must fail in his task, and that of the Messiah who can accomplish it."[17] Scholem reads the "angel of history" that would like to but cannot repair what is broken as a would-be Messiah, since in "the Lurianic *kabbalah* the awaking of the dead and the joining together and restoring of what has been smashed and broken is the task not of an angel but of the Messiah."[18] As in the *kabbalah*, so too in Benjamin's theses, in this respect: Scholem writes that what the angel wants to do "can be fulfilled, in the last thesis of this sequence, only by the Messiah, who might enter through the 'strait gate' of every fulfilled second of historical time, as Benjamin says in an exposition concerning the relationship of the Jews to time and the future."[19] What Scholem sees as a division of the "function of the Messiah" might also be seen, suggests Brüggemann, in terms of the refiguring of Grünewald's resurrected Messiah as angel in both Klee's picture and Benjamin's ninth thesis.

The previous two chapters reinforce Brüggemann's suggestions that Klee was playing off of Grünewald's Resurrection panel and that Benjamin caught that play. But if it now seems more firmly established that Grünewald's Resurrection is in some sense an interpicture both for Klee's *Angelus novus* and for Benjamin's "angel of history," it seems also more pressing to acknowledge the most obvious problem thereby introduced. While Benjamin himself, in a casual sketch, drew a crucified "Angelus" taking on iconographic features of Christian images of Jesus, it will not do to slide too easily between the messiah of Grünewald's altarpiece and that of Benjamin's "On the Concept of History."

Brüggemann's discussion risks assimilating traditions of Jewish to Christian messianism. In doing so, it might perhaps be said to complement Scholem's contrary emphasis on the Jewish elements of Benjamin's writings in relation to the angel. Scholem could certainly be said to follow Benjamin's lead at many moments (Benjamin calls the *Angelus* a "good Jew," a "messenger of the Kabbalah," and so on), but he also tends to suppress what does not fit, obscuring the way the *Angelus novus* may have served as a kind of emblem of theological montage, to draw again on Jennings's discussion.[20]

We can see this kind of montage in "On the Concept of History," which draws both on Jewish and on Christian figurations of the messiah. In one thesis, specifically Christian eschatology is cited: "The Messiah comes not only as the redeemer; he comes as the victor over the Antichrist."[21] In another, he speaks specifically of how "Jews" understood the future, in which "every second was the small gateway in time through which the Messiah might enter."[22]

Agamben, in his *The Time That Remains: A Commentary on the Letter to the Romans*, elaborates a reading of "On the Concept of History" as permeated by Paul's writings as translated by Luther, cued by what Agamben sees as a "citation without citation marks" of Luther's translation of 2 Corinthians in Benjamin's phrase "w e a k messianic power" in the second thesis: "the entire vocabulary of the theses appears to be truly stamped Pauline. It will not come as a surprise then that the term *redemption* (*Erlösung*)—an absolutely critical concept in Benjamin's notion of historical knowledge—is the term that Luther uses to convey Pauline *apolytrosis*, just as crucial to the Letters."[23] Agamben's reading builds on *The Political Theology of Paul*, by Scholem's former student Jacob Taubes, in which the latter reads Paul as a Jewish figure whose messianism negates Roman and Jewish values and Benjamin's "Theological-Political Fragment" (ca. 1921) in relation to Paul's letter to the Romans.[24] Further, Agamben speculates that Scholem may have been both aware of and troubled by "the discovery of a Pauline inspiration in aspects of his friend's messianic thought."[25]

Brian Britt criticizes Agamben's reading of "On the Concept of History" and the way it hinges on "a single figure and genius (Paul) to account for messianic tradition," pointing out Benjamin's "deliberate avoidance of specific religious citations" as demonstrating "that biblical tradition pervades language and thought, even in modernity." Britt proposes that a "better way of understanding biblical reception and biblical tradition, one that is reflected in Benjamin's deliberately ambiguous religious references, might be to describe them as a constellation of allusions."[26] In "On the Concept of History," Benjamin might be seen not as searching for a shared past in Jewish Christianity, in a figure like Paul, but as juxtaposing latter-day polarizations, which have already gone through processes of reciprocal differentiation. If, following Jennings and Britt, we might see Benjamin as juxtaposing elements from both Jewish and Christian traditions without attempting to undo the historical processes of mutual polarization that make these combinations so tense, it may make sense to see Klee's *Angelus novus* as modeling juxtaposition as the making of an image.

In "Walter Benjamin and His Angel," Scholem decries the neglect, on the part of Benjamin's "New Left" interpreters, of Benjamin's "ties to the mystical tradition and to a mystical experience which nevertheless was a far cry from the experience of God. . . . Benjamin knew that mystical experience is many-layered (*mystische Erfahrung vielschichtig ist*), and it was precisely this many-layeredness (*Vielschichtigkeit*) that played so great a role in his thinking and in his productivity."[27] Perhaps the layers (not many, just a few) of the eminently material artifact that Benjamin cites in the ninth thesis—this angelic figuration made of paper, cardboard, cheap engraving, and paint—played a role, too.

Acknowledgments

This book could never be but for the generosity of Rebecca Quaytman. She kindly welcomed first my tagging along with her on the last leg of her investigation into the mystery of the *Angelus novus*, and then my follow-up inquiries, which were nourished by her curiosity and encouragement.

I thank Brigid Doherty, Michael Jennings, Lisa Florman, Mark Haxthausen, Marie Kakinuma, Paul Mendes-Flohr, Peter Parshall, Martin Schawe, and Jennifer Nelson for indispensable aid.

Lisa Lee, Ralph Ubl, Angela Lampe, Mark Godfrey, Gregor Wedekind, Kate Nesin, Johanna Függer-Vagts, Joyce Tsai, Maureen Chun, Spyros Papapetros, Hal Foster, and Yve-Alain Bois made crucial contributions of various kinds, for which I thank them. Thanks to Michael Baumgartner, Fabienne Eggelhöffer, Graham Bader, Malika Maskarinec, and Megan R. Luke for questions and comments.

I was exceptionally lucky to air the early versions of sections of this book before engaged audiences who helped me to advance and refine my claims; the earliest versions were very rough indeed. The questions and comments I received at a 2015 workshop at eikones, Universität Basel, at the 2016 Klee colloquium at the Centre Pompidou, at the 2017 Lovis Corinth Colloquium on German Modernism at Emory University, at the Princeton University Humanities Council, and at the 2019 conference of the International Walter Benjamin Society and Walter Benjamin Kolleg der Philosophisch-historischen Fakultät der Universität Bern were formative.

I thank Susan Bielstein for guiding me in shaping this project into a book.

Thanks to Ronit Sorek and Michael Maggen of the Israel Museum for answering many questions; thanks to Cathrin Klingsöhr-Leroy for inviting me to the Schloss Suresnes, and to the Bayerisches Hauptstaatsarchiv for welcoming me. The Zentrum Paul Klee was very helpful.

At the beginning of this project, I was fortunate to enjoy the support of the Alexander von Humboldt-Stiftung, and of Susanne von Falkenhausen's generosity as a host; I am grateful for their bearing with me when my plans took an entirely unanticipated course.

The support of the David Baumgardt Memorial Fellowship of the Leo Baeck Institute enabled a critical portion of my research; I thank Frank Mecklenburg for graciously welcoming me out of my depth.

I thank my students and my colleagues at the School of the Art Institute of Chicago for their encouragement. I am grateful for the Faculty Enrichment Grant from the School that helped me with the costs of images. Alivé Piliado was a great help with securing images and permissions.

Generous support from the Dedalus Foundation made the completion of this project possible; a subvention from the Barr Ferree Foundation Publication Fund of the Department of Art and Archaeology, Princeton University, made it possible for this book to take the form it should have. This book was finished under difficult conditions in 2020 and 2021; I would not have been able to prevail in the end without the heroic efforts of Holly Dankert and Olive Jenkins. My thanks as well to Joseph Leo Koerner for a last-minute kindness.

I thank my children for their patience, their grandparents for making possible the travels involved in making this book, and my husband, Ben Lytal, for his unstinting faith.

Notes

CHAPTER 1

1. R. H. Quaytman, "Engrave," and Annie Bourneuf, "The Margins of the *Angelus novus*," in *Chapter 29: Haqaq* (Tel Aviv: Tel Aviv Museum of Art, 2016), 51–61 and 35–41. Gregor Wedekind, "Ein neuer Engel? Walter Benjamins Bilddenken und Paul Klees Philosophie der Unzulänglichkeit," in *Vom Ende der Geschichte her: Walter Benjamins geschichtsphilosophische Thesen*, ed. Thomas Schröder and Jonas Engelmann (Mainz: Ventil, 2017), 183–85.

2. Walter Benjamin, *Selected Writings*, trans. Edmund Jephcott and others, ed. Howard Eiland and Michael W. Jennings (Cambridge, MA: Belknap Press of Harvard University Press, 2003), 4:392.

3. Quaytman, "Engrave," 53.

4. Annie Bourneuf, *Paul Klee: The Visible and the Legible* (Chicago: University of Chicago Press, 2015).

5. Usually the dark border is applied directly to the mount around a watercolor; see, for example, *Gartenhäuser* (1919, 8) or *Vogel = Inseln* (1921, 20) or *Kristall-Stufung* (1921, 88) or *Bild aus dem Boudoir* (1922, 14). Sometimes it is applied to a separate sheet of paper, the margins of which are visible all around, as in *Der Blick des Ahriman* (1920, 148). Sometimes Klee used a metallic paper as a border, as in *Hoffmanneske Geschichte* (1921, 18); in one instance, *Burglandschaft m. d. schwarzen Blitz* (1920, 83), he used a piece of paper printed with regular, horizontal, parallel lines, black on white, related to but distinct from the parallel lines of the engraving interleaved in the *Angelus*. Note that the captions for most of Paul Klee's works reproduced in this book include a second number after the date; at times I use this number in the text as well. The second number is part of Klee's own system for ordering his work: it corresponds to the sequence in which he entered the object into the oeuvre-catalog he used to keep track of his production.

6. Walter Benjamin, "The Work of Art in the Age of Its Technological Reproducibility: Second Version," in *The Work of Art in the Age of Its Technological Reproducibility and Other Writings on Media*, ed. Michael W. Jennings, Brigid Doherty, and Thomas Y. Levin (Cambridge, MA: Belknap Press of Harvard University Press, 2008), 21; Rolf Tiedemann and Hermann Schweppenhäuser, eds., *Gesammelte Schriften* (Frankfurt: Suhrkamp, 1991), 7:352 (hereafter *Gesammelte Schriften*).

7. Leopold Zahn, *Paul Klee: Leben, Werk, Geist* (Potsdam: Gustav Kiepenheuer, 1920); Wilhelm Hausenstein, *Kairuan, oder eine Geschichte vom Maler Klee und von der Kunst dieses Zeitalters* (Munich: Kurt Wolff, 1921); Elizabeth Kaiser Schulte, Margaret Holben Ellis, and Antoinette King, "An Approach to the Conservation Treatment of Paul Klee Drawings," *Book and Paper Group Annual* 5 (1986): 19–32.

8. See the moiré in Johann Konrad Eberlein, *"Angelus novus": Paul Klees Bild und Walter Benjamins Deutung* (Freiburg: Rombach, 2006). The most probable explanation for the peculiar appearance of the engraved area in the reproduction in the Klee catalogue raisonné noted by Quaytman ("Engrave," 54) is that it resulted from a botched attempt to get rid of a moiré without cropping.

9. Klee, "Beitrag für den Sammelband *Schöpferische Konfession* (1920)," in *Schriften: Rezensionen und Aufsätze*, ed. Christian Geelhaar (Cologne: DuMont, 1976), 120; Klee, *Pädagogisches Skizzenbuch*, Faksimile-Nachdruck nach der Ausgabe von 1925 (Berlin: Gebr. Mann, 1997), 23.

10. Quaytman, "Engrave," 58–59.

11. Andreas Andresen, *Handbuch für Kupferstichsammler oder Lexicon der Kupferstecher, Maler-Radirer und Formschneider aller Länder und Schulen nach Massgabe ihrer geschätztesten Blätter und Werke*, vol. 2 (Leipzig: T. O. Weigel, 1873), s.v. "Friedrich Müller"; M. Ch. Le Blanc, *Manuel de l'amateur d'estampes* (Paris: P. Jannet, 1857), s.v. "MULLER (*Johann Friedrich*)." Friedrich Müller is not to be confused with the celebrated engraver Johann Friedrich Wilhelm Müller (1782–1816).

12. In remarks on the "location of images in Protestant life," Morgan comments on their especially important role in the spaces of Protestant education, in homes and schools, as well as on portraiture as a favored genre. David Morgan, *The Forge of Vision: A Visual History of Modern Christianity* (Oakland: University of California Press, 2015), 51–52. See also Hofmann's discussion of the crucial role of an image's location in Luther's and Zwingli's judgments about its propriety. Werner Hofmann, "Die Geburt der Moderne aus dem Geist der Religion," in *Luther und die Folgen für die Kunst*, ed. Werner Hofmann (Munich: Prestel, 1983), 28.

13. A few "avant la lettre" proofs were pulled before this quotation was added; Le Blanc, *Manuel de l'amateur d'estampes*, s.v. "MULLER (*Johann Friedrich*)."

14. Quaytman, "Engrave," 60.

15. Werckmeister, *Icons of the Left: Benjamin and Eisenstein, Picasso and Kafka after the Fall of Communism* (Chicago: University of Chicago Press, 1999), 8–35.

16. Paul Rohrbach's lithograph of Rudolf Jordan's painting *The Pilots' Exam* serves as the support for Klee's *Pathos der Fruchtbarkeit*. See the Metropolitan Museum of Art online collection record: https://www.metmuseum.org/art/collection/search/483145. Thanks to Marie Kakinuma for pointing out this comparison.

17. Benjamin, "Rigorous Study of Art" (1932), in *Selected Writings*, vol. 2, *1927–1934*, ed. Michael W. Jennings, Howard Eiland, and Gary Smith (Cambridge, MA: Belknap Press of Harvard University Press, 1999), 668–69; Ernst Bloch, "Recollections of Walter Benjamin," trans. Michael W. Jennings, in *On Walter Benjamin*, ed. Gary Smith (Cambridge, MA: MIT Press, 1988), 40; "Erinnerungen," in Theodor Adorno, *Über Walter Benjamin*, ed. Rolf Tiedemann (Frankfurt: Suhrkamp, 1968), 17.

18. Klee's words may be found in a 1915 postcard in "Briefe von Paul Klee an Alfred Kubin," in *Paul Klee: Das Frühwerk, 1883–1922*, ed. Armin Zweite (Munich: Städtische Galerie im Lenbachhaus, 1979), 87. Peter Parshall pointed out this aspect of the *Angelus* as I was corresponding with him about the as-yet-unidentified print, speaking of the "appeal of the patterned backdrop as a 'found' frame/border with the signature as a teaser." "I take it . . . that nobody in Jerusalem is about to lift the drawing to find out," he continued. "If I were the

curator I wouldn't authorize it. In a sense, if it *was* left as a teaser it would be cheating to take it up. More sporting to play by his rules." Email to the author, March 20, 2015.

19. As Nathan Stoltzfus explains, the order stipulated that schools and other public buildings must remove "ecclesiastical and other religious symbols"—the Luther portraits and the crucifixes that served as signs of Protestant and Catholic affiliation, respectively (Stoltzfus speaks of the image of Hitler fighting on a "school-wall battlefield" against traditional symbols of the largest confessions, "the crucifix, the pope, and the German icon Martin Luther"). Because of the protests launched by the Catholics of Oldenburg in response to it, the Oldenburg order has received a good deal of scholarly attention (the Protestants, in contrast, mostly complied, replacing Luther with Hitler portraits as directed.) Nathan Stoltzfus, *Hitler's Compromises: Coercion and Consensus in Nazi Germany* (New Haven, CT: Yale University Press, 2016), 91–108; Jeremy Noakes, "The Oldenburg Crucifix Struggle of November 1936: A Case Study of Opposition in the Third Reich," in *The Shaping of the Nazi State*, ed. Peter D. Stachura (London: Croom Helm, 1978), 218, 220. Cranach's Luther portraits continue to be very much in circulation within the Lutheran denominations: a contemporary Lutheran publishing house in Missouri sells posters of Cranach portraits with the words "Every Lutheran church and home needs a print of Martin Luther!" Concordia Publishing House, "Worship Resources," https://www.cph.org/c-3239-prints.aspx. More broadly, the image of Luther remains in heavy use in Germany in particular: the German toy line Playmobil's figure of Luther with black gown and Bible, introduced in the lead-up to the five hundredth anniversary of the Reformation, is the well-known manufacturer's fastest-selling figure of all time. Rose Troup Buchanan, "Martin Luther Toy Becomes Fastest Selling Playmobil Figurine of All Time," *The Independent*, February 17, 2015, https://www.independent.co.uk/news/world/europe/martin-luther-toy-becomes-fastest-selling-playmobil-figurine-of-all-time-10051834.html.

20. Martin Warnke, *Cranachs Luther: Entwürfe für ein Image* (Frankfurt: Fischer, 1984).

21. Joseph Leo Koerner, *Reformation of the Image* (Chicago: University of Chicago Press, 2004), 391–92. Koerner is discussing works incorporating portraits of Reformation figures including Luther, such as Cranach's Wittenberg and Weimar altarpieces and the triptych of Luther portraits that Veit Thim, possibly Lucas Cranach the Younger's assistant, made for the Stadtkirche in Weimar.

22. Thomas Albert Howard, *Remembering the Reformation: An Inquiry into the Meanings of Protestantism* (Oxford: Oxford University Press, 2016), 71.

23. Howard, 94–99.

24. Scholem, "Walter Benjamin and His Angel" (1972), in Scholem, *On Jews and J udaism in Crisis: Selected Essays*, ed. Werner J. Dannhauser (Philadelphia: Paul Dry Books, 2012), 198–236.

25. Adam Kirsch, "Seeing Double," review of Samantha Baskin and Larry Silver, *Jewish Art: A Modern History*, *Tablet*, October 11, 2011, https://www.tabletmag.com/jewish-arts-and-culture/80442/seeing-double.

26. Benjamin writes in a February 1940 letter to Horkheimer of "un certain nombre de thèses sur le concept d'Histoire." Christoph Gödde and Henri Lonitz, eds., *Gesammelte Briefe* (Frankfurt: Suhrkamp, 2000), 6:400 (hereafter *Gesammelte Briefe*). Gershom Scholem, *The Fullness of Time: Poems*, trans. Richard Sieburth, introduced and annotated by Steven M. Wasserstrom (Jerusalem: Ibis Editions, 2003), 64–67.

27. Benjamin, "On the Concept of History," trans. Harry Zohn, in *Selected Writings*, ed. Howard Eiland and Michael W. Jennings (Cambridge, MA: Belknap Press of Harvard University Press, 2003), 4:392–93.

> Mein Flügel ist zum Schwung bereit
> *ich kehrte gern zurück*
> denn blieb' ich auch lebendige Zeit
> ich hätte wenig Glück.
>
> *Gerhard Scholem, Gruß vom Angelus*
>
> Es gibt ein Bild von Klee, das Angelus novus heißt. Ein Engel ist darauf dargestellt, der aussieht, als wäre er im Begriff, sich von etwas zu entfernen, worauf er starrt. Seine Augen sind aufgerissen, sein Mund steht offen und seine Flügel sind ausgespannt. Der Engel der Geschichte muß so aussehen. Er hat das Antlitz der Vergangenheit zugewendet. Wo eine Kette von Begebenheiten vor *uns* erscheint, da sieht *er* eine einzige Katastrophe, die unablässig Trümmer auf Trümmer häuft und sie ihm vor die Füße schleudert. Er möchte wohl verweilen, die Toten wecken und das Zerschlagene zusammenfügen. Aber ein Sturm weht vom Paradiese her, der sich in seinen Flügeln verfangen hat und so stark ist, daß der Engel sie nicht mehr schließen kann. Dieser Sturm treibt ihn unaufhaltsam in die Zukunft, der er den Rücken kehrt, während der Trümmerhaufen vor ihm zum Himmel wächst. Das, was wir den Fortschritt nennen, ist *dieser* Sturm.

Benjamin, "Über den Begriff der Geschichte," in *Gesammelte Schriften*, 1:691–704. While Scholem adopted the Hebrew name Gershom, Benjamin addressed him by his birth name, Gerhard.

28. Dieter Roelstraete, "*Kleeblätter*: A Selection of Annotated Book Covers," and Susan Bielstein, "Judging a Book," in Roelstraete, *Kleine Welt* (Chicago: Neubauer Collegium for Culture and Society, 2019), 13–95, 97–101.

29. Quaytman, "Engrave," 59.

30. Ernst Troeltsch, *The Social Teachings of the Christian Churches*, trans. Olive Wyon (Chicago: University of Chicago Press, 1981), 2:521; Debbie Lewer, "Hugo Ball, Iconoclasm and the Origins of Dada in Zurich," *Oxford Art Journal* 32, no. 1 (2009): 17–35.

31. See *"Überall Luthers Worte . . .": Martin Luther im Nationalsozialismus* (Berlin: Stiftung Topographie des Terrors and Gedenkstätte Deutscher Widerstand, 2017); Richard Steigmann-Gall, *The Holy Reich: Nazi Conceptions of Christianity, 1919–1945* (New York: Cambridge University Press, 2003).

32. Steigmann-Gall, *Holy Reich*, 134–37.

33. Paul Klee, "Bildnerische Form- und Gestaltungslehre," 1921–1931, Zentrum Paul Klee, Bern, http://www.kleegestaltungslehre.zpk.org/ee/ZPK/Archiv/2011/01/25/00001/.

34. Paul Klee, "On Modern Art," trans. David Farrell Krell, in *Philosophical Vision: From Nature to Art,* ed. John Sallis (Chestnut Hill, MA: McMullen Museum of Art, Boston College, 2012), 10.

35. Hal Foster, Rosalind Krauss, Yve-Alain Bois, Benjamin H. D. Buchloh, and David Joselit, *Art since 1900*, 2nd ed. (New York: Thames and Hudson, 2011), 140.

36. Godfrey, "Angels, Boulders, and Tongues," in *Chapter 29: Haqaq* (Tel Aviv: Tel Aviv Museum of Art, 2016), 16–17.

37. Quaytman, "Engrave," 52.

38. Quaytman, 53.

39. Quaytman, 53.

40. Quaytman, 54.

41. Quaytman, 52.

42. Quaytman and Godfrey, conversation, Friends of the Tel Aviv Museum of Art in Israel, Tel Aviv, May 18, 2015.

43. Quaytman, *Spine* (New York: Sequence Press, 2011), back cover ("Collection").

44. Quaytman, "Engrave," 54.

45. Quaytman, 54.

46. Quaytman, 55.

47. R. H. Quaytman, "de Fem," in Daniel Birnbaum and Ann-Sofi Noring, eds., *The Legacy of Hilma af Klint: Nine Contemporary Responses* (London: Koenig Books; Stockholm: Moderna Museet, 2013).

48. Rebentisch, "Reflections and Refractions: Notes on R. H. Quaytman," in Quaytman, *Morning: Chapter 30* (Los Angeles: Museum of Contemporary Art, 2016), 134.

49. Trodd, *The Art of Mechanical Reproduction: Technology and Aesthetics from Duchamp to the Digital* (Chicago: University of Chicago Press, 2015), 19–22.

50. Josef Helfenstein and Christian Rümelin, eds., *Paul Klee: Catalogue raisonné* (Wabern: Benteli, 1998–2004), vol. 3, nos. 2377 and 2414; Trodd, *Art of Mechanical Reproduction*, 24.

51. Trodd, *Art of Mechanical Reproduction*, 264n21.

52. Sarah Ganz Blythe, "R. H. Quaytman: Archive to Ark, the Subjects of Painting," *Afterall* 38 (Spring 2015): 77.

53. Blythe, "Quaytman: Archive to Ark," 77. See images in Quaytman, *Chapter 29: Haqaq*, 71–73.

54. Christine Smallwood, "The Mother-Daughter Thing," *T Magazine*, March 24, 2015.

55. Quaytman, "Engrave," 56.

56. Quaytman, 55.

57. Benjamin, "Eduard Fuchs, Collector and Historian," in *Selected Writings*, 3:261–62; Benjamin, "Eduard Fuchs, der Sammler und der Historiker," in *Gesammelte Schriften*, 2:467.

58. Benjamin, *Selected Writings*, 3:262.

59. See the comments that Hans-Friedrich Geist reports Klee as having made when Geist visited the artist's studio in 1930: "Meine Zeichen sind keine gewollten Träger von Inhalten. . . . Der Beschauer deutet, verbindet Lineares, Flächiges, Hell-Dunkles, Farbiges mit 'Erinnerungen.' Ich bin zum Schluß selber Beschauer und lasse mich beschenken." Ludwig Grote, ed., *Erinnerungen an Paul Klee* (Munich: Prestel, 1959), 90. See Charles W. Haxthausen's discussion in "Zur 'Bildsprache' des Spätwerkes," in *Paul Klee: Das Schaffen im Todesjahr*, ed. Josef Helfenstein and Stefan Frey (Stuttgart: Gerd Hatje, 1990), 28–29.

60. Benjamin's death plays a major role in influential accounts of his work, such as Scholem's "Walter Benjamin," in Scholem, *On Jews and Judaism in Crisis*, 172.

61. On the "tragic tangle of obstruction" faced by Jews seeking to emigrate from Vichy France, see Michael Robert Marrus and Robert O. Paxton, *Vichy France and the Jews* (Stanford, CA: Stanford University Press, 1995), 161–64.

62. Gregor Wedekind, "Kosmische Konfession. Kunst und Religion bei Paul Klee," in *Paul Klee: Kunst und Karriere*, ed. Oskar Bätschmann and Josef Helfenstein (Bern: Stämpfli, 2000), 226–27.

63. He articulated his thoughts about responding to the Nazis in a letter of April 6, 1933, to his wife, Lily, explaining that their son Felix will "sein Christentum nachweisen. Wenn es von mir officiell verlangt wird, dann muß ich es auch tun. Aber von mir aus etwas gegen so plumpe Anwürfe zu unternehmen, scheint mir unwürdig. Denn: wenn es auch wahr wäre, daß ich Jude bin und aus Galizien stammte, so würde dadurch an dem Wert meiner Person und meiner Leistung nicht ein Jota geändert. Diesen meinen persönlichen Standpunkt, der meint, daß ein Jude und ein Ausländer an sich nicht minderwertiger ist als ein Deutscher und Inländer, darf ich von mir aus nicht verlassen." Paul Klee, *Briefe an die Familie, 1893–1940*, ed. Felix Klee, vol. 2, *1907–1940* (Cologne: DuMont, 1979), 1234.

64. For a detailed and well-documented chronology, see Stefan Frey and Andreas Hüneke, "Paul Klee, Kunst und Politik in Deutschland 1933: Eine Chronologie," in *Paul Klee 1933*, by Pamela Kort (Cologne: Verlag der Buchhandlung Walther König, 2003), 268–300.

65. Sorg, "Der Engel der Engel," 114–33; Howard Eiland and Michael W. Jennings, *Walter Benjamin: A Critical Life* (Cambridge, MA: Belknap Press of Harvard University Press, 2014), 677–78. Klee's reputation also increased in the postwar decades—reproductions of Picasso, Renoir, and Klee decorate the walls of Patricia's place in Godard's *Breathless*—though less dramatically than Benjamin's, and the contours are different, as he was already a well-known artist in the 1920s and 1930s. Christine Hopfengart, *Klee, vom Sonderfall zum Publikumsliebling: Stationen seiner öffentlichen Resonanz in Deutschland, 1905–1960* (Mainz: Phillip von Zabern, 1989).

66. O. K. Werckmeister, "Walter Benjamin's Angel of History, or the Transfiguration of the Revolutionary into the Historian," *Critical Inquiry* 22, no. 2 (Winter 1996): 242.

67. Scholem, "Walter Benjamin and His Angel," 210.

68. Scholem, *Walter Benjamin und sein Engel: Vierzehn Aufsätze und kleine Beiträge* (Frankfurt: Suhrkamp, 1983); Scholem, *Walter Benjamin: The Story of a Friendship*, trans. Harry Zohn (New York: New York Review Books, 2003).

69. Sorg, "Der Engel der Engel," 128.

70. Scholem, "Walter Benjamin und sein Engel," in *Zur Aktualität Walter Benjamins: Aus Anlaß des 80. Geburtstags von Walter Benjamin*, ed. Siegfried Unseld (Frankfurt: Suhrkamp, 1972), 87–138; Scholem, *Walter Benjamin und sein Engel*, 223.

71. Sorg, "Der Engel der Engel," 128.

72. Scholem, "Walter Benjamin and His Angel," 210. "Als er im Juni 1940 aus Paris floh . . . schnitt Benjamin das Bild aus dem Rahmen und stopfte es noch in einen der Koffer." Scholem, *Walter Benjamin und sein Engel*, 45.

73. Sorg, "Der Engel der Engel," 127.

74. It should be kept in mind that in 1940 Scholem was living in Jerusalem and that he reckons that a letter he sent to Benjamin in February 1940 was "probably the last direct communication" between the two of them. Scholem, ed., *The Correspondence of Walter Benjamin and Gershom Scholem, 1932–1940*, trans. Gary Smith and André Lefevere (New York: Schocken, 1989), 264–67.

75. Scholem, "Walter Benjamin and His Angel," 210.

76. Sorg, "Der Engel der Engel," 127.

77. In 1969, Gretel Adorno wrote to the Swiss dealer Eberhard W. Kornfeld for an estimate of the value of the *Angelus*; Kornfeld replied: "Im Prinzip handelt es sich um ein sehr schönes Werk aus Klee's gesuchtester Zeit, dessen Wert, Echtheit und gute Erhaltung vorausgesetzt, sich sicher auf ca. Fr. 80'000.- beläuft, eventuell auch mehr." Letters reproduced in Carl Djerassi, *Four Jews on Parnassus—A Conversation* (New York: Columbia University Press, 2008), 83.

78. Meyer, "Die Verwandlung des Sichtbaren: Die Bedeutung der modernen bildenden Kunst für Rilkes späte Dichtung," in *Zarte Empirie: Studien zur Literaturgeschichte* (Stuttgart: J. B. Metzlersche Verlagsbuchhandlung, 1963), 287–334, 418.

79. Sorg, "Der Engel der Engel," 128–29; Benjamin, "Mein Testament," in *Gesammelte Briefe*, 4:122; Elke Morlok und Frederek Musall, "Die Geschichte *seiner* Freundschaft—Gershom Scholem und die Benjamin-Rezeption in der Bonner Republik," in *Gershom Scholem in Deutschland: Zwischen Seelenverwandtschaft und Sprachlosigkeit*, ed. Gerold Necker, Elke Morlok, and Matthias Morgenstern (Tübingen: Mohr Siebeck, 2014), 115–43.

80. Sorg, "Der Engel der Engel," 128.

81. See Djerassi, *Four Jews on Parnassus*, 82–84.

82. Scholem, “Walter Benjamin and His Angel,” 201.

83. Scholem, “Walter Benjamin and His Angel,” 231, 215–16.

84. Scholem, “Walter Benjamin and His Angel,” 201, 231, 202.

85. Scholem, 199. “Der Gestus des Esoterikers, den Adorno und ich an ihm wahrgenommen haben, war der des Produzenten autoritärer, und das freilich heißt auch: von vornherein und ihrem Wesen nach zitierbarer und deutbarer Sätze.” Scholem, *Walter Benjamin und sein Engel*, 35.

86. Weidner, “Reading Gershom Scholem,” *Jewish Quarterly Review* 96, no. 2 (Spring 2006): 203.

87. Weidner, 203.

88. Scholem, “Walter Benjamin and His Angel,” 202.

89. Eberlein, *“Angelus novus,”* 21; Scholem, “Walter Benjamin and His Angel,” 209. Helfenstein and Rümelin, in *Paul Klee: Catalogue raisonné*, no. 2377, mention no exhibitions whatsoever except for the 1920 Munich exhibition.

90. Bourneuf, *Paul Klee*, 27–30. Charles W. Haxthausen, “Paul Klee, Wilhelm Hausenstein, and ‘the Problem of Style,’” *Kritische Berichte* 42, no. 1 (2014): 47–67. Heinz Brüggemann, *Walter Benjamin über Spiel, Farbe und Phantasie* (Würzburg: Königshausen & Neumann, 2007), 15–16, 330–31. Benjamin’s “Verzeichnis der gelesenen Schriften” lists Leopold Zahn’s *Paul Klee* (1920) as item 747 but makes no mention of Hausenstein’s *Kairuan*. *Gesammelte Schriften*, 7:448. There are a handful of citations of Hausenstein’s *Vom Geist des Barock* in Benjamin’s *Trauerspiel* book.

91. Bourneuf, *Paul Klee*, 66–82.

92. Gershom Scholem and Theodor W. Adorno, eds., *The Correspondence of Walter Benjamin, 1910–1940*, trans. Manfred R. Jacobson and Evelyn M. Jacobson (Chicago: University of Chicago Press, 1994), 165.

93. Scholem and Adorno, 181; *Gesammelte Briefe*, 2:167–68. This amounts to roughly fourteen US dollars at that time. The prices Benjamin lists in his letters of used books he bought or wanted to buy give another sense of the value of one thousand marks at that time: the same letter mentions a history of the Catholic index of forbidden books for sixty-five marks, one a couple of weeks later mentions the theologian Ignaz von Döllinger’s “essays on the sectarian history of the Middle Ages” for ten marks. Scholem and Adorno, *Correspondence of Walter Benjamin*, 184; *Gesammelte Briefe*, 2:174. Bloch is also mentioned several times in the first letter in the *Gesammelte Briefe* in which the *Angelus* is mentioned, the June 16, 1921, postcard from the Benjamins to Scholem. *Gesammelte Briefe*, 2:160–62. Helfenstein and Rümelin, *Paul Klee*, no. 2377, cites Klee’s own oeuvre catalog that he used to keep track of his production: “Verkauft Goltz Juni 1921.”

94. Bloch, *Thomas Münzer als Theologe der Revolution* (Munich: Kurt Wolff, 1921). Speaking of a “very cautious” and “Machiavellian” rapprochement with Bloch, Benjamin writes to Scholem in 1921 that he began reading Bloch’s book. Scholem and Adorno, *Correspondence of Walter Benjamin*, 196. Later that year, Benjamin would describe this book to Scholem as “einfach furchtbar, ein in sternheimsches Idiom eingedeutschter Max Weber.” *Gesammelte Briefe*, 2:226.

95. Scholem, “Walter Benjamin and His Angel,” 209.

96. Scholem, 209–10.

97. Scholem, 209.

98. Scholem and Adorno, *Correspondence of Walter Benjamin*, 197; *Gesammelte Briefe*, 2:223. Benjamin appears to misspell Burchhardt’s name.

99. Scholem and Adorno, *Correspondence of Walter Benjamin*, 187. It is clear from *Gesammelte Briefe*, 2:180–82, that this letter to Scholem was written by Benjamin and

Burchhardt together, whereas it appears as solely a letter from Benjamin to Scholem in Walter Benjamin, *Briefe 1*, ed. Gershom Scholem and Theodor Adorno (Frankfurt: Suhrkamp, 1978), 272–73.

100. Scholem and Adorno, *Correspondence of Walter Benjamin*, 199; *Gesammelte Briefe*, 2:269.

101. Scholem, "Walter Benjamin and His Angel," 211; *Gesammelte Briefe*, 2:160–62.

102. Scholem and Adorno, *Correspondence of Walter Benjamin*, 196; *Gesammelte Briefe*, 2:216.

103. Scholem, "Walter Benjamin and His Angel," 210–11; Scholem, "Lyrik der Kabbalah?" *Der Jude* 6, no. 1 (1921–22): 55–69; Meïr Wiener, *Die Lyrik der Kabbala: Eine Anthologie* (Vienna: R. Löwit: 1920).

104. Sander L. Gilman, *Jewish Self-Hatred: Anti-Semitism and the Hidden Language of the Jews* (Baltimore: Johns Hopkins University Press, 1986), 270–71. Michael Brenner, *The Renaissance of Jewish Culture in Weimar Germany* (New Haven, CT: Yale University Press, 1996), 142.

105. Brenner, *Renaissance of Jewish Culture*, 70.

106. Scholem, *From Berlin to Jerusalem: Memories of My Youth*, trans. Harry Zohn (Philadelphia: Paul Dry Books, 2012), 40.

107. Brenner, *Renaissance of Jewish Culture*, 3; Jay Howard Geller, *The Scholems: A Story of the German-Jewish Bourgeoisie from Emancipation to Destruction* (Ithaca, NY: Cornell University Press, 2019), 85.

108. On Benjamin's attempts to learn Hebrew in 1920 and in 1929, see Scholem, *Story of a Friendship*, 110, 113, 198–99. See Robert Alter, "On Not Knowing Hebrew," in *Necessary Angels: Tradition and Modernity in Kafka, Benjamin and Scholem* (Cambridge, MA: Harvard University Press, 1991), 42–52; Howard Eiland, "Walter Benjamin's Jewishness," in *Walter Benjamin and Theology*, ed. Colby Dickinson and Stéphane Symons (New York: Fordham University Press, 2016), 113–43.

109. Geller, *Scholems*, 105–6; Brenner, *Renaissance of Jewish Culture*, 3. While study of Hebrew was traditionally understood as a male prerogative, Jewish girls' opportunities for formal religious instruction in Germany increased beginning in the mid-nineteenth century. The neo-Orthodox leader Samson Raphael Hirsch played a major role in this development; it is possible that Burchhardt benefited.

110. Gershom Scholem, "The Curious History of the Six-Pointed Star: How the 'Magen David' Became the Jewish Symbol," trans. Milton Himmelfarb, *Commentary* 8 (1949): 250–51. Scholem's article, written in the wake of the declaration of the State of Israel, dismisses what he sees as a lot of hooey about the Magen David as an ancient religious symbol, stressing instead its modern origin as a differential marker: "The Jews of the era of Emancipation, seeing the 'symbol of Christianity' everywhere, sought a 'symbol of Judaism.' If Judaism is the 'Mosaic religion,' why should it not properly have a striking and simple sign of recognition, like the other religions?" Djerassi, *Four Jews on Parnassus*, 124.

111. On the comparison between *Angelus descendens* and *Angelus novus*, see Eberlein, *"Angelus novus,"* 49–52.

112. Cited in Schlemmer, "Flugblatt der Üecht-Gruppe: Kritik als Kunst—der Lüge" (1919), in Karin v. Maur, *Oskar Schlemmer und die Stuttgarter Avantgarde 1919* (Stuttgart: Staatliche Akademie der bildenden Künste, 1975), 11.

113. Bourneuf, *Paul Klee*, 209n13; Kerry Wallach, *Passing Illusions: Jewish Visibility in Weimar Germany* (Ann Arbor: University of Michigan Press, 2017), 34–35.

114. Bourneuf, *Paul Klee*, 118–25.

115. The 1931 letter discussed below would in fact seem to implicitly group Klee's 1916

watercolor with the Christian *Heiligenbilder* of Benjamin's collection, in contrast to the *Angelus*, which is distinguished from the others as the "einziger Botschafter der Kabbala."

116. Scholem and Adorno, *Correspondence of Walter Benjamin*, 197, 195; *Gesammelte Briefe*, 2:223, 211. On Agnon and Hebrew literature in the Weimar Republic, see Brenner, *Renaissance of Jewish Culture*, 205–8.

117. "Man bettet ihn auf Rosenzweigen / Doch lieber wird er schwebend bleiben." *Gesammelte Briefe*, 2:209; Scholem and Adorno, *Correspondence of Walter Benjamin*, 194.

118. Scholem, "Walter Benjamin and His Angel," 212.

119. See Benjamin's letters to Scholem of October 27 and November 8, 1921; Scholem and Adorno, *Correspondence of Walter Benjamin*, 191–93; *Gesammelte Briefe*, 2:203, 207.

120. Benjamin, *Selected Writings*, 1:296.

121. Benjamin, "Agesilaus Santander (First Version)," in *Selected Writings*, 2:712–13.

122. Benjamin, "Experience and Poverty," in *Selected Writings*, 2:733.

123. Scholem, "Walter Benjamin and His Angel," 210.

124. Scholem, 210.

125. Alice Henkes, "Engel auf Stippvisite," *St. Galler Tagblatt*, June 10, 2008, https://www.tagblatt.ch/leben/engel-auf-stippvisite-ld.162014.

126. Email to the author, January 8, 2015.

127. Quaytman, "Engrave," 54.

128. Bourneuf, "The Margins of the *Angelus novus*," 35.

129. Bourneuf, 35.

130. Email to the author, March 20, 2015.

131. Email to the author, July 7, 2015.

132. Email to the author, March 20, 2015.

133. Quaytman, "Engrave," 58.

134. Beatrice Hanssen, "Portrait of Melancholy (Benjamin, Warburg, Panofsky)," *MLN* 114, no. 5 (December 1999): 998.

135. Benjamin, *Origin of German Tragic Drama*, trans. John Osborne (London: Verso, 1998), 246.

136. Eberlein, *"Angelus novus,"* 73–74; Djerassi, *Four Jews on Parnassus*, 95–97.

137. Adorno links these caricatures with the *Angelus* in "Commitment" (1962), trans. Francis McDonagh, in Adorno et al., *Aesthetics and Politics* (London: Verso, 2007), 194.

138. Hitler's most prominent appearance prior to the making of the *Angelus novus* would have been his speech introducing the "Program of the German Workers' Party" to an estimated audience of around two thousand at the Hofbräuhaus on February 24, 1920. It seems very implausible that Klee would have attended such a gathering; not only was he uninvolved in the far-right political groups that thrived in postrevolutionary Munich, but his actions the previous year suggest that he was not unjustifiably afraid of them. In the spring of 1919, Klee had joined Munich's Action Committee of Revolutionary Artists in backing Munich's first short-lived *Räterepublik*; the far-right paramilitary units' bloody suppression of the *Räterepublik* prompted Klee to flee briefly to Switzerland. Werckmeister, *The Making of Paul Klee's Career, 1914–1920* (Chicago: University of Chicago Press, 1989), 175.

139. There is no mention of a print in Eberlein's remarks on the picture's dark border in a chapter undertaking a close description of the *Angelus* itself. Opposite a reproduction of the *Angelus* in which all three layers are visible (although the area reproducing the dark engraving is marred by a moiré, presumably caused by the engraving's fine lines), Eberlein writes: "Das Blatt ist auf einen Karton vor einem dunkelbraunen Grund so montiert, daß sich in Zusammenhang mit dem unregelmäßigen Rand der Fläche der im Oeuvre Klees in jener Zeit häufig gesuchte Eindruck eines wie auf einer Holzwand angebrachten, schon leicht verwitterten Blattes ergibt." Eberlein, *"Angelus novus,"* 43.

140. "Wie bisher verschmäht er es, Einflüsterungen—nach Art der Orakel—zu geben." *Gesammelte Briefe*, 2:211; Scholem and Adorno, *Correspondence of Walter Benjamin*, 195.

141. Scholem, *Fullness of Time*, 66–67.

142. Quaytman, "Engrave," 57; Scholem, "Yeẓirah, Sefer," in *Encyclopaedia Judaica*, ed. Michael Berenbaum and Fred Skolnik, 2nd ed. (New York: Macmillan Reference USA, 2007), 21:328–31.

143. Quaytman, *Spine* (New York: Sequence Press, 2011), back cover ("Collection").

144. Godfrey, "Angels, Boulders, and Tongues," 18–20.

145. Quaytman, "Engrave," 61.

146. Quaytman, "Engrave," 60.

147. Michael Baxandall, *Patterns of Intention: On the Historical Explanation of Pictures* (New Haven, CT: Yale University Press, 1985), 8.

148. Baxandall, 8–9.

149. Benjamin, *Selected Writings*, 2:456; *Gesammelte Schriften*, 2:367.

150. *Gesammelte Schriften*, 2:1112. See Giorgio Agamben, "Walter Benjamin and the Demonic: Happiness and Historical Redemption," in *Potentialities: Collected Essays in Philosophy*, ed. and trans. Daniel Heller-Roazen (Stanford, CA: Stanford University Press, 1999), 142.

151. Benjamin, "The Work of Art in the Age of Its Technological Reproducibility: Second Version," in *The Work of Art in the Age of Its Technological Reproducibility*, 36.

152. "Noch hängt nicht alles, aber schon gebe ich mir mit Schrecken Rechenschaft, daß in meiner Kommunistenzelle . . . nur Heiligenbilder hängen!" "[d]er alte Dreiköpfe Christus . . . eine Nachbildung eines byzantinischen Elfenbeinreliefs, ein Trickbild—drei verschiedene Heiligendarstellungen, je nachdem wie man draufblickt—aus dem bayrischen Wald, ein Sebastian." Walter Benjamin, *Gesammelte Briefe*, vol. 4, ed. Christoph Gödde and Henri Lonitz (Frankfurt: Suhrkamp, 1998), 62. Benjamin, *Correspondence*, 386. See also Scholem, *Story of a Friendship*, 47.

153. Brigid Doherty, "'The History of Art is a History of Prophecies.' Or, the Beginnings of Benjamin's Artwork Essay," keynote address, *Benjamin's Beginnings*, Bern, 29 June 2019.

154. Though it is translated thus in Benjamin, *Correspondence*, 386, a "*kommunistische Zelle*" would be the normal term for a clandestine revolutionary group and would make little contextual sense, though Benjamin might well have enjoyed the echo of that phrase.

155. Jacob Grimm und Wilhelm Grimm, *Deutsches Wörterbuch*, s.v. "Zelle," accessed March 28, 2021, https://www.woerterbuchnetz.de/DWB.

156. See Benjamin's comment on Thomas Mann's novel as "fascinating purely because of its sovereign workmanship" in *Correspondence of Walter Benjamin*, 262. In Mann's novel *Magic Mountain* (1924), the sinister Jesuit Naphta, a Jewish convert to Catholicism, argues on behalf of "modern communism," rails against democracy and enlightenment, and made his own living quarters into a private sanctum of art with his anonymous fourteenth-century carved *pietà* "in the corner to the left of the sofa-group . . . mounted on a red-covered dais." Mann, *The Magic Mountain*, trans. H. T. Lowe-Porter (London: Secker and Warburg, 1971), 392–94, 403–5. It is well known that Mann himself saw Naphta as modeled on Georg Lukács; see Alasdair MacIntyre, "Marxist Mask and Romantic Face: Lukács on Thomas Mann," in *Alasdair MacIntyre's Engagement with Marxism: Selected Writings, 1953–1974*, ed. Paul Blackledge and Neil Davidson (Leiden: Brill, 2008), 317–28.

157. "Der Kultwert als solcher scheint heute geradezu daraufhinzudrängen, das Kunstwerk im Verborgenen zu halten: gewisse Götterstatuen sind nur dem Priester in der cella zugänglich." Benjamin, *Selected Writings*, 4:257; *Gesammelte Schriften*, 1:483.

158. Benjamin, "The Work of Art in the Age of Its Technological Reproducibility: Second Version," in *The Work of Art in the Age of Its Technological Reproducibility*, 24.

159. Benjamin, "The Work of Art in the Age of Its Technological Reproducibility: Second Version," in *The Work of Art in the Age of Its Technological Reproducibility*, 25.

160. Brigid Doherty, "'The History of Art is a History of Prophecies.' Or, the Beginnings of Benjamin's Artwork Essay," keynote address, *Benjamin's Beginnings*, Bern, 29 June 2019. Benjamin, "The Work of Art in the Age of Its Technological Reproducibility: Third Version," trans. Harry Zohn and Edmund Jephcott, in Benjamin, *Selected Writings*, vol. 4, 257, 273–74n15.

161. Apropos "On the Concept of History," Djerassi writes: "His confusion of 'debris' with Klee's then newly discovered oil transfer technique, which subsequently was used in dozens of works, none of which in any way related to debris, is only one mistake. Philosophically, what Benjamin wrote is perfectly acceptable, but artistically it borders on the risible." Letter to the editors, *New York Review of Books* 61, no. 14 (September 25, 2014). http://www.nybooks.com/articles/2014/09/25/walter-benjamins-angel-hitler/. While I have learned so much from Weigel's writing on Benjamin and the *Angelus novus*, evidence does not support her surprising assertion that Benjamin "had few opportunities to contemplate [the *Angelus*] in real time" because "most of the time it was Scholem who cared for the picture." Sigrid Weigel, *Walter Benjamin: Images, the Creaturely, and the Holy*, trans. Chadwick Truscott Smith (Stanford, CA: Stanford University Press, 2013), 215, 217.

162. Similarly, Klee wrote the title on the mount of the pencil version of the *Angelus novus*—in black ink that is easier to see than the graphite lines making up the angel's body.

163. Bourneuf, *Paul Klee*, 82.

164. Bourneuf, 66–82.

165. Bourneuf, 24–27.

166. Quaytman, "Engrave," 56.

167. Quaytman, 59.

168. Quaytman, 58.

CHAPTER 2

1. Quaytman, 60.

2. Gregor Wedekind, "Kosmische Konfession. Kunst und Religion bei Paul Klee," in *Paul Klee: Kunst und Karriere*, ed. Oskar Bätschmann and Josef Helfenstein (Bern: Stämpfli, 2000), 226–27. Klee was christened in 1880 in the Protestant Evangelisch-reformierten Kirche des Kantons Bern, a church in the Reformed (Zwinglian), not the Lutheran ("Evangelisch-lutherische"), tradition.

3. "Paul Zion ist nicht richtiger, sondern ganz falsch, ohne dass ich im Judentum irgend ein Manco zu erblicken vermöchte. Immerhin meine legitimen Väter und Grossväter waren Protestanten." Klee, letter to Oskar Schlemmer, November 11, 1919, cited in Schlemmer, "Flugblatt der Üecht-Gruppe: Kritik als Kunst—der Lüge" (1919), in Karin v. Maur, *Oskar Schlemmer und die Stuttgarter Avantgarde 1919* (Stuttgart: Staatliche Akademie der bildenden Künste, 1975), 10–11.

4. Klee, *Briefe*, 1:237, 587. "Zeitgenosse von Luther . . . reformatorisch gesinnt, aber weit über den blöden Luther hinausgehend."

5. Corrinth, *Potsdamer Platz oder die Nächte des neuen Messias: Ekstatische Visionen* (Munich: G. Müller, 1919); O. K. Werckmeister, *The Making of Paul Klee's Career, 1914–1920* (Chicago: University of Chicago Press, 1989), 147–56; Lisa Marie Anderson, *German Expressionism and the Messianism of a Generation* (Amsterdam: Rodopi, 2011).

6. Heinz Brüggemann, in his *Walter Benjamin über Spiel, Farbe und Phantasie* (Würzburg: Königshausen & Neumann, 2007), 335–36, asks whether Klee's work might not be seen as a "entstaltende, defigurierende, zugleich destruierende und konstruierende Auseinandersetzung mit Grünewalds *Auferstehung*." Eberlein, *"Angelus novus,"* 55–58. Thanks to Angela Lampe for urging me to explore the connection between Grünewald's panel and the *Angelus* in relation to Quaytman's discovery. Eberlein also discusses the retable's general importance for modernism in Germany as well as the German nationalism tied up with the intensity of the response to its 1918–1919 exhibition, writing that Klee "muß durch den Mißbrauch Grünewalds durch die konservative Propaganda zu einer Art kultureller Dolchstoßlegende tief getroffen worden sein" (57). For Eberlein, the connection between Grünewald's Christ and the *Angelus* is marshaled to support his hypothesis, discussed in the previous chapter, that the *Angelus* should be seen as Klee's response to Hitler.

7. Crucial articulations of the Reformation as initiating modernity include Hegel's *Lectures on the Philosophy of History* and Max Weber's *The Protestant Ethic and the Spirit of Capitalism* (1905), although Weber also points out the many traditionalist features of Luther's thought in counterdistinction to the still greater capitalist affinities of Calvinism and the "Protestant sects." See Hegel's section 3, "The Modern Time," in his *Lectures on the Philosophy of History*—"the period of Spirit conscious that it is free, inasmuch as it wills the True, the Eternal—that which is in and for itself Universal"—that begins with Luther's Reformation. Hegel, *The Philosophy of History*, trans. J. Sibree (New York: Colonial Press, 1900), 412–15.

8. Andrew Zimmerman, "Race and World Politics: Germany in the Age of Imperialism, 1878–1914," in *The Oxford Handbook of Modern German History*, ed. Helmut Walser Smith (Oxford: Oxford University Press, 2011), 360.

9. I owe a great deal to Charles W. Haxthausen, who, in a May 2016 conversation about Quaytman's discovery, urged me to consider how the contradiction between the sixteenth-century date and the syntax in which it is written might have been key to Klee's interest in it, and more broadly how the layers of the *Angelus* engage in a paradoxical play with markers of art's historicity akin to that of Klee's mock-"auratic" parodies discussed by Haxthausen in "'Abstract with Memories': Klee's 'Auratic' Pictures," in *Paul Klee: Philosophical Vision; From Nature to Art*, ed. John Sallis (Chestnut Hill, MA: McMullen Museum of Art, Boston College, 2012). My research since then has both confirmed and elaborated on Haxthausen's insights. See also Haxthausen, "Paul Klee, Wilhelm Hausenstein, and 'the Problem of Style,'" *Kritische Berichte* 42, no. 1 (2014): 47–67.

10. Inventory of Klee's library provided by the Zentrum Paul Klee, Bern.

11. Worringer, *Lukas Cranach* (Munich: R. Piper, 1908), 114–16.

12. "Uns sind Dürers Apostel, Rembrandts Porträts, Beethovens Symphonien die eigentlich protestantischen Kunstwerke."

13. "Man braucht nur die religiösen Darstellungen Cranachs vor der Reformation mit den nachreformatorischen zu vergleichen, um den ganzen Kontrast zu erfassen. Dort sinnliche Anschaulichkeit, Ausdrucksfülle und geschlossene Bildwirkung, hier ein jeder bildlichen Geschlossenheit spottendes Nacheinander von allegorischen Szenen, die Anschaulichkeit und Zusammenhang erst durch die rationalistische Interpretation gewinnen. Statt Bilder erhalten wir theologische Traktate."

14. Inventory of Klee's library provided by the Zentrum Paul Klee, Bern. Wilhelm Hausenstein, *Der Isenheimer Altar des Matthias Grünewald* (Munich: Walther C. F. Hirth, 1919). On Hausenstein's changing interpretations of Klee's work, see my *Paul Klee: The Visible and the Legible* (Chicago: University of Chicago Press, 2015).

15. Werckmeister, *Making of Paul Klee's Career*, 175; David Clay Large, *Where Ghosts Walked: Munich's Road to the Third Reich* (New York: W. W. Norton & Co., 1997).

16. For a reasonably clear narrative of the complex succession of events in Munich between Eisner's proclamation of the Bavarian Republic on November 7, 1918, and the entry of the Whites into Munich on May 1, 1919, see David Clay Large, *Where Ghosts Walked: Munich's Road to the Third Reich* (New York: W. W. Norton & Co., 1997), 73–122.

17. See Paul Mendes-Flohr, "Messianic Radicals: Gustav Landauer and Other German-Jewish Revolutionaries," in *Gustav Landauer: Anarchist and Jew*, ed. Mendes-Flohr and Anya Mali (Berlin: Walter de Gruyter, 2015), 14–44; Michael Brenner, "Between Hermann Cohen and Karl Marx: The Jewish Dimension of Kurt Eisner's Revolution in Bavaria, 1918–19," *Modern Judaism* 40, no. 1 (February 2020): 17–36; Victor Klemperer, *Munich 1919: Diary of a Revolution* (Cambridge, UK: Polity Press, 2017).

18. Gustav Landauer, *Aufruf zum Sozialismus*, Revolutionsausgabe (Berlin: Paul Cassirer, 1919), xvii.

19. Wilhelm Hausenstein, *Kairuan, oder eine Geschichte vom Maler Klee und von der Kunst dieses Zeitalters* (Munich: Kurt Wolff, 1921), 9–18.

20. Weinstein, *The End of Expressionism: Art and the November Revolution in Germany, 1918–1919* (Chicago: University of Chicago Press, 1990), 223–24. For Klee's letter of support to the Action Committee of Revolutionary Artists, see Justin Hoffmann, "Künstler und ihre Revolution," in *Süddeutsche Freiheit: Kunst der Revolution in München 1919*, ed. Helmut Friedel (Munich: Städtische Galerie im Lenbachhaus, 1993), 32. See also Werckmeister, *Making of Paul Klee's Career*, 171–80.

21. "So wenig dauerhaft diese kommunistische Republic von Anfang an schien, so gab sie doch Gelegenheit zur Überprüfung der subjektiven Existenz-Möglichkeiten in einem solchen Gemeinwesen. Ohne positives Ergebnis war sie nicht. Natürlich eine zugespitzte, individualistische Kunst ist zum Genuß durch die Gesamtheit nicht geeignet, sie ist kapitalistischer Luxus. Aber wir sind doch wohl mehr als Kuriositäten für reiche Snobs. Und das was an uns irgendwie darüber hinaus Ewigkeitswerten zustrebt, das würde im kommunistischen Gemeinwesen eher Förderung erfahren können." Letter to Alfred Kubin, May 12, 1919, in *Paul Klee: Das Frühwerk, 1883–1922*, ed. Armin Zweite (Munich: Städtische Galerie im Lenbachhaus, 1979), 93.

22. Weber, *The Vocation Lectures*, ed. David Owen and Tracy B. Strong, trans. Rodney Livingstone (Indianapolis: Hackett Publishing Co., 2004). See also Mendes-Flohr, "Messianic Radicals," 14–17.

23. Weber, *The Vocation Lectures*, 92.

24. Karl-Ulrich Gelberg and Ellen Latzin, *Historisches Lexikon Bayerns*, s.v. "Ordnungszelle Bayern," March 7, 2007, https://www.historisches-lexikon-bayerns.de/Lexikon/Ordnungszelle_Bayern. Large, *Where Ghosts Walked*, 137–42.

25. Friedrich Engels, "The Peasant War in Germany," trans. Moissaye J. Olgin, in *The German Revolutions*, ed. and introduced by Leonard Krieger (Chicago: University of Chicago Press, 1967), 43; Abraham Friesen, "Thomas Müntzer in Marxist Thought," *Church History* 34, no. 3 (1965): 306–27: http://www.jstor.org/stable/3162805.

26. Hausenstein, *Isenheimer Altar*, 68–69. On Hausenstein's politics, see Charles W. Haxthausen, "A Critical Illusion: 'Expressionism' in the Writings of Wilhelm Hausenstein," in *The Ideological Crisis of Expressionism: The Literary and Artistic German War Colony in Belgium, 1914–1918*, ed. Rainer Rumold and O. K. Werckmeister (Columbia, SC: Camden House, 1990).

27. Martin Schawe, "Vor 100 Jahren: Die Bayerischen Staatsgemäldesammlungen im Ersten Weltkrieg," *Bayerische Staatsgemäldesammlungen: Jahresbericht* (2018): 198–201.

28. Undated note, Bayerisches Hauptstaatsarchiv, Akt 25/7, No. 700.

29. Martin Schawe, "Vor 100 Jahren: Die Bayerischen Staatsgemäldesammlungen im Ersten Weltkrieg," 201–2. On the reception of the Isenheim Altarpiece in Germany, see also

Ann Stieglitz, "The Reproduction of Agony: Toward a Reception-History of Grünewald's Isenheim Altar after the First World War," *Oxford Art Journal* 12, no. 2 (1989): 87–103, and Peter Selz, *German Expressionist Painting* (Berkeley: University of California Press, 1974), 16–19. Werckmeister, *Making of Klee's Career*, 175.

30. Minaty's volume compiles many responses to Grünewald, whose modern reputation was first established by such figures as Clemens Brentano and Jacob Burckhardt in the first half of the nineteenth century. Wolfgang Minaty, *Grünewald im Dialog: 500 Jahre Isenheimer Altar in Kunst, Literatur und Musik* (Regensburg: Schnell & Steiner, 2016), 17–20. Huysmans's extended discussion of the altarpiece appeared in 1905 in *Trois Primitifs*; Klee wrote appreciatively about Grünewald in 1906. Scholem, *Story of a Friendship*, 47. The next chapter includes a discussion of Benjamin's interest in the altarpiece.

31. Hendrik Ziegler, "Le musée de Colmar pendant la Première Guerre mondiale," in *Histoire du musée d'Unterlinden et de ses collections: De la Révolution à la Première Guerre mondiale*, ed. Sylvie Lecoq-Ramond (Colmar: Société Schongauer, 2003), 319–20.

32. Ziegler, 320.

33. Ziegler speaks of a "conspiration munichoise" (Ziegler, 322), citing correspondence in the Bayer. Hauptstaatsarchiv, Abt. III, Geh. Hausarchiv, Nachlaß Kronprinz Rupprecht, 231, 233, and 635. Some details of this correspondence suggest that Georgii in particular was quite willing to let the supreme end of getting the panels to Munich justify somewhat underhanded means and anticipated Rupprecht's approval in doing so: in a letter to Rupprecht of June 1, 1916, he recounts how he and some other artists stationed in the area wrote a report stating that, given the fragile condition of the panels, a journey to Berlin would risk serious damage—a report that blocked the transfer—while remarking a couple of sentences later that Munich (which would also be a long journey by rail from Colmar, though not as far as Berlin) had more right to the work, and adding that, if the Berliners got the altarpiece, they would surely try to keep it by claiming that its condition would not tolerate the journey back. Bayer. Hauptstaatsarchiv, Abt. III, Geh. Hausarchiv, Nachlaß Kronprinz Rupprecht, 635.

34. Rudolf Oldenbourg refers to the first rumor in his article "Der Grünewald-Altar und die Kopisten," *Münchner Neueste Nachrichten*, No. 66, February 7, 1919, in the folder "Grünewald-Kopien" in Akt 25/7 [alt: 26/6a], Rückgabe der Isenheimer Altartafeln nach Kolmar 1919, Archiv-Nr. 700. In a letter from the mayor of Colmar to Dörnhöffer, February 20, 1920, the mayor reassures the museum director that the latter rumor is groundless. Akt 25/7 [alt: 26/6a], Rückgabe der Isenheimer Altartafeln nach Kolmar 1919, Archiv-Nr. 700, Folder 2: "Leihgabe Isenheimer Altar."

35. *Der Reichsbote*, Berlin, 30 September 1919, Akt 25/7 [alt: 26/6a], Rückgabe der Isenheimer Altartafeln nach Kolmar 1919, Archiv-Nr. 700; Oldenbourg, "Der Grünewald-Altar und die Kopisten," *Münchner Neueste Nachrichten*, No. 66, February 7, 1919, in the folder "Grünewald-Kopien" in Akt 25/7 [alt: 26/6a], Rückgabe der Isenheimer Altartafeln nach Kolmar 1919, Archiv-Nr. 700.

36. See the folder "Grünewald-Kopien" in Akt 25/7 [alt: 26/6a], Rückgabe der Isenheimer Altartafeln nach Kolmar 1919, Archiv-Nr. 700. On the practice of painting copies in the Alte Pinakothek and on how the museum regulated the practice, which was common up to the Second World War, see Martin Schawe, "Kopien und Kopieren," in *Dürer und das Nürnberger Rathaus: Aspekte von Ikonographie, Verlust und Rekonstruktion*, ed. Thomas Schauerte (Petersberg: Michael Imhof, 2013), 9–29.

37. Max Doerner, *Münchner Neueste Nachrichten*, February 18, 1919, in the folder "Grünewald-Kopien" in Akt 25/7 [alt: 26/6a], Rückgabe der Isenheimer Altartafeln nach Kolmar 1919, Archiv-Nr. 700.

38. Oldenbourg, "Der Grünewald-Altar und die Kopisten," *Münchner Neueste Nachrichten*, No. 66, February 7, 1919, in the folder "Grünewald-Kopien" in Akt 25/7 [alt: 26/6a], Rückgabe der Isenheimer Altartafeln nach Kolmar 1919, Archiv-Nr. 700.

39. On the display as leading especially to its nationalist appropriation as exemplar of the "Gothic," see Stieglitz. Further complicating how this altarpiece was understood as relating to art history (continuing an earlier "Gothic," anticipating Expressionism), it was also sometimes seen as proto-Baroque: the Expressionist art historian Wilhelm Niemeyer described the panel representing the resurrection as anticipating the Baroque compositionally. Niemeyer, *Matthias Grünewald, der Maler des Isenheimer Altars: Gemälde und Zeichnungen des Meisters* (Berlin: Furche-Verlag, 1921), 16.

40. Hausenstein, *Der Isenheimer Altar*, 109, trans. in Stieglitz, "Agony," 93. I have amended Stieglitz's translation.

41. Quaytman, "Engrave," 60.

42. The way in which Klee's *Angelus* engages with the Protestant Reformation as well as with Dada iconoclasm might be seen as picking up on aspects of Hugo Ball's "thinking about iconoclasm, Müntzer, the radical Reformation and the German Peasants' War"; on Ball's (as well as his then friend Ernst Bloch's) engagement with religiopolitical chiliasms of the sixteenth century during and after the war, and how it might have mattered for Zurich Dada, see Debbie Lewer, "Hugo Ball, Iconoclasm and the Origins of Dada in Zurich," *Oxford Art Journal* 32, no. 1 (2009): 17–35.

43. Werner Hofmann, "Die Geburt der Moderne aus dem Geist der Religion"; Koerner, "*Homo Interpres in Bivio*: Cranach and Luther," in *The Moment of Self-Portraiture* (Chicago: University of Chicago Press, 1993), 363–410; Koerner, "The Icon as Iconoclash," in *Iconoclash: Beyond the Image Wars in Science, Religion, and Art*, ed. Bruno Latour and Peter Weibel (Cambridge, MA: MIT Press, 2002), 164–213; Koerner, *Reformation of the Image* (Chicago: University of Chicago Press, 2004).

44. Koerner, *Reformation of the Image*, 155.

45. Koerner, 153–60.

46. Hofmann, "Die Geburt der Moderne aus dem Geist der Religion," 23, 35, 39.

47. Martin Warnke, *Cranachs Luther: Entwürfe für ein Image* (Frankfurt: Fischer, 1984), 33.

48. Koerner, *Reformation of the Image*, 196.

49. Scribner, "Incombustible Luther: The Image of the Reformer in Early Modern Germany," *Past and Present* 110 (February 1986): 68.

50. Warnke, *Cranachs Luther*, 67–68; Koerner, *Reformation of the Image*, 115.

51. Kirchner, "Chronicle of the Brücke" (1913), translated in Rose-Carol Washton Long, ed., *German Expressionism: Documents from the End of the Wilhelmine Empire to the Rise of National Socialism* (New York: G. K. Hall, 1993), 24.

52. Klee, *Briefe*, 237; Koerner, *Reformation of the Image*, 30, 237–38. It was not only avant-garde opinion around 1900 that found fault with Cranach; for instance, the liberal nationalist art journal *Der Kunstwart*, heavily invested in German Renaissance artists, published "Artist-Portfolios" of reproductions of works by Dürer and Grünewald, but Cranach did not get one. Insert in the *Dürer-Portfolio* (Munich: Kunstwart-Verlag, G. D. W. Callwey, 1902).

53. "Vergangenen Generationen war Cranach vor allem der Freund der Reformatoren, der Maler des Luthertums. Sein künstlerischer Ruhm basierte auf seinem Stoffgebiet. Heute ist es diese Seite seiner Kunst, die ihn am meisten diskreditiert." Worringer, *Cranach*, 114.

54. Worringer, 114.

55. See the list of subjects of Müller's prints in Andresen, *Handbuch für Kupferstichsammler*; Le Blanc, *Manuel de l'amateur d'estampes*.

56. David Morgan, *The Forge of Vision: A Visual History of Modern Christianity* (Oakland: University of California Press, 2015), 54–55.

57. Warnke, *Cranachs Luther*.

58. Lyndal Roper, "Martin Luther's Body: The 'Stout Doctor' and His Biographers," *American Historical Review* 115, no. 2 (April 2010): 351–84. See the many examples of the "Typus ab 1539" produced by the Cranach workshop in the Cranach Digital Archive maintained by the Stiftung Museum Kunstpalast and CICS Institut für Restaurierungs- und Konservierungswissenschaft Technische Hochschule Köln, at the website https://lucascranach.org/AT_KHM_GG845.

59. This made it possible to use, for instance, the same torso template to make Venus and Lucretia. Koerner, *Reformation of the Image*, 240–43.

60. Koerner, *Reformation of the Image*, 27–37.

61. Hegel, *Aesthetics: Lectures on Fine Art*, trans. T. M. Knox (Oxford, UK: Clarendon Press, 1975), 1:103. See also Hofmann on Hegel's account of the artistic consequences of the Reformation, of Luther's counting pictures among *adiaphora*, things of indifference, neither prohibited nor necessary for salvation, which Hofmann reads as the beginning of artistic modernity, of art's "Frag-Würdigkeit." "Die Geburt der Moderne," 48–49.

62. Hegel, *Aesthetics*, trans. Knox, 1:11.

63. Hegel, 2:885.

64. "Es bedarf nur des einen Namens, Matthias Grünwald, um den 'Maler' Cranach auf den Platz zurückzuweisen, der ihm gebührt. Man spricht Grünwalds Namen aus und eine Erinnerung, stark wie eine Offenbarung, richtet sich auf. Wie ein Sturm heult es im Ohr. Ein Sturm der lebendigen Farbe. Leben, Leben schreit es aus den düstern Gluten heraus, die grosse Befreiertat, die Erweckung der toten Farbe durch den Geist, den Geist des raumgestaltenden Lichtes, war getan. Mit unerhörter Wucht wälzten sich die zurückgehaltenen Kräfte hinaus und drängten in wildem Ansturm gegen ihre Grenzen, die zu zerbersten drohten. Wie wenig sagt uns nach diesem Erlebnis Cranachs glitzernde Buntheit." Worringer, *Cranach*, 85.

65. Koerner, *Reformation of the Image*, 27–37.

66. "Es kommt darauf an, daß der 'Expressionismus' sich true bleibe. Dann baut er zu seinem Teil mit an dem Fundament einer Gesinnung, welche die neuen Symbole schaffen soll, die uns heute noch gänzlich fehlen und durch welche das Christentum erst seine neue Daseinsform gewinnen wird. Erst wenn dieses Dasein gesichert ist, wird auch die neue religiöse Kunst geboren sein." G. F. Hartlaub, *Kunst und Religion: Ein Versuch über die Möglichkeit neuer religiöser Kunst* (Leipzig: Kurt Wolff Verlag, 1919), 103. David Morgan, "The Enchantment of Art: Abstraction and Empathy from German Romanticism to Expressionism," *Journal of the History of Ideas* 57, no. 2 (April 1996): 317–41; James Elkins and David Morgan, eds., *Re-Enchantment* (New York: Routledge, 2009).

67. "Grünewald hat noch einmal, freilich fast als letzter, den Mut zu einem Altar größten Stils aufgebracht." Hausenstein, *Isenheimer Altar*, 50.

68. "Der letzte Altarmaler, im tiefen Sinn des Altarkunstwerks, der letzte, der die Maltafel ganz als Glied des Altaraufbaus, als Auswirkung des Altargedankens nimmt." Niemeyer, *Matthias Grünewald, der Maler des Isenheimer Altars: Gemälde und Zeichnungen des Meisters* (Berlin: Furche-Verlag, 1921), 37.

69. A posthumous inventory of Grünewald's possessions in 1528 included Lutheran tracts. Alexander Nagel, "Altarpiece" (2003), *Grove Art Online*, https://www.oxfordartonline.com/groveart/view/10.1093/gao/9781884446054.001.0001/oao-9781884446054-e-7000002082.

70. Altarpieces for Lutheran churches created by Cranach and others are the crux of

Koerner's book *The Reformation of the Image*; on pre-Reformation altarpieces and the "play of [visual] access and restriction," see Koerner, *Reformation of the Image*, 358–59.

71. "So viel Emanzipationen von der alten Kirche, so viel neue Hemmungen der Kunst" (64). See Koerner's historical explanation of the Hegelian origins of "the art-historical animus against Reformation art" in *Reformation of the Image*, 32–37.

72. Koerner, 28–29.

73. Florman, *Concerning the Spiritual and the Concrete in Kandinsky's Art* (Stanford, CA: Stanford University Press, 2014), 5–32.

74. Marc, "Die 'Wilden' Deutschlands," in *Der Blaue Reiter*, ed. Wassily Kandinsky and Franz Marc, Dokumentarische Neuausgabe (Munich: Piper, 1984), 31.

75. Quaytman suggests that the monogram could be read as a CL standing, as it were, for Klee. Email to the author, March 17, 2015.

76. Tamara Trodd, *The Art of Mechanical Reproduction: Technology and Aesthetics from Duchamp to the Digital* (Chicago: University of Chicago Press, 2015), 2, 22.

77. Koerner, *Reformation of the Image*, 240–43.

78. Trodd, *Art of Mechanical Reproduction*, 34.

79. Hartmut Kühne, "Der Agent des Antichristen: Die Entstehung der Tetzellegende im 16. und 17. Jahrhundert," in *Johann Tetzel und der Ablass*, ed. Hartmut Kühne, Enno Bünz, and Peter Wiegand (Berlin: Lukas Verlag, 2017), 107.

80. Scholem speaks of the Jewish conception of an angel as "the messenger who transmits a message" in his "Walter Benjamin and His Angel," in *On Jews and Judaism in Crisis: Selected Essays*, ed. Werner J. Dannhauser (New York: Schocken, 1976), 213.

81. Scholem, 225. The inscribed head of Klee's *Angelus descendens* (1918), very much related to the *Angelus novus*, might also be seen as resonating with Scholem's remark. Klee not infrequently made use of these scroll-like forms; see, for instance, his *Demon above the Ships* (1916, 65).

82. Hartman, "Benjamin in Hope," *Critical Inquiry* 25, no. 2 (1999): 346.

83. Hegel's *Lectures on the Philosophy of History* is here again a crucial text.

84. Curiously, a Luther portrait of 1698 that depicts the reformer with an angel bears an inscription pointing out a similar contrast: "The angel flies and Luther stands." Both Klee and this obscure portrait are riffing, of course, on Luther's legendary words at the Diet of Worms. Scribner, "Incombustible Luther," 59.

85. On the relation of both pictures to the panel of the Isenheim Altarpiece, see Eberlein, 55–58.

86. Courbet's remark appears as follows in the 1906 German translation of Vincent van Gogh's letters: "Engel malen! Ja, wer hat denn je Engel gesehen?" Vincent van Gogh, *Briefe*, trans. Margarete Mauthner (Berlin: Bruno Cassirer, n.d.), 21. On Klee's engagement with this first German publication of van Gogh's letters in book form, see Josef Helfenstein, "'Ein kleines Publikum aus feinen Köpfen': Klees Bildertausch mit befreundeten Künstlern," in *Paul Klee: Kunst und Karriere*, ed. Oskar Bätschmann and Helfenstein (Bern: Stämpfli, 2000), 125.

87. Klee, *Schriften: Rezensionen und Aufsätze*, ed. Christian Geelhaar (Cologne: DuMont, 1976), 118. Klee drafted the essay in 1918 in response to the Expressionist writer Kasimir Edschmid's invitation to write about his own work for an anthology that Edschmid was gathering of statements by artists, which Edschmid published under the title *Schöpferische Konfession* (*Creative Confession*) (Berlin: Erich Reiss, 1920). In the larger context of the relations among art and religion around 1920, it should be understood that Edschmid uses the word *Konfession* not in the sense of an admission of guilt or of an account of the extremely personal (as in confessional poetry), but in the sense of a declaration of articles of faith (as in the Augsburg Confession). Edschmid transposes the word from a post-

Reformation religious usage to art conceived as creation. For more on Klee's contribution, see Bourneuf, *Paul Klee*, 30 57.

88. *Cranach*, 114.

89. Klee, "On Modern Art," 12.

90. See Brigid Doherty's analysis of *Knave Child* in her "Between the Artwork and Its 'Actualization': A Footnote to Art History in Benjamin's 'Work of Art' Essay," *Paragraph* 32, no. 3 (2009): 351–55.

91. Doherty, 354.

92. Doherty, 354.

93. Benjamin, "One-Way Street" (1928), in *Selected Writings*, 2:171.

94. Hartlaub, *Kunst und Religion*, 103.

95. "Das Abstrakte unsrer Kunst hat nur einen Sinn, wenn es die Vorstufe neuer Gegenständlichkeit im Bilde ist. Unsre spekulative Graphik wird nur fruchtbar, wenn sie ein Prolegomenon zu künftigen Altarbildern ist. In der Hand Grünewalds wurde die Kunst noch einmal vollständig: Altar. . . . Dann war die große Kluft. Erhob sich aber nicht diesseits ein Anspruch von ähnlichen Maßen?" Hausenstein, *Isenheimer Altar*, 110.

96. On the use of "speculative" and "graphic art" (*Graphik*) as key terms in Klee's own writing (including an autobiographical text he prepared for Hausenstein in 1919) and in Hausenstein's writing about Klee at the time, see Bourneuf, *Paul Klee*.

97. Hausenstein, *Kairuan*, 126–27; the plate of the *Angelus* comes directly after 128. The secondary supports of works are cropped off in the reproductions throughout Hausenstein's book.

98. Haxthausen, "Walter Gropius and Lyonel Feininger, Bauhaus Manifesto, 1919," in *Bauhaus 1919–1933: Workshops for Modernity*, ed. Leah Dickerman and Barry Bergdoll (New York: Museum of Modern Art, 2009), 64–67; Marcel Franciscono, *Walter Gropius and the Creation of the Bauhaus in Weimar: The Ideals and Artistic Theories of Its Founding Years* (Urbana: University of Illinois Press, 1971).

99. Georg Dehio, *Geschichte der deutschen Kunst* (Berlin: Vereinigung wissenschaftlicher Verleger, 1921), 2:117. It should be noted that Dehio and Pinder used the term in an explicitly nationalist project of German art history. Panofsky, "'Imago Pietatis': Ein Beitrag zur Typengeschichte des 'Schmerzensmannes' und der 'Maria Mediatrix'" (1927), in Panofsky, *Deutschsprachige Aufsätze*, ed. Karen Michels and Martin Warnke (Berlin: Akademie Verlag, 1998), 1:190–91; Karl Schade, *Andachtsbild: Die Geschichte eines kunsthistorischen Begriffs* (Weimar: Verlag und Datenbank für Geisteswissenschaften, 1996), 35–87.

100. Schade, *Andachtsbild*, 35–40.

101. *Heiligenbild* and *Andachtsbild*, but especially the former, could both be applied to modern mass-produced images marketed to Catholics in particular, such as the chromolithographic holy cards published by Josef Müller in Munich. Schade, *Andachtsbild*, 44, 46. See also Scholem's characterization of the picture as serving Benjamin as a *Meditationsbild*—a related but distinct term. Scholem, "Walter Benjamin and His Angel," 210.

102. O. K. Werckmeister, "Benjamin's Angel," *Critical Inquiry* (Winter 1996): 242.

103. "Der Begriff des 'Andachtsbildes' . . . läßt sich . . . nach zwei Seiten hin abgrenzen: zum einen gegen den Begriff des szenischen 'Historienbildes,' zum andern gegen den des hieratischen oder kultischen 'Repräsentationsbildes.' Von beiden . . . Formen unterscheidet sich das 'Andachtsbild' . . . durch die Tendenz, dem betrachtenden Einzelbewußtsein die Möglichkeit zu einer *kontemplativen Versenkung* in den betrachteten Inhalt zu geben . . . Das kann (und will) weder das szenische Historienbild, das seine Darstellungselemente zu einer mehr oder weniger momentanen, jedenfalls aber auf eine bestimmte Zeitspanne eingeschränkten Handlung verbindet, noch auch das Repräsentationsbild, das umgekehrt die Darstellungselemente in einem zeitlosen und seelisch gleichsam undurchdringlichen

Dasein vor uns hinstellt. . . . In der Tat entstehen denn auch die neuen Typen des Andachtsbildes entweder dadurch, daß aus geeigneten szenischen Darstellungen bestimmte Einzelgruppen oder Einzelgestalten herausgelöst werden, in denen die Handlung selbst zum Stillstand gebracht, dafür aber dem mit der Handlung verbundenen Gefühlserlebnis eine der kontemplativen Versenkung zugängliche Dauer verliehen erscheint." Or, alternatively, static, hieratic "representational images" may be made moving and approachable. Panofsky, "'Imago Pietatis,'" 190–91. If one takes as echoing Panofsky Benjamin's use of the phrase "contemplative immersion" in the artwork essay to describe the form of reception invited by Derain or Rilke but ruled out by the Dadaists—a form that became, he says, "as the bourgeoisie degenerated . . . a breeding ground for asocial behavior" (39)—it would seem to be an attempt to further his argument that the basis of practices of valuing "the 'authentic' work of art" from the Renaissance through modernism (24) is ultimately cultic, however secularized, by comparing the behavior of an admirer of, for instance, Fauvist painting, with that of a pious user of devotional images in the late Middle Ages in Panofsky's account. Benjamin, "Work of Art in the Age of Its Technological Reproducibility: Second Version," in *The Work of Art in the Age of Its Technological Reproducibility*, 39, 24.

104. Kakinuma, "Die Serie der 'Selbstbildnisse' im Jahr 1919 von Paul Klee," *Zwitscher-maschine.org*, no. 3 (Spring 2017), 30n4; Large, *Where Ghosts Walked*, 119–21.

105. Kakinuma reads *Mister Sol* as representing the face of the sun god Sol (Kakinuma, 28). See Bloch's repudiation of attempts to link Jesus with "the entire myth of the solar god's decline and his ascent that also rescues us." Bloch, *The Spirit of Utopia*, trans. Anthony A. Nassar (Stanford, CA: Stanford University Press, 2000), 215; Bloch, *Geist der Utopie* (Munich: Duncker & Humblot, 1918), 377–78.

106. Kakinuma, "Die Serie der 'Selbstbildnisse,'" 22–32; Kakinuma, "Transparency and Opacity: Recto-Verso Works by Paul Klee," *Die Zwitscher-Maschine. Journal on Paul Klee / Zeitschrift für internationale Klee-Studien* 7 (2019): 4–23, https://www.zwitscher-maschine.org/no-7-2019.

107. Bourneuf, *Paul Klee*, 66–82.

108. Trodd, "Drawing in the Archive," 80.

109. Haxthausen, "'Abstract with Memories,'" 72.

110. "Im Anfang ist wohl die Tat, aber darüber liegt die Idee. Und da die Unendlichkeit keinen bestimmten Anfang hat, sondern kreisartig anfanglos ist, so mag die Idee für primär gelten. Im Anfang war das Wort, übersetzt Luther." Klee, *Schriften*, 119.

111. Friedrich A. Kittler, *Discourse Networks 1800/1900*, trans. Michael Metteer, with Chris Cullens (Stanford, CA: Stanford University Press, 1990), 7–24.

112. Klee, *Tagebücher 1898–1918*, Textkritische Neuedition, ed. Wolfgang Kersten (Stuttgart: Gerd Hatje, 1988), 400–402. See Werckmeister, *Making of Paul Klee's Career*, 76–80.

113. Bourneuf, *Paul Klee*, 183–86.

114. Marc, "Zwei Bilder," in *Der Blaue Reiter*, 33–34. See Koerner, *Moment of Self-Portraiture in German Renaissance Art*, 34–42.

CHAPTER 3

1. "Symbol," "Bedeutung," "Zeichen (Siegel)," "Darstellung" "Wie verhält sich zu diesen das Kunstwerk (z. B. Klee)?" Benjamin, *Selected Writings*, 1:269; *Gesammelte Schriften*, 6:21.

2. Peter Fenves, "Diverging Correspondences Concerning the Problem of Identity: Russell-Wittgenstein and Benjamin-Scholem," *MLN* 127, no. 3 (April 2012): 559. See also Eiland and Jennings, *A Critical Life*, 139.

3. "Luther: Das Brot *ist* der Leib Christi. . . . Statt ist 'bedeutet' zu sagen, wäre noch falscher." *Selected Writings*, 1:270; *Gesammelte Schriften*, 6:22.

4. As discussed in chapter 1.

5. "Im Lauf der Zeit kamen verschiedene kleine Figurinen und Bilder, meistens Reproduktionen, dazu. Schon damals und noch lange hing in seinem Arbeitszimmer eine solche von Grünewalds Altarbildern aus Colmar, um deretwillen er als Student 1913 eigens nach Colmar gefahren war. Beziehungen auf diese Bilder, an denen ihn das 'Ausdruckslose,' wie er es zu nennen pflegte, überwältigte, kamen in seinen Aufzeichnungen aus diesen Jahren oft vor." Scholem, *Story of a Friendship*, 47; Scholem, *Walter Benjamin—die Geschichte einer Freundschaft* (Frankfurt: Suhrkamp, 1975), 51–52.

6. Scholem, "Walter Benjamin and His Angel," 212.

7. *Gesammelte Briefe*, 2:207; Scholem and Adorno, *Correspondence of Walter Benjamin*, 193.

8. Benjamin, *Selected Writings*, 1:296.

9. As Scholem recounts, in 1921 he "told Benjamin what the Talmud and the mystics [of the Kabbalah] had to say about the hymns of angels, and my words fell on very fruitful soil." Scholem, *Story of a Friendship*, 123.

10. John 19:1–7.

11. Benjamin, *Selected Writings*, vol. 1, *1913–1926*, ed. Marcus Bullock and Michael W. Jennings (Cambridge, MA: Belknap Press of Harvard University Press, 1996), 292.

12. Eiland and Jennings, *A Critical Life*, 184. An important moment for both Buber and Rang, which appears to have been an impetus for both men's pursuit of Jewish-Christian dialogue, took place at the August 1914 meeting of the Forte-Circle; see Buber, "Zwiesprache," in *Die Kreatur* 3 (1929–30), 205. See also Brenner, *Renaissance of Jewish Culture*, 53.

13. Martin Buber, "Jüdische Renaissance," *Ost und West* 1 (1901): 7–10; Brenner, *Renaissance of Jewish Culture*, 4–5.

14. Letter to Scholem of June 15, 1919, *Correspondence of Walter Benjamin*, 142. Scholem writes of Benjamin's activities in the spring of 1919: "In his conversation with Bloch and Ball, Benjamin was confronted with the question of political activity, and he declined to engage in such activity the way they urged him to. The Munich soviet republic of April 1919 came into his purview only because Felix Noeggerath, whom he highly esteemed as a philosopher, was arrested for participating in it—something that greatly excited Benjamin." Scholem, *Story of a Friendship*, 98. Noeggerath served as "Volkskommissar beim Zentralkommissariat für politisch Verfolgte und auswärtige Revolutionäre" in the short-lived republic. Joachim Lilla, s.v. "Noeggerath, Felix," in Lilla, *Staatsminister, leitende Verwaltungsbeamte und (NS-)Funktionsträger in Bayern 1918 bis 1945*, 2014, https://verwaltungshandbuch.bayerische-landesbibliothek-online.de/noeggerath-felix. Benjamin, *Selected Writings*, 1:288–90. On Benjamin's use of Landauer, see Werner Hamacher, "Guilt History: Benjamin's Sketch 'Capitalism as Religion,'" trans. Kirk Wetters, *Diacritics* 32, nos. 3–4 (2002): 92–95.

15. Hermann Cohen, "Deutschtum und Judentum" (1915), trans. Jeffrey Verhey and Roger Chickering in *German History in Documents and Images*, http://ghdi.ghi-dc.org/sub_document.cfm?document_id=947; Brenner, *Renaissance of Jewish Culture in Weimar Germany*, 89–90, 94–96.

16. Brenner, *Renaissance of Jewish Culture*, 36–37.

17. Brenner, 31–36; Werner Bergmann and Ulrich Wyrwa, s.v. "Antisemitism," *International Encyclopedia of the First World War*, https://encyclopedia.1914-1918-online.net/article/antisemitism.

18. Scholem, "Walter Benjamin and His Angel," 212, 231.

19. "Mich setzten die Erwartungen, die Benjamin mit meiner Mitarbeit verband,

in nicht geringe Verlegenheit. Ich konnte ihm ja nicht verhehlen, daß ich keine Berufung empfand, mich in einer, wie mir schien, besonders sichtbaren Weise an einer deutschen Zeitschrift zu beteiligen, während mein Sinn nach ganz anderen Dingen und Zielen stand, was er ja wissen mußte." Scholem, *Story of a Friendship*, 126; Scholem, *Walter Benjamin—die Geschichte einer Freundschaft*, 131.

20. Scholem, "Against the Myth of the German-Jewish Dialogue," in *On Jews and Judaism*, 63.

21. Scholem, "Walter Benjamin," in *On Jews and Judaism*, 193.

22. Scholem, "Walter Benjamin," in *On Jews and Judaism*, 192; Scholem, *Story of a Friendship*, 70.

23. Scholem and Adorno, *Correspondence of Walter Benjamin*, 119–20.

24. Taubes, *Political Theology of Paul*, trans. Dana Hollander (Stanford, CA: Stanford University Press, 2004), 62–70. The connection between antisemitism and the historicist "higher criticism" represented by Harnack was clear long before the war. Solomon Schechter mentioned Harnack in particular in his 1903 address "Higher Criticism—Higher Anti-Semitism." Schechter, *Seminary Addresses and Other Papers* (Cincinnati, OH: Ark, 1915), 36–37.

25. The first volume of Harnack's *Lehrbuch der Dogmengeschichte* contains a thorough analysis of Marcion in a chapter titled "Das Unternahmen des Marcion, die ATliche Grundlage des Christenthums zu beseitigen, die Tradition zu reinigen und auf Grund des paulinischen Evangeliums die Christenheit zu reformiren," 2nd ed. (Freiburg: J. C. B. Mohr, 1888), 226–43. See also Taubes, "Walter Benjamin—A Modern Marcionite? Scholem's Benjamin Interpretation Reexamined," in *Walter Benjamin and Theology*, ed. Colby Dickinson and Stéphane Symons (New York: Fordham University Press, 2016), 164–78; Adolf von Harnack, *Marcion: The Gospel of the Alien God*, trans. John E. Steely and Lyle D. Bierma (Durham, NC: Labyrinth Press, 1990).

26. Eiland cites the work of Taubes and Agamben on "an idiosyncratic 'Christian' dimension to Benjamin's thinking" as positing "a less absolute division between Jewish and Christian scriptural traditions" than Scholem wants to see, quoting Agamben speaking of Benjamin as placing himself "at the singular intersection of Christianity and Judaism." Taubes's argument connecting the messianism of Paul's Epistle to the Romans and that of Benjamin's "Theological-Political Fragment" is to be found in his *Political Theology of Paul*, 70–76; Agamben's argument, building on Taubes, for a Pauline dimension in "On the Concept of History" is to be found in his *The Time That Remains: A Commentary on the Letter to the Romans*, trans. Patricia Dailey (Stanford, CA: Stanford University Press, 2005), 138–45. Eiland, "Walter Benjamin's Jewishness," 122–29.

27. Scholem, "Walter Benjamin and His Angel," 213, 223, 233.

28. Jennings, "Towards Eschatology: The Development of Walter Benjamin's Theological Politics in the Early 1920s," in *Walter Benjamins anthropologisches Denken*, ed. Carolin Duttlinger, Ben Morgan, and Tony Phelan (Freiburg: Rombach, 2012), 48, 42.

29. "Werdenden religiösen Ordnungen." Benjamin, *Selected Writings*, 1:294–95; *Gesammelte Schriften*, 2:244.

30. Marc, "Zwei Bilder," in *Der Blaue Reiter*, 33–34; Benjamin, *Selected Writings*, 2:488. Benjamin writes that he ordered the almanac from the publisher when he was living in Switzerland, which would imply that he acquired it between 1917 and 1919.

31. Benjamin, *Selected Writings*, 1:294–95; *Gesammelte Schriften*, 2:244.

32. Benjamin, *Selected Writings*, 2:732.

33. Benjamin, *Selected Writings*, 1:295.

34. Bloch, *Geist der Utopie* (Munich: Duncker & Humblot, 1918), 33–34.

35. Scholem and Adorno, *Correspondence of Walter Benjamin*, 186.

36. On the 1912 "Dialogue" and Benjamin's contemporaneous letters to Ludwig Strauss, see Eiland, "Benjamin's Jewishness," 114–22.

37. "Man wird den Dualismus von sozialer Sittlichkeit und Persönlichkeit anerkennen. Aus dieser Not wird eine Religion wachsen." *Gesammelte Schriften*, 2:26; Benjamin, *Early Writings, 1910–1917*, ed. and trans. Howard Eiland (Cambridge, MA: Belknap Press of Harvard University Press, 2011), 71, translation slightly altered.

38. *Gesammelte Schriften*, 2:28–29.

39. *Gesammelte Briefe*, 1:73. See Anson Rabinbach, "Between Apocalypse and Enlightenment: Benjamin, Bloch, and Modern German-Jewish Messianism," in Rabinbach, *In the Shadow of Catastrophe: German Intellectuals between Apocalypse and Enlightenment* (Berkeley: University of California Press, 1997), 27–65; Paul Mendes-Flohr, *German Jews: A Dual Identity* (New Haven, CT: Yale University Press, 1999), 48–55.

40. Benjamin, *Early Writings*, 203; Brod, "Unsere Literaten und die Gemeinschaft," *Der Jude* 1, no. 7 (October 1916): 460–61; "Franz Werfels 'Christliche Sendung,'" *Der Jude* 1, no. 11 (Feb. 1917): 717. More broadly on café culture and modern Jewish culture during this period, see Sigrid Bauschinger, "The Berlin Moderns: Else Lasker-Schüler and Café Culture," in *Berlin Metropolis: Jews and the New Culture, 1890–1918*, ed. Emily D. Bilski (Berkeley: University of California Press, 1999), 58–101; Shachar M. Pinsker, *A Rich Brew: How Cafés Created Modern Jewish Culture* (New York: New York University Press, 2018).

41. *Gesammelte Briefe*, 1:71.

42. "Kultur-Zionismus, der die jüdischen Werte *allerorten* sieht und für sie arbeitet." *Gesammelte Briefe*, 1:72.

43. "Sie haben ihre ernste Mission darin, aus der Kunst, die sie selbst nicht machen können, Geist für das Leben der Zeit zu gewinnen." *Gesammelte Briefe*, 1:63–64.

44. *Gesammelte Briefe*, 1:71. Perhaps Benjamin's reference is to the second of Buber's *Three Addresses on Judaism*, "Das Judentum und die Menschheit." Benjamin explains in a subsequent letter to Strauß that Jews constitute "eine Elite . . . in der Schar der Geistigen" and that he understands Jewishness not as a "Selbstzweck," but instead as "eine vornehmster Träger und Repräsentant des Geistigen." *Gesammelte Briefe*, 1:75.

45. *Gesammelte Briefe*, 1:72.

46. Britt, *Postsecular Benjamin: Agency and Tradition* (Evanston, IL: Northwestern University Press, 2016), 10.

47. Gershom Scholem, *Tagebücher nebst Aufsätzen und Entwürfen bis 1923*, ed. Karlfried Gründer, Herbert Kopp-Oberstebrink, et al., vol. 2, *1917–23* (Frankfurt: Jüdischer Verlag, 2000), 300–306; Daniel Weidner, "Reading Gershom Scholem," *Jewish Quarterly Review* 96, no. 2 (Spring 2006): 208–9.

48. See Scholem's comments on Luther's translation of Job in Scholem, *Tagebücher*, 2:295n4 and 2:497. For line-by-line comparison of Luther's and Scholem's translations of portions of Job and Ezekiel, see Lina Barouch and Paula Schwebel, "Translators' Introduction," in *Lament in Jewish Thought: Philosophical, Theological, and Literary Perspectives*, ed. Ilit Ferber and Paula Schwebel (Berlin: Walter de Gruyter, 2014), 310–11.

49. Scholem, *A Life in Letters, 1914–1982*, ed. and trans. Anthony David Skinner (Cambridge, MA: Harvard University Press, 2002), 118.

50. Leora Batnitzky, "Translation as Transcendence: A Glimpse into the Workshop of the Buber-Rosenzweig Bible Translation," *New German Critique* 70 (Winter 1997): 87–116; Peter Eli Gordon, "Rosenzweig and Heidegger: Translation, Ontology, and the Anxiety of Affiliation," *New German Critique* 77 (Spring–Summer 1999): 113–48; and Lawrence Rosenwald, "On the Reception of Buber and Rosenzweig's Bible," *Prooftexts* 14, no. 2 (May 1994): 141–65.

51. Franz Rosenzweig, *Die Schrift und Luther* (Berlin: Lambert Schneider, 1926), 8–12.

52. Benjamin, *Selected Writings*, 1:294.

53. *Gesammelte Schriften*, 2:987.

54. *Der Jude* 8 (1924), 1: 38–57.

55. "Historische Psychologie des Karnevals," *Die Kreatur* 2, no. 2 (1927–28): 311–43. See Debbie Lewer, "Dada, Carnival, and Revolution," in *Regarding the Popular: Modernism, Avant-Garde and High and Low Culture*, ed. Sascha Bru et al. (Berlin: Walter de Gruyter, 2012), 99–114.

56. Rang, "Goethe's Selige Sehnsucht," *Neue Deutsche Beiträge* 1, no. 1 (1922), 83–125.

57. Charles Baudelaire, *Tableaux Parisiens: Deutsche Übertragung mit einem Vorwort über die Aufgabe des Übersetzers von Walter Benjamin* (Heidelberg: Richard Weissbach, 1923).

58. Scholem and Adorno, *Correspondence of Walter Benjamin*, 79–81.

59. Quoted in Daniel Weidner, "'Going Together without Coming Together': *Die Kreatur* (1926–1929) and Why We Should Read German Jewish Journals Differently," *Naharaim* 10, no. 1 (2016): 122.

60. Weidner, 112.

61. Rosenzweig, *Briefe und Tagebücher*, 947–48; Weidner, "'Going Together without Coming Together,'" 124.

62. *Gesammelte Briefe*, 2:280; Scholem and Adorno, *Correspondence of Walter Benjamin*, 203.

63. Rang, letter to Hofmannsthal of November 8, 1922, quoted in *Gesammelte Schriften*, 2:994.

64. Witte, *Walter Benjamin: An Intellectual Biography*, trans. James Rolleston (Detroit: Wayne State University Press, 1991), 66.

65. Witte, 66.

66. *Gesammelte Schriften*, 2:983.

67. Quoted in Alys X. George, "Editing Interwar Europe: *The Dial* and *Neue Deutsche Beiträge*," *Austrian Studies* 23 (2015): 16; *Gesammelte Schriften*, 2:982.

68. Scholem and Adorno, *Correspondence of Walter Benjamin*, 228.

69. Hofmannsthal, "Vorwort," *Neue Deutsche Beiträge* 1, no. 1 (1922): 4.

70. *Gesammelte Schriften*, 2:245. Quoted in George, "Editing Interwar Europe," 31.

71. George, "Editing Interwar Europe," 34, 22–23, 31. See Steinberg, *The Meaning of the Salzburg Festival: Austria as Theater and Ideology, 1890–1938* (Ithaca, NY: Cornell University Press, 1990).

72. Benjamin, *Selected Writings*, 1:294, translation slightly altered. *Gesammelte Schriften*, 2:243–44.

73. *Neue Deutsche Beiträge* appears not to have published contributions explicitly dealing with Jewish topics. Discussions of Hofmannsthal's own vexed dealings with religion, identity, and his Jewish ancestry include Abigail Gillman, *Viennese Jewish Modernism: Freud, Hofmannsthal, Beer-Hofmann, and Schnitzler* (University Park: Pennsylvania State University Press, 2009); Peter C. Pfeiffer, "1893: Hugo von Hofmannsthal Worries about His Jewish Mixed Ancestry," in *Yale Companion to Jewish Writing and Thought in German Culture, 1096–1996*, ed. Sander L. Gilman and Jack Zipes (New Haven, CT: Yale University Press, 1997), 212–18.

74. See *Der Potsdamer Forte-Kreis: Eine utopische Intellektuellenassoziation zur europäischen Friedenssicherung*, ed. Richard Faber and Christine Holste (Würzburg: Königshausen & Neumann, 2001). See also Wedekind, "Kosmische Konfession," 227.

75. Eiland and Jennings, *A Critical Life*, 184.

76. Scholem, *Story of a Friendship*, 38.

77. "Der Altar," *Die weissen Blätter* 1, no. 5 (1914): 443–46; Buber, *Ereignisse und Begegnungen* (Leipzig: Insel-Verlag, 1917); Martin Buber, "The Altar," trans. Marion Picker, *Journal of Visual Culture* 4, no. 1 (2005): 116.

78. "In *jeder* Hinsicht . . . von einer noch nicht dagewesenen Abscheulichkeit." Scholem, *Tagebücher nebst Aufsätzen und Entwürfen bis 1923*, ed. Karlfried Gründer, Herbert Kopp-Oberstebrink, et al., vol. 2, *1917–23* (Frankfurt: Jüdischer Verlag, 2000), 71–72.

79. Scholem, *Tagebücher nebst Aufsätzen und Entwürfen*, 71, 73. See Buber's own distancing of himself from an emphasis on *Erlebnis* as such in the 1923 preface to his *Reden über das Judentum*, in Buber, *On Judaism*, ed. Nahum N. Glatzer (New York: Schocken, 1972), 7–8.

80. "Über Gott, die Welt . . . den Leib, Grünwalds Altar, und was sonst noch grade in der Sauce schwamm." Scholem, *Tagebücher nebst Aufsätzen und Entwürfen*, 71–72.

81. See, for instance, Kasimir Edschmid, quoted in Minaty, *Grünewald im Dialog*, 22.

82. Buber, "The Altar," 116.

83. Buber, 116–17.

84. Paul Mendes-Flohr, *From Mysticism to Dialogue: Martin Buber's Transformation of German Social Thought* (Detroit: Wayne State University Press, 1989), 57–67.

85. Mendes-Flohr, 49.

86. Buber, "Ekstase und Bekenntnis," in *Ekstatische Konfessionen, gesammelt von Martin Buber* (Jena: Eugen Diederichs Verlag, 1909), xi–xxvi; Buber, "Introduction: Ecstasy and Confession," in *Ecstatic Confessions*, ed. Paul Mendes-Flohr, trans. Esther Cameron (San Francisco: Harper & Row, 1985), 1–11.

87. Buber, "The Altar," 122.

88. Scholem, "Martin Buber's Conception of Judaism" (1967), in *On Jews and Judaism in Crisis*, 170.

89. See Mendes-Flohr, "Martin Buber's Reception among Jews," in *Modern Judaism* 6, no. 2 (May 1986): 117–18. Klee, incidentally, owned a copy of *Die Legende des Baal Schem*, now in the collection of the Zentrum Paul Klee in Bern.

90. Buber, "The Altar," 117, translation altered; Martin Buber, *Ereignisse und Begegnungen* (Leipzig: Insel-Verlag, 1917), 14.

91. Minaty, *Grünewald im Dialog*, 76–87. Modern responses to the Isenheim Altarpiece most often concentrate on the Crucifixion and Resurrection panels. To adduce a further example from someone whom this chapter has already cited in other connections, Rosenzweig wrote in 1906 a lengthy discussion of the Colmar panels ("die einfach zum Allergrößten gehören, was es in deutscher Malerei gibt. Ich mag nichts weiter darüber schreiben . . . Ich will *doch* versuchen, im Kunstgeschichtsstil davon zu sprechen"), emphasizing the painter's "Farben und Beleuchtungen," especially with reference to the Resurrection ("den Auferstehenden Christus malt er so mit der Glorie in eins, daß man nur die Augen und Wundmale als gleichmäßig brennende rote Flecken sieht") and the expressive power of the painted figures' hands ("Die Hände sind das Ausdrucksvollste"), especially with reference to the Crucifixion. Letter of October 21, 1906, Rosenzweig, *Briefe und Tagebücher*, ed. Rachel Rosenzweig and Edith Rosenzweig-Scheinmann (The Hague: Martinus Nijhoff, 1979), 1:59.

92. Buber, "The Altar," 117.

93. Buber, 117.

94. Buber, 122.

95. Buber, 122.

96. Buber, 122.

97. Buber, 122.

98. Brenner, *Renaissance of Jewish Culture*, 23–31. See also Matthew B. Hoffman, *From Rebel to Rabbi: Reclaiming Jesus and the Making of Modern Jewish Culture* (Stanford,

CA: Stanford University Press, 2007), Taubes's comments in *Political Theology*, 5, and Löwy, *Redemption and Utopia: Jewish Libertarian Thought in Central Europe*, trans. Hope Heaney (London: Verso, 2017), 132–33, 142.

99. Scholem, "Martin Buber's Conception of Judaism" (1967), 138.

100. "Die stellvertretende Genugtuung mittelst der Kreuzes- und Opfertodsmagie." Bloch, *Geist der Utopie* (Munich: Duncker & Humblot, 1918), 374–76. The way in which Bloch's thinking here counters Friedrich Delitzsch's school of thought is implicit in the 1918 edition, but less so in the second edition (*The Spirit of Utopia*, trans. Anthony A. Nassar, 214–15), and similar and completely explicit in his much later *Atheism in Christianity: The Religion of the Exodus and the Kingdom*, trans. J. T. Swann (New York: Herder and Herder, 1972), 202–7. See Bill T. Arnold and David B. Weisberg, "A Centennial Review of Friedrich Delitzsch's 'Babel und Bibel' Lectures," *Journal of Biblical Literature* 121, no. 3 (Autumn 2002): 441–57.

101. Scholem, "Martin Buber's Conception of Judaism" (1967), 138.

102. Buber, *On Judaism*, 92.

103. Lisa Marie Anderson, *German Expressionism and the Messianism of a Generation* (Amsterdam: Rodopi, 2011).

104. Helmer Ringgren, s.v. "Messianism," *Encyclopedia of Religion*, 2nd ed., 5972.

105. Scholem, *The Messianic Idea in Judaism and Other Essays on Jewish Spirituality* (New York: Schocken, 1971), 2.

106. Scholem, 2.

107. Scholem, 1.

108. Scholem, 2.

109. Scholem, 16.

110. Benjamin, letters to Scholem, January 13, 1920, and January 1921, in *Correspondence of Walter Benjamin*, 156 and 174.

111. "Die politische Bedeutung der Theokratie mit aller Intensität geleugnet zu haben ist das größte Verdienst von Blochs *Geist der Utopie*." As Rabinbach writes, this sentence "can be read against the grain of Bloch's own revolutionary messianism, which amalgamates politics and messianism in a way that Benjamin explicitly rejects." Rabinbach, *In the Shadow of Catastrophe*, 59.

112. Bloch, "Symbol: Die Juden" (1912/13), in Bloch, *Durch die Wüste: Frühe kritische Aufsätze* (Frankfurt: Suhrkamp, 1964), 122–40. This section disappeared from the 1923 edition of *Spirit of Utopia* but was published in Bloch, *Durch die Wüste: Kritische Essays* (Berlin: Cassirer, 1923). The significantly different 1923 edition appeared with the following note at the beginning: "Dies Buch liegt hier zum zweiten Mal vor. Es wurde begonnen April 1915, beendet Mai 1917, erschien Sommer 1918. Die damalige Ausgabe ist jedoch lediglich als vorläufige Fixierung, als gedrucktes Konzept zu betrachten. Mit der hier vorliegenden neuen Ausgabe erst erscheint der '*Geist der Utopie*' in endgültiger, systematischer Form." Bloch, *Geist der Utopie* (Berlin: Paul Cassirer, 1923).

113. "Neu erwacht der Stolz, jüdisch zu sein." Bloch, *Durch die Wüste: Frühe kritische Aufsätze* (Frankfurt: Suhrkamp, 1964), 122.

114. Bloch, 133.

115. "Fast allen Juden des jüngeren Geschlechts gleitet der Name Jesu leicht über die Lippen. . . . [D]ie abergläubische Scheu vor dem nazarenischen Ereignis ihrer Geistesgeschichte verschwindet, Jesus kehrt endlich zu seinem Volk zurück . . . Sie fühlen und verstehen, daß nur sie und niemand sonst, wie sie die Geschichte Josefs und die Psalmen miterlebt haben, so auch die frühchristliche Gemeinde und die Evangelien bilden konnten. Es hat den Anschein, als ob die Juden an der Stelle angelangt wären, wo sie es wieder als ihre eigenste Sache ansehen müssen, was als Christentum und in der entweichenden Substanz

des Christentums vor sich geht, nachdem sich die anderen, die fremden Völker am Christentum müde und vielleicht zu Ende gearbeitet hat." Bloch, 128.

116. "In unserem tiefsten, noch namenlosen Inneren schläft der letzte, unbekannte Christus . . . von Moses geahnt, von Jesus umgeben, der selber einen noch künftigen Parakleten ankündet . . . So ist es immer noch denkbar und aus der Kurve der bisherigen Geschichte zu begreifen, anders, es muß wieder denkbar werden . . . daß durch die tausendfachen Energien, durch die äonenweite Optik einer neuen Proklamation das Judentum mit dem Deutschtum nochmals eine Letztes, Gotisches, Barockes zu bedeuten hat, um solchergestalt, mit Rußland vereint, diesem dritten Rezipienten des Wartens, des Gottesgebärertums und Messianismus,—die absolute Zeit zu bereiten." Bloch, 140.

117. Salomo Friedlaender, "Der Antichrist und Ernst Bloch," *Das Ziel: Jahrbücher für geistige Politik* 4 (1919): 103–16. On Bloch's later thinking about the fascist uses of the Christian apocalyptic thought of, for instance, Joachim of Fiore—sources with which the *Spirit of Utopia* very much engaged—see Rabinbach, "Unclaimed Heritage: Ernst Bloch's *Heritage of Our Times* and the Theory of Fascism," *New German Critique* 11 (Spring 1977): 5–21.

118. Friedlaender, "Der Antichrist und Ernst Bloch," 114.

119. Friedlaender, 114.

120. Hiller, "Nachwort," *Das Ziel: Jahrbücher für geistige Politik* 4 (1919): 116–17. On Benjamin's views on Hiller and *Das Ziel*, see Scholem, *Story of a Friendship*, 22.

121. Hiller, "Nachwort," 117.

122. Scholem, *Story of a Friendship*, 108; Scholem, *Geschichte einer Freundschaft*, 113.

123. Scholem, *Story of a Friendship*, 109; Scholem, *Geschichte einer Freundschaft*, 113–14, translation slightly altered.

124. Letter to Scholem, 13.2.1920. *Gesammelte Briefe*, 1:75; Scholem and Adorno, *Correspondence of Walter Benjamin*, 159. In the same 1932 will in which Benjamin bequeathed the *Angelus* to Scholem, he left "den dreiköpfigen Christus" to Bloch. Benjamin, "Mein Testament," in *Gesammelte Briefe*, ed. Christoph Gödde and Henri Lonitz (Frankfurt: Suhrkamp, 1998), 2:122.

125. Benjamin, *Selected Writings*, 1:294–95; *Gesammelte Schriften*, 2:244.

126. Buber, *Vom Geist des Judentums* (Leipzig: Kurt Wolff Verlag, 1916), 8.

127. Buber, "The Altar," 116.

128. Ivan Davidson Kalmar and Derek J. Penslar, "Orientalism and the Jews: An Introduction," in *Orientalism and the Jews*, ed. Ivan Davidson Kalmar and Derek J. Penslar (Waltham, MA: Brandeis University Press, 2005), xviii; on Buber's Orientalism specifically, see Abigail Gillman, *Viennese Jewish Modernism: Freud, Hofmannsthal, Beer-Hofmann, and Schnitzler* (University Park: Pennsylvania State University Press, 2009), 138–41.

129. Buber, *On Judaism*, 56–61, 44; Buber, *Vom Geist des Judentums*, 9–10. See Mendes-Flohr, *From Mysticism to Dialogue*, 69–70.

130. Buber, "The Spirit of the Orient and Judaism," in *On Judaism*, 58–59.

131. Buber, 68.

132. Buber, "The Altar," trans. Picker, 116, translation slightly altered.

133. Buber, *Vom Geist des Judentums* (Leipzig: Kurt Wolff Verlag, 1916), 45–48.

134. As Mendes-Flohr writes, "The indictment of pre-Holocaust generations of German Jews for courting peril by endorsing the myth of a German-Jewish symbiosis is burdened by the fallacy of retrospective judgment." Mendes-Flohr, *German Jews: A Dual Identity* (New Haven, CT: Yale University Press, 1999), 91–92.

135. Buber, *Vom Geist des Judentums*, 47.

136. Mendes-Flohr, *German Jews*, especially 42–43.

137. Buber, *On Judaism*, 63.

138. Mendes-Flohr, *From Mysticism to Dialogue*, 99–102. I quote Mendes-Flohr's translation of Buber's note, 102.

139. "Der Altar," *Die weissen Blätter* 1, no. 5 (January 1914): 443–46. See Heinz Brüggemann, *Walter Benjamin über Spiel, Farbe und Phantasie* (Würzburg: Königshausen & Neumann, 2007), 185–86.

140. John Gage, *Color and Culture: Practice and Meaning from Antiquity to Abstraction* (Berkeley: University of California Press, 1999), 94.

141. Heinrich Wölfflin, *Die Kunst Albrecht Dürers* (Munich: F. Bruckmann, 1905), 295.

142. Benjamin, *Early Writings*, 220; *Gesammelte Schriften*, 7:25. See my discussion of Scholem's and Benjamin's dealings with color in *Paul Klee*, 66–82.

143. Benjamin, *Early Writings*, 234; *Gesammelte Schriften*, 2:130, translation slightly altered.

144. Erwin Panofsky, "On the Problem of Describing and Interpreting Works of the Visual Arts," trans. Jaś Elsner and Katharina Lorenz, *Critical Inquiry* 38, no. 3 (2012): 467–82, at 476, https://doi.org/10.1086/664547.

145. Pantxika Béguerie-De Paepe, *The Isenheim Altarpiece: The Masterpiece of the Musée Unterlinden* (Paris: Éditions Artlys, 2015), 86.

146. J. R. C. Cousland, in *The New Oxford Annotated Bible*, ed. Michael D. Coogan, 5th ed. (New York: Oxford University Press, 2018), 1783.

147. Scholem, *Story of a Friendship*, 47.

148. Scholem, "Walter Benjamin and His Angel," 209.

149. "Künstler-Mappen" in *Kunstwartarbeit: Eine Übersicht zum praktischen Gebrauch über die von Ferdinand Avenarius begründeten und geleiteten Unternehmungen* (Munich: Georg D. W. Callwey, 1908), 36–37. Advertisement for "Farbige Künstlermappen u. Alben aus dem Verlage von E. A. Seemann in Leipzig" in *Kunstchronik* 25, no. 44 (September 25, 1914), n.p., https://digi.ub.uni-heidelberg.de/diglit/kunstchronik1914/0335. A 1920 list of publications of all of the altarpiece's panels includes also H. H. Josten, *Matthias Grünewald* (Bielefeld: Velhagen & Klasing, 1913); Schmid, *Die Gemälde und Zeichnungen von Matthias Grünewald* (Strassburg: W. Heinrich, 1911); and Ernst Heidrich, *Die altdeutsche Malerei* (Jena: Eugen Diederichs, 1909). Alfred Martin, "Der Pestteufel in der Versuchung des hl. Antonius auf dem Isenheimer Altargemälde von Matthias Grünewald," *Münchener medizinischen Wochenschrift* 34 (1920): 992–95. This last article by Martin includes the 1920 list of publications; the Josten, Schmid, and Heidrich are all items on the list.

150. Jennings, "Towards Eschatology," 48.

151. Benjamin, *Selected Writings*, 1:296; *Gesammelte Schriften*, 2:246, translation modified.

152. Scholem, "Über Klage und Klagelied," in *Tagebücher, 1917–1923*, 128–33.

153. *Talmud, Chagigah*, 14a. Quoted in Peter Fenves, *Arresting Language: From Leibniz to Benjamin*, 257; see also the William Davidson Talmud available digitally on Sefaria.org.

154. Lamentations 3:21–23. *Tanakh, a New Translation of the Holy Scriptures according to the Traditional Hebrew Text* (Philadelphia: Jewish Publication Society, 1985). Scholem's translation of these lines from Hebrew into German is as follows: "Dies will ich erwidern meinem Herzen, / Darum hare ich aus: / Gottes Gnade, / Daß wir nicht ganz zu Grunde gingen, / Nicht sein Erbarmen ganz dahin ist. / Neu an jedem Morgen, / Groß ist deine Treue." Scholem, *Tagebücher, 1917–1923*, 120.

155. Scholem, "Walter Benjamin and His Angel," 213.

156. Isidore Singer, ed., *Jewish Encyclopedia* (New York: Funk and Wagnalls, 1906), s.v. "Angelology." See Geoffrey Hartman, *The Third Pillar: Essays in Judaic Studies* (Philadelphia: University of Pennsylvania Press, 2011), 124–28.

157. Benjamin, *Selected Writings*, 1:296; *Gesammelte Schriften*, 2:246, translation modified.

158. Or that he had any awareness of them. While Klee did own *Die Legende des Baal Schem*, Buber's collection of Hasidic lore, it makes no reference to these ephemeral angels of the Talmud.

159. *Gesammelte Schriften*, 2:246; *Selected Writings*, 1:295–96.

160. As Barber writes, "At the start of [the twentieth] century a basic Jewish antipathy to images was a dominant assumption. . . . This understanding, based largely in verbal sources, was, however, undermined by a series of discoveries," such as the 1932 discovery of the Dura Europos synagogue. Charles Barber, "The Truth in Painting: Iconoclasm and Identity in Early-Medieval Art," *Speculum* 72, no. 4 (October 1997): 1021; Joseph Gutmann, ed., *No Graven Images: Studies in Art and the Hebrew Bible* (New York: Ktav, 1971).

161. Kalman P. Bland, *The Artless Jew: Medieval and Modern Affirmations and Denials of the Visual* (Princeton, NJ: Princeton University Press, 2001), 13–32; Martin Buber, ed., *Juedische Kuenstler* (Berlin: Juedischer Verlag, 1903), n.p. On the first page of the unpaginated preface Buber wrote for an illustrated collection of essays on the work of six contemporary Jewish artists, Buber asserts that such activity in the visual arts is a new development in the history of the Jews and undertakes an explanation of the "Unfruchtbarkeit" prevailing, according to Buber, until very recently: "Dass der Jude des Altertums keine Bildkunst hatte, kann aus seinen Rasseneigenschaften erklärt werden. Allerdings soll man nicht vergessen, dass diese Rasseneigenschaften nicht etwas Letztes und nicht weiter Zurückführbares sind, sondern nur das Produkt des Bodens und seiner klimatischen Bedingungen, der wirtschaftlichen und sozialen Struktur der Gemeinschaft, der Lebensformen und des historischen Schicksals . . . So mögen wir es uns erklären, dass der Jude des Altertums mehr Ohrenmensch als Augenmensch und mehr Zeitmensch als Raummensch ist. Von allen seinen Sinnen trägt sein Gehör am meisten dazu bei, sein Weltbild zu formen."

162. Bourneuf, *Paul Klee: The Visible and the Legible*, 66–82.

163. For instance, Shalom Sabar explores the frequent use in decorated Jewish marriage contracts (*ketubot*) in seventeenth- and eighteenth-century Italy of Christian as well as Greco-Roman motifs, including human figures, angels, and heavenly bodies often borrowed from Gentile sources including "title-pages, allegorical handbooks, and majolica plates" (62). Sabar also cites rabbinic criticism of such decorated *ketubot*, based on interpretations of the Second Commandment (47). To suggest how Italian Jews of the period negotiated with such criticism, Sabar quotes Rabbi Leone da Modena of Venice (1571–1648): "In Italy a great many [Jews] take the liberty to keep . . . pictures in their houses, especially if they are not in *relievo* nor a whole body but only the face" (47n3). Sabar, "The Use and Meaning of Christian Motifs in Illustrations of Jewish Marriage Contracts in Italy," *Journal of Jewish Art* 10 (1984): 47–63. See also the large number of European *ketubot* from the seventeenth through the nineteenth century featuring angels and cherubs in Shalom Sabar, *Mazal Tov: Illuminated Jewish Marriage Contracts from the Israel Museum Collection* (Jerusalem: Israel Museum, 1993).

164. Bourneuf, *Paul Klee: The Visible and the Legible*, 66–82; Martin Buber, ed., *Juedische Kuenstler* (Berlin: Juedischer Verlag, 1903), n.p.; Michael Stanislawski, *Zionism and the Fin de Siècle: Cosmopolitanism and Nationalism from Nordau to Jabotinsky* (Berkeley: University of California Press, 2001); Michael Berkowitz, *Zionist Culture and West European Jewry before the First World War* (New York: Cambridge University Press, 1993).

165. As Weigel writes, "Benjamin's use of the word refers to a meaning of *Bild* that precedes the distinctions among mental, visual, and material images as well as the differentiation of scripture and pictures and the separation of concept (*Begriff*) and metaphor." Sigrid Weigel, "The Flash of Knowledge and the Temporality of Images," *Critical Inquiry* 41 (Winter 2015): 344.

166. Benjamin, October 1, 1922, *The Correspondence of Walter Benjamin, 1910–1940*,

ed. Gershom Scholem and Theodor W. Adorno, trans. Manfred R. Jacobson and Evelyn M. Jacobson (Chicago: University of Chicago Press, 1994), 199–200; *Gesammelte Briefe*, 2:269.

167. *Gesammelte Schriften*, 2:990–91; Scholem and Adorno, *Correspondence of Walter Benjamin*, 200, 201–3.

168. Letter to Hofmannsthal, quoted in *Gesammelte Schriften*, 2:994.

169. Scholem, *Story of a Friendship*, 126.

170. Scholem, 138.

171. Scholem and Adorno, *Correspondence of Walter Benjamin*, 219–20; *Gesammelte Briefe*, 2:376–78.

172. Scholem and Adorno, *Correspondence of Walter Benjamin*, 217–18; *Gesammelte Schriften*, 4:791–92.

173. "Die Menschen dieser Gruppe bilden schon eine Gemeinschaft, wie sie zum Aufbau des Volkskörpers nottut . . . Aus der Kraft dieser Gemeinschaft heraus rede ich." Rang, *Deutsche Bauhütte: Ein Wort an uns Deutsche über mögliche Gerechtigkeit gegen Belgien und Frankreich und zur Philosophie der Politik*, Reprint der Erstausgabe, ed. Uwe Steiner (Göttingen: Wallstein, 2015), 6; Steiner, "Nachwort," *Deutsche Bauhütte*, 220.

174. Rang, *Deutsche Bauhütte*, 185–86.

175. Benjamin to Rang, November 18, 1923, in Scholem and Adorno, *Correspondence of Walter Benjamin*, 214–15; *Gesammelte Briefe*, 2:367–71.

176. Benjamin, *Selected Writings*, 2:456–57.

177. Scholem, "Against the Myth of the German-Jewish Dialogue," 61.

178. "Diese nicht geschriebne Zeitschrift könnte mir nicht wirklicher und nicht lieber sein, wenn sie vorläge." Benjamin to Rang, October 14, 1922, in Scholem and Adorno, *Correspondence of Walter Benjamin*, 203; *Gesammelte Briefe*, 2:279–80.

EPILOGUE

1. Benjamin himself referred to the text as "theses"; see note 26 in chapter 1 of this book. On the poetics of citation in Scholem's by-no-means-straightforward text, see Weidner, "Reading Gershom Scholem," 208–15.

2. Weigel, *Body- and Image-Space: Re-reading Walter Benjamin*, trans. Georgina Paul, with Rachel McNicholl and Jeremy Gaines (London: Routledge, 1996), 46–56. Gerhard Richter, *Thought-Images: Frankfurt School Writers' Reflections from Damaged Life* (Stanford, CA: Stanford University Press, 2007); Andreas Huyssen, *Miniature Metropolis: Literature in an Age of Photography and Film* (Cambridge, MA: Harvard University Press, 2015), 10–17.

3. Weigel, s.v. "Angelus Novus," *Enzyklopädie jüdischer Geschichte und Kultur*, ed. Dan Diner (Stuttgart: J. B. Metzler, 2011), 98.

4. Benjamin, *Selected Writings*, 4:392–95.

5. Benjamin, *Selected Writings*, 4:393. See Scholem, "Walter Benjamin and His Angel," 231.

6. Quaytman, "Engrave," 61.

7. Godfrey, "Angels, Boulders, and Tongues," 17.

8. Bloch, *Spirit of Utopia*, 235–36.

9. Bloch, 236, 1–2.

10. Benjamin, *Selected Writings*, 4:395.

11. Benjamin, *The Arcades Project*, trans. Howard Eiland and Kevin McLaughlin (Cambridge, MA: Belknap Press of Harvard University Press, 1999), 461.

12. Benjamin, *Arcades Project*, 462.

13. Benjamin, 462.

14. Brüggemann, *Benjamin über Spiel, Farbe und Phantasie*, 338.

15. Brüggemann, 335–36.

16. Brüggemann, 337–38.

17. Scholem, "Walter Benjamin and His Angel," 235.

18. Scholem, 233–34.

19. Scholem, 234. On the echo that many have heard in Benjamin's "kleine Pforte" of Luther's translation of Matthew 7:13–14, see Andrew Benjamin, *Working with Walter Benjamin: Recovering a Political Philosophy* (Edinburgh: Edinburgh University Press, 2013), 194–95.

20. Jennings, "Towards Eschatology," 42–48.

21. Benjamin, *Selected Writings*, 4:391.

22. Benjamin, 397.

23. Agamben, *The Time That Remains: A Commentary on the Letter to the Romans*, trans. Patricia Dailey (Stanford, CA: Stanford University Press, 2005), 139–40, 144.

24. Taubes, *Political Theology of Paul*, 10–11, 70–76.

25. Agamben, *Time That Remains*, 144–45.

26. Britt, *Postsecular Benjamin*, 282.

27. Scholem, "Walter Benjamin and His Angel," 201.

Index

Page numbers in *italics* refer to illustrations.